IN SARDINIA

IN SARDINIA

An Unexpected Journey in Italy

JEFF BIGGERS

MELVILLE HOUSE
BROOKLYN · LONDON

In Sardinia: An Unexpected Journey in Italy

First published in 2023 by Melville House
Copyright © Jeff Biggers, 2022
All rights reserved
First Melville House Printing: March 2023

Melville House Publishing
46 John Street
Brooklyn, NY 11201
and
Melville House UK
Suite 2000
16/18 Woodford Road
London E7 0HA

mhpbooks.com
@melvillehouse

ISBN: 978-1-68589-026-1
ISBN: 978-1-68589-027-8 (eBook)

Library of Congress Control Number: 2022949372

Designed by Patrice Sheridan

Printed in the United States of America

10 9 8 7 6 5 4 3 2 1

A catalog record for this book is available from the Library of Congress

Per Carla, per sempre

A Valerio e Angela

A Sardonicus

The Sardes are almost all born poets.

—Charles Dickens, "Conductor," *Household Words* magazine, 1856

Since in this report the compiler assumes that Sardinia is not known, except for unfaithful geographic maps, and that the Sardinian is an unknown being . . . I think it is my duty to note that neither Sardinia nor its inhabitant is so unknown, as the aforementioned compiler indicates. Ancient stories from all ages of the world often mention Sardinia.

—Giuseppe Cossu, *Descrizione geografica della Sardegna*, 1799

CONTENTS

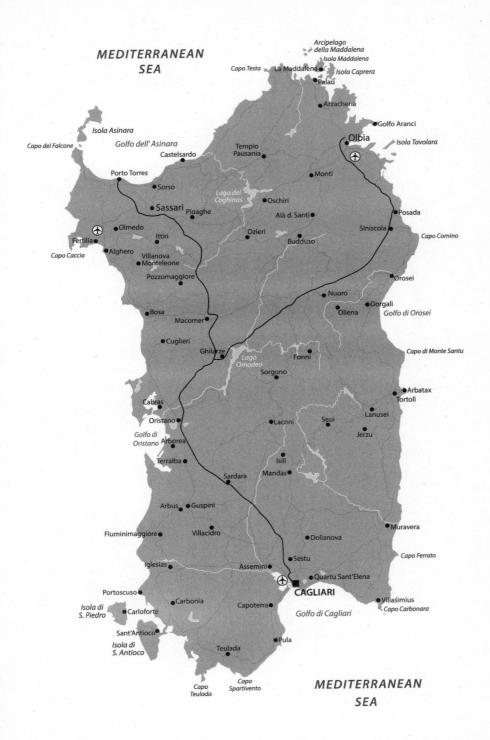

CROSSING OVER TO SARDINIA

cola su mare, e cando in sa fiorida
America nche ses a tottus nara
chi s'isula 'e Sardigna isettat galu
de esser iscoperta e connoschida.

cross the sea, and when you are in flowering
America tell everyone
that the island of Sardinia is still waiting
to be discovered and known.

—Grazia Deledda, "America and Sardinia," 1893

SARDINIA BLUES

And always, everywhere, it meant, even to those who heard it for the first time, distance, exile, the desire to return.

—Salvatore Cambosu, *Miele Amaro*, 1954

In 1979, renowned Sardinian artist Maria Lai was summoned by the mayor of her mountain village of Ulassai. She was residing in Rome. They had raised funds to commission a war memorial. Having lived away from Sardinia for decades, conflicted with her village over the murder of her brother, Lai turned down the town councilors. "I was convinced I would never return there," she wrote. Lai suggested a monument "to the living by the living," as part of a celebration of a resurgent Sardinian culture. If you want to make history, she declared, you must create history.

The villagers agreed. Lai's sculpture and textile work drew on Sardinian traditions of weaving and storytelling; in secondary school, she had been a student of author Salvatore Cambosu, whose poems and stories had taught her how to "follow the rhythm."

On a fall day in 1981, Lai led the entire village in wrapping Ulassai with sixteen miles of blue ribbons, lacing the doors of houses and balconies of apartments, church spires and shops, winding up the warrens until they reached Mount Gedili, a craggy ridge that overlooked the valley. Some neighbors tied a knot of friendship among themselves; others left it straight. But all were connected. The blue ribbon recalled a folktale of a young girl who had survived a mountain landslide by following the trace of the ribbon. *Legarsi alla montagna*—binding oneself to the mountain—turned into an internationally recognized avant-garde work of performance art that sought to heal divisions in the village and reconnect the residents to their rugged natural habitat.

"A town far from the fashionable cultural circuit was able to give the world a fresh insight into what art can be," Lai mused.

It also brought Lai back to the island.

Lai's neighbor in Rome was acclaimed Sardinian novelist Giuseppe Dessí, whose work Lai would embroider into canvas in her exhibition of "sewn books," her art functioning as a way to connect the island to the world. For Dessí, Sardinia was a state of mind, a "land of permanence, and not of travel."

Travelers and islanders alike, Sardinian author Marcello Serra once declared, shared a longing to return to the island—a kind of "sortilege" that runs in your veins with a "sweet and bitter languor." In 1956, Serra named it in his travel guide as *mal di Sardegna*—the Sardinia blues—as real for native islanders as those who visit. It wasn't simply nostalgia; it was more like an unyielding yearning to return.

When you leave "the island of the Sardinians, with dense memories of fabulous encounters, of landscapes timeless and ancient," Serra wrote, "then the heart, overseas brother, will weigh you down like a ripe fruit."

Not every visitor, of course, feels this longing. Cicero, the ancient Roman statesman, once displayed his oratory skills: "Sardinia was a bad island, everything in the island was ugly and even its abundant honey was bitter."

Yet, it was that special honey, *miele amaro* or *miele di corbezzolo*, bitter honey from the strawberry tree, that gave Sardinia its special flavor, according to Cambosu and other writers, for those wishing to see the reality of the island.

THREE MAPS AND A PHOTO

So I set out from Venice and went along Greek Street, and thence by road through the kingdom of Garbo and through Baldacca, thence reaching Parione, and afterwards at some expense of thirst—Sardinia.

—Giovanni Boccaccio, *The Decameron*, 1353

The work of Lai and Cambosu, among so many other writers and artists, returns to me now as I look at three maps of Sardinia on the wall of my office, as if some boat awaits me outside.

One map, titled "Mediterranean without Borders," by French cartographer Sabine Réthoré, turns our view ninety degrees to the right, the "west" facing up—imagine North Africa to the left and Europe into Turkey to the right with equal stature, the Levant stretching to Egypt at the bottom, and the Rock of Gibraltar at top. Our perspective shifts, the Mediterranean Sea unfolding almost like a lake, the shores mirroring each other along these ancient corridors dotted by islands and waterways. It's a busy thoroughfare. The Mediterranean is "probably the most vigorous place of interaction," as eminent historian David Abulafia observed, "between different societies on the face of this planet."

There in the upper reaches, the island of Sardinia sits in the middle,
a focal point of entry and inspection. Instead of being on the periphery
of empires or a nebulous island west of the Italian mainland, Sardinia
is central to the Mediterranean story and a nexus for navigators heading in any direction. The idea of isolation, as one medieval historian
would note, no longer appears "tenable."

The second map is of Sardinia itself: the main island with its many
islets. It is not a floating green mountain with a defining valley that
splices along the south by southwest, as a topographical map would
show. Instead, this map is as colorful as a neon strip of nightlife you
might download on a cell phone for the latest cultural events. In fact,
devised as a geoportal and online app by a volunteer organization
called Nurnet in 2013, the map pinpoints the thousands of Neolithic
and Bronze Age monuments across the islands with the fanfare of an
open museum.

As part of Nurnet's mission to "promote a different image of
Sardinia in the world," the map is nothing less than astounding. If
you actually illuminated all of these ancient monuments, from the
Neolithic array of Stonehenge-like dolmens and menhir stone forma-
tions to the thousands of burial tombs, Bronze Age towers and complexes called *nuraghes* or *nuraghi*, the entire island would light up like a
prehistoric hotspot. The vastness of the uninterrupted cycles of civilizations and their architectural marvels still standing today would be incomparable with any place in Europe on that first Mediterranean map.

The Sardinians call it the "endless museum."

The third is a wine map of Sardinia, at least the official "DOC"
(designation of controlled origins) varieties that make it into the official
registers. The unmarked bottles of wine in the secret cellars of connois-
seurs, Cannonau or Vernaccia or Vermentino or Semidano, have their
own registry for the fortunate, but this map displays the five provinces

on the island that don't vary too much from the original kingdoms or *judicadus* that ruled in the Middle Ages with a degree of independence. The names have changed or been consolidated; the wine remains the same, in the north of Sassari (and Gallura), the west of Oristano, the central Barbagia mountains and east of Nuoro, the south of the Sulcis and Campidano valley. The fifth province is the capital city of Cagliari.

Wine, of course, makes any journey a delight—or an adventure. Plutarch invoked Gaius Gracchus's words that the Romans drank wine in Sardinia and returned with their amphoras filled with gold and silver. In Sardinia, wines are also a portal into the island's cultures, like the popular berry-tone Cannonau, with its high level of flavonoids and artery-scrubbing antioxidants. It is the drink in the holy grail of the Blue Zones' research on the island's phenomenon as the home of the most centenarians in the world. This was an old story; in 1639, Sardinian historian Francisco Angelo de Vico noted the extraordinary number of islanders that lived until one hundred years old or more. In fact, evidence of the oldest wine-making press and cultivation of domestic grapes in western Europe was discovered in recent excavations at Nuragic sites, dating back to 1,500 B.C.

Alongside these maps, I also have a framed photo of a young boy in shorts and a beret, probably from the 1890s, sitting with his legs dangling off the thick walls on the medieval bastion in the northern port of Alghero, Sardinia, reading a book. Fishing boats line the shores below, dwarfed by the mainmasts of three ships, the sails folded, the walls of the city's fortress in the background.

There on the bastion walls of Alghero, I imagine the young boy reading a travel story, for some reason; in the photo he's watched over by two other kids who don't seem to know what to make of the scene. I see this boy turning the page on the story of the first European crossing of the Mississippi River in North America by Spanish conquistadors in

1541, and their attacks on indigenous populations. In the end, it was thanks to a Sardinian boat maker who fashioned caulk from hemp to rebuild a new vessel to descend the great river in 1543, that the crew survived to tell Europe the story of this other world.

I have sat on those same walls in the morning, gazing out at the sea and the spellbinding cliffs of Capo Caccia in the distance, over many years. In 2017, my wife Carla and I packed up our two young boys (ages twelve and fifteen, actually) and moved to Alghero, as part of a university sabbatical from our work and lives in the United States. We had no plans other than to rest and explore the island and its fabled beaches, travel the winding back roads into its mountains and villages, and sample the varieties of food and wine; we were still dealing with the last details of a particularly grueling year of assignments, deadlines, and demands. Having raised our children as Italians and Americans, our main goal was to give them another chance to experience a school system in Italian and an opportunity to live in a different part of Italy.

But something almost unexplainable happened in Sardinia. The island had its own plans, as if a traveler couldn't simply pass through its confines with a little sand in one's shoes. We arrived as Sardinia was on the cusp of "re-storying" its history in a raucous debate, undergirded by an extraordinary range of poets, writers, musicians, artists, historians, and everyday storytellers. The formal recognition of some huge archaeological discoveries in the last half century was forcing scholars from around the world to reconsider a certain narrative about Sardinia and rewrite the history of the Mediterranean.

Picking up D. H. Lawrence's *Sea and Sardinia* one day, the defining book on the island in English over the past century, I opened the first pages to this passage: "Sardinia, which has no history, no date, no race, no offering." Lawrence's legendary provocateur role aside, that seemed like an incredibly outdated notion. The rest of the book, based on his six-day tour, seemed equally antiquated. One hundred years after its publication in 1921, *Sea and Sardinia* still remained on the bookshelves as the main window in English into one of the most beguiling and complex regions in Italy.

While Sardinian authors, like Giuseppe Cossu in 1799, had been lamenting the oversight of the island's history and "unfaithful geographic maps" for centuries, there still seemed to be a lingering narrative of historical ambivalence, as if the island had been an empty stage until the arrival of Phoenicians and Romans; as if Sardinians had no ancient civilization or role in their own destiny—or, more importantly, as if they had no role in shaping Italy and the worlds beyond their island. I couldn't help but wonder if we were missing the most vital parts of the island and its history; that perhaps we needed to understand Sardinia if we were to truly understand the rest of Italy.

In fact, it might be more accurate to speak of "le Sardegne," as in plural, instead of "la Sardegna," a singular entity, with a singular culture or set of ways. The "fundamental misunderstanding" in the Mediterranean, as historian Abulafia wrote in *The Great Sea*, was the illusive search for some sense of unity and clarity in such a place. Instead, he suggested, "we should note diversity," among the shores in a "constant state of flux."

When we arrived in Sardinia, festivals of all types abounded across the island—food, folk, dance, music, literature, theatre, sports, and archaeology. The range of political parties joyfully clashed, with the nationalist party now aligned with the right-wing parties on the Italian mainland. (We heard a frequent refrain in every town: Emilio Lussu, the great Sardinian patriot of the twentieth century, would be turning in his grave.) The traditional processions and events continued to grow, including those that had marked Sardinia's unique cultures for centuries, such as the extreme S'Ardia horse race in Sedilo, recalling a battle under the Byzantine Emperor Constantine or the elaborate Sant'Efisio procession that re-walks a forty-mile journey from Cagliari to Nora, celebrating the end of the plague in 1656.

Along the shores, plains, and mountains in Sardinia, that fine line between unity and diversity had been an old rub on the island, we would find out. In an interview with *Rolling Stone* magazine, legendary jazzman Paolo Fresu, the son of a shepherd who grew up in the village of Berchidda, referred to an old adage of Sardinia's factions and feuds: *centu concas, centu berritas*, a hundred heads, a hundred caps. But Sardinia was an island, he added. "Despite the sea, it is mainly one of land, and that forges us together."

Sardinian singer Claudia Aru, from the southern town of Villacidro, who sang like a mix tape of Bessie Smith, Lila Downs, and Maria Carta, added her own version of that theme during the COVID-19 pandemic, releasing a single titled "Centu Concas," as a hymn to multiculturalism. She was joined by iconic Sardinian singer and comic entertainer Benito Urgu. She called her song "a critical reading of a certain Sardinian identity that is too dusty," because "Sardità," the identity or state of being Sardinian, was not a given concept, or acquired with birth, "but is rather a choice of life, a fruit of behavior. Sardinia is, for me, an act of love."

This book is my chronicle of our sojourn in Alghero in 2017, and our subsequent journeys across Sardinia through 2022. While the COVID quarantine prevented any trip in 2020, I found myself with the time to finally read all the books I had collected on the island. In an attempt to wade into the scholarly world of archaeology, I even signed up on the academia.edu website, which sent me an article on ancient Sardinia each evening. But that had its limits. When I received notification of an article by "D. Trump," one of the leading British scholars on prehistoric Sardinia, I nearly spilled my coffee. His middle name was Hilary.

This book is not intended to be a sweeping history or tourist guide, but more of what the older Sardinians call *s'arrogliu*, a storytelling gathering, when folks from the neighborhood would come out of their houses carrying a chair, a bottle of wine, and a glass, arrange themselves in a circle, and spend hours telling each other stories about their life's adventures.

Years after our first journey, the longing to return often tugs at me in the evening, like some beckoning call of the waves off the coast of Porto Ferro, straddling the high cliffs to one side as we meandered along the dirt path between the thick mounds of myrtle and rosemary, the sun setting into the sea with its threads. I would take a seat in a clearing for a moment, in the shadows of the medieval ruins of Torre Bandine Sale, which teeter, wishing to crumble into the terra cotta earth like another layer of clay. I often brought along a bag of *seadas*, the deep-fried shepherd pastries filled with pecorino cheese and smothered in miele amaro.

Following the dramatic coastal trail along the cliffs, my memory can still trace the history of the coves—Cala del Turco, Cala del Vino, Cala Porticciolo, Cala Viola—until land's end at the sheer cliffs of Capo Caccia on the northwestern flank of the island.

At the end of the trail to Capo Caccia, there is another trail, where the submerged caverns of Grotta Verde have disappeared with the remains of burial grounds from seven thousand years ago, and where the tide comes and goes with travelers out to sea.

The sea—and then there is the sea.

An Italian romance may begin in a gondola amid the marvel of Venice, but a traveler looking for the great stories of Italy will board a sailboat amid the gale force of mistral winds, confront the rough seas and warnings of "the insane mountains" that have addled visitors for thousands of years, and then traverse the Strait of Bonifacio in search of Sardinia.

PART ONE

S'ABBA TENET MEMORIA
THE WATER REMEMBERS

The water was still cool and clear after the night and through it you could see the colored pebbles and the pieces of coral and green and blue glass. The waves that reached the shore were light and frail and their splashing so pleasant that it seemed that it could be held in one's mouth like a pebble and sucked with gusto.

—Maria Giacobbe, *Il Mare*, 1997

1 | THE SHIP

I am weary of being wedded to the waves of the Venetian gulf, and purpose in the course of a few days to embark upon a wider sea. I have so long cherished a wish to visit the islands of Corsica and Sardinia, that I cannot tell when it first originated.

—Lord Byron,
Narrative of Lord Byron's Voyage to Corsica and Sardinia, 1821

Carla had insisted that we arrive by boat from Corsica, even if symbolically in this age when a discount flight from Bologna to Alghero was only an hour and a glass of wine away. We were embarking on a longer sojourn in the port town of Alghero, our two kids in tow, our baggage still full of a lot of misperceptions about Sardinia, and she wanted to start it on the sea.

"After all, is it not the sea that makes an island?" Sardinian author Marcello Fois wondered. (But he titled his book the opposite, *In Sardegna non c'é il mare.*) In 1572, cartographer Tommaso Porcacchi featured a sailboat heading to "Sardigna," declaring "the earth is an island, if you look at the sea." He included sea monsters on his map, too.

No monsters or gods or water defined our arrival as much as the wind. The mistral wind came down from the north in a fury, *bentu maistru*, the Sardinians called it. Even before we arrived in Sardinia, we understood the force of its meaning. (Little did we know the role it would eventually play in our lives, living in the port in the northwest.) The thump of a squall brought down the sails of our thirty-six-foot rig, as we watched our able captain Maurizio from Rome hold on to the wheel with both hands with a certain delight. He recounted stories of shipwrecks in the infamous strait, called the *Buccas* (mouth) *de Bonifatziu* in Sardinian. The kids removed themselves from the deck. The late summer skies were draped in clouds. The waves sprayed us with a challenge.

In 1734, French painter Claude-Joseph Vernet demanded to be tied to the mainmast during such a storm off Sardinia, so he could witness "the angry sea." His storm masterpieces ended up at the Metropolitan Museum of Art in New York and national galleries around the world.

We made the first sighting of Sardinia. Our captain insisted you could actually see Sardinia from Corsica on a clear day. The Strait of Bonifacio ran less than seven miles from one island to the next, a distance so close that some even deemed Corsica and Sardinia an impeded archipelago.

While the captain pointed out a century-old obelisk that alerted sailors of the demarcation line between France and Italy, I only saw the dark blue lines of water that spoke of eternal corridors.

The strait granted passageway between the Tyrrhenian Sea and the Italian coast, the Sea of Sardinia and the Balearic islands of Spain—and then, if we kept going, the Atlantic.

The sea did not swirl with borders, but channels of connection, even in a storm. "Between a dark line and a light line," Sardinian poet Giovanni Dettori wrote, is "a strong line."

The winds continued to whip. The white caps rolled. The outcropping of rocks along the coastline emerged as if scattered with islets and coves and fringing shoals. Everything bent to the winds, the mastic trees in an arch; the broom and myrtle and lavender clutched to the shelves of rocks. Even the boulders appeared to have been sculpted and slanted by the mistral force.

Due to an even larger storm forming, our destination to the coastal town of Palau was diverted to the island of La Maddalena.

When we finally eased our sailboat into the dock, we could hear the echo of a concert in the town square as the wind roared off the sea like a spectator. Across the port from Cala Gavetta stood a building that fronted as a bank now, but it had its own history with an English ship captain and Lord Byron's schooner, Bolivar, which had arrived on the island without him. While Byron did visit the city of Cagliari in 1821 on the southern end of Sardinia, greeted by a twelve-gun salute and escorted by an honor guard, his tragic death in Greece in 1824 left his new boat in the eventual hands of Captain Daniel Roberts, an English sailor and shipbuilder with a gift for drawing. The Captain never quite resolved his grief over Bryon's close friend Percy Shelley, who had died at sea in a storm, on a boat Roberts had also designed and built. So, Roberts sailed Byron's vessel to La Maddalena, fell in love with the island, and eventually took his place on the corner of the port as a beloved raconteur until his death.

Things had a way of turning out differently in Sardinia.

2 | THE LOVE OF ITALY

Oh! To live and to die / While the herring swim by / Where the Delicatessen flows.

—George Gershwin, "In Sardinia," *Tell Me More*, 1925

The love of Italy is an acquired affair.

Like most travelers to Italy, I had stuck to Lord Byron's nineteenth century "Grand Tour" tradition of Venice to Florence to Rome, as if we had to follow some infallible guidebook of beauty in a country of limitless artistic and architectural wonders.

In my case, it started with a late night stroll along the narrow canals in Venice in the late 1980s, somewhere between spellbound and weak in the knees, and it continued across the medieval Ponte Vecchio into renaissance Florence, in awe of its treasuries of art—and that museum jar with Galileo's middle finger.

I will always recall walking for the first time through the triumphal arches in the Roman Forum *in Rome*, hearing the stories of the decadence of spectacles and vomitoriums in the Colosseum, across the limestone steps of royal processions before the sackings by Goths and Vandals started the collapse of the Roman Empire.

I ended up moving to Florence in the spring of 1989, and then to Bologna when I met Carla. Within a short time, I began to transcend the "Grand Tour" constraints and venture out into other parts of Italy, from the Carso plateau of Gorizia on the Slovenian border to Portapalo di Capo Passero, the southernmost tip of Sicily.

The marbled-floor corridors of Bologna's porticos, where Carla had attended the university, eventually became our adopted home in northern Italy, as much as any place we had called home in the last three decades. We married in Spoleto, in central Italy, the ancestral home of her family, and I spent many summers wandering the back alleys of that Umbrian hill town with Nonna Gigia, the family matriarch who ran a bar in the *Piazza del Mercato* for half a century. Rome, where I had based one of my plays with a theatre group on the life of Emperor Septimius Severus and the edicts of *damnatio memoriae* (the act of destroying and removing history from public memory), was forever the "eternal city." Even when we moved back to the States, and pursued work elsewhere, we always returned "home" to Bologna for the summers or holidays, the one constant in our itinerant lives.

We all become time travelers of sorts in Italy. No matter where we find ourselves, the irresistible splendor of ancient Italy is always around the corner, shadowing the modern literary itineraries of food, fashion, religious pilgrimages, and romantic travel.

Archaeology is only a layer of dust away from the dinner table or the evening stroll. In the "seven churches" of Santo Stefano in Bologna, one of my favorite places in that city, an engraved stone from the first century A.D. reminds you that the temple was first dedicated to Iside or Isis, the Egyptian goddess. Traces of the foundations of Bologna, called Felsina by the Etruscans, dated back to the sixth century B.C.

As far as the shores of Sicily and its delicious sweets, ancient Greek theatres like Segesta sprawl across the ribs of Mount Barbaro with an intact stone stage for thousands, still resounding with the perfect acoustics for dramas and comedies set in centuries before Imperial Rome was even founded. Among the dreamy Tuscan villas are the Etruscan tombs and their wonderful frescos from the Iron Age.

And then there is Sardinia—*the Autonomous Region of Sardinia*—where a civilization even older than ancient Rome or Magna Grecia or the Etruscans had evolved over thousands of years, turning it into one of the cradles of the Bronze Age in the Mediterranean and the staging ground for some of the most important historical episodes in Italy.

It took me thirty years to cross over to Sardinia.

I don't really know why it took us so long to make the journey. I can't really blame it on the inconvenience of taking a ship in those early years, before the era of the discount air flights. We took plenty of ships to Sicily, even Greece and ex-Yugoslavia. Even *National Geographic* magazine, back in 1916, waxed poetic on the "comfort" of taking a night ship to Sardinia, the beauty of waking up to the sunrise on the cliffs of the Golfo degli Aranci. In retrospect, I now realize the American author, the wife of a mining baron, wrote this in the throes of World War I.

In 1341, encountering a violent tempest of a storm that even the oldest mariner aboard had never seen, German priest Ludolph Von Suchem wrote about his ship's landing in Sardinia. The priest found the island to be "very noble," with fertile soil and "abounding in flocks, herds and dairies." He seemed amazed most by the size of giant fish off Sardinia that puffed out water "further than a crossbow could shoot" and made "noise like thunder."

Not that we knew much more about the island—or islands—than Von Suchem, outside of the fame of the breathtaking beaches. To be honest, we visited Sardinia briefly in advance of our sojourn in Alghero as tourists, lounging on its sand dunes at Capo Comino and along the

Gulf of Orosei. We checked out the setting for Lina Wertmüller's classic movie, *Swept Away*. Our beach towels and knowledge of the islands were not far from where Disney would eventually film its remake of *The Little Mermaid*, and actor and director George Clooney would set his miniseries adaptation of the *Catch-22* novel, a similar quagmire of history set on loop.

En route to the airport outside of Alghero, on our return trip to Bologna, we saw Alghero from the distance for the first time. Perhaps it was the time of day, the sun setting over the bay of Alghero in grand fashion, the promontory of Capo Caccia plopped on the horizon like a sleeping giant. The fortress of Alghero caught the afterglow. We made our decision in an instant: let's go live there.

Like many Americans, we had heard about the "Blue Zone" movement for health and longevity, which got its groove in Sardinia. The "blue" in the Blue Zone had its origins in the blue check marks from researchers in mountain communities on the island, which recorded the highest rates of centenarians on the planet. Actor Zac Efron's top-rated Netflix series, *Down to Earth*, had explored the Blue Zone phenomenon of the island, based on the bestselling series of books by Dan Buettner, but the images of older men in berets and their miracle habits almost seemed otherworldly. So did the media stories on the "Robinson Crusoe of Italy," another elder who had lived alone on a smaller Sardinian islet for three decades in a former military shack, protecting its glittering pink beaches.

And, of course, there were the constant clickbait stories of homes for sale for $1 in Italy, inevitably in a remote Sardinian village. I must admit, they did look tempting.

The interior of the main island, like Sardinia's complex history, however, remained just beyond our tourist reach. The memory of Sardinia in Carla's family came from our Zio Vittorio, who had served in the Italian Air Force, and grounded his plane on the island when World War II came to an end. Zio Vittorio picked up malaria; the images of wartime poverty haunted him for years.

I think I had first heard about Sardinia from an interview with legendary American musician Frank Zappa in the late 1980s or 1990s. Zappa had been "astonished" by the recordings of the *cantu a tenore*, the chilling polyphonic singing quartets fashioned traditionally by shepherds. UNESCO enshrined the vocal skills and ancient songs as part of the "intangible cultural heritage of humanity." I have a vague recollection of hearing the raves about the "Tenores di Bitti," and seeing a photo of them standing in a huddle, dressed in their white shirts and black vests, and wondering where on earth was this "Bitti."

Back in 1992, in my early years in Italy, the *New York Times* ran a story on Sardinia, titled "Where Kings of the Mountains Are Kidnappers," which remained in the back of my mind with an air of skepticism and wonder. But didn't criminal gangs even kidnap the beloved Italian folk-rock icon Fabrizio De André in 1979, who had made his home on the island—and remained on the island, forever enchanted?

Some might say our American and Italian views had not progressed since Henri Cartier-Bresson's photographs immortalized Sardinia for *Vogue* in 1963 as "a unique island hovering between old-fashioned banditry and jets."

Decades later, our Italian and expatriate friends still shook their heads at our choice to live in Sardinia for our sabbatical. *And not Rome! Not even Sicily!* They saw it as some sort of sleepy outpost, trapped between the images of quaint pastoral villages, gritty films about shepherds and their unfortunate sons and daughters, and endless stories about impoverished villages or bloody family feuds. Or, of course, they spoke about the glittering beaches in a handful of resorts on the Costa

Smeralda set up by the Aga Khan, the spiritual leader of a small sect of Ismaili Muslims, who made the northeastern corner of Sardinia a hotspot for the rich and famous of the world.

Writing in *The Atlantic Monthly* about her travels in Sardinia in 1900, expatriate writer Mary Argyle Taylor had experienced the same reaction. She met an Italian captain who had not spoken to a woman in eighteen months, or so it seemed. He didn't understand why she wanted to visit the island. Sardinia was "no less a foreign country to the cultured, progressive Milanese than to my American eyes."

British Vice Admiral Horatio Nelson fell in love with La Maddalena and the Sardinian islands off the Strait of Bonifacio, making it his military base in the early 1800s. He wrote that he enjoyed the local wines. In 1805, Nelson hailed Sardinia as the most important island in the Mediterranean: "It has for sure, at its northern end, the most beautiful port in the world."

But he didn't get to appreciate Sardinia. He soon died in the epic Battle of Trafalgar, as if the island intended on vexing his expectations as well.

3 | *BALLU TONDU*

We called ourselves S'ard, which in the ancient language means
dancers of the stars.

—Sergio Atzeni, *Passavamo sulla terra leggeri*, 1996

We didn't stay in Alghero on our first night in Alghero. We ended up
in Villanova Monteleone (*Biddas Noas*, in Sardinian), a town just a few
miles from Alghero—and it was glorious.

The dancers spread out single file on the stage, women and men in
alternating positions, their colors a blend of black, white, and reddish-
purple in a stark display. The older man with an *organetto*, like a small
accordion, stood to the side. The crowd leaned in, as if to measure the
costumes, and then counted off the beginning steps of the *ballu tondu*,
the round dance.

The women attracted my attention first, statuesque in their white
veils, *su mucaloru*, and tight-fitting jackets, white aprons spilling over
their long reddish skirts. As the dancers began to move across the stage
in short steps, assembling into a circle, the intricate dance steps of the
women became clearer with a hop and then a swirl. The black *berrita*
of the men, meanwhile, dominated their attire, perched on their heads
like stockings folded back. Their black jackets covered the sleeveless

vests, coordinated with black pleated skirts atop their white pants. Matching perfectly with their caps, all the men wore the black *ghettas*, or leggings, of horsemen.

Sardigna mia, ca cara mi sese, balla sempre su tundu ballu antigu, ballos anzenos in usu no lese, the legendary oral poet Remundu Piras beseeched his hometown of Villanova Monteleone in northwestern Sardinia: "Dance our ancient round dance, do not include among your customs the dances of foreigners."

Since our apartment in Alghero wasn't quite ready, amid the last throngs of high season tourism, we had taken the southern road out of town, watching the sun set over the bay as we eventually turned inland a few miles out and found ourselves climbing the Scala Piccada, a narrowish road sculpted from the hillsides. The Sardinian passion for tailgating and passing on these narrow mountain roads, switch-backing on hairpin turns, was in full display for the six-kilometer stretch. We would soon adapt.

The overlook was spellbinding at the top. We pulled over. The last lines of the day sank into the sea, etching out silhouettes of the coastal cliffs. Unfolding westward, the sea reminded us that this side of Sardinia had its back to Italy, facing Spain. The mountains plunged into the sea at dusk, and that must have made for a Sisyphean task for whatever bitter invader happened to scale the dramatic shores below. Not far from our stretch of the road was the *sa pigada 'e sos turcos*—the ascent of "the Turks," a reference to pirates—recognizing a bloody invasion and a heroic response in 1582 that is still commemorated every summer.

Two centuries earlier, when the Catalans captured Alghero in the late 1390s, expelling indigenous Sardinians from the town and fortress, many had also fled for the villages on this plateau.

We weren't the only ones to stare at the expanse of the western sea, as if the sun had been extinguished by the tide. Our handy Nurnet geoportal told us the nearby Nuraghe Appiu tower hugged the Chentu Mannas plateau, surrounded by two hundred village stone huts, and recorded its own sunsets in the same way, three thousand years before our arrival. In this seemingly remote hillside, the Nuragic ruins, among others, were always a reminder that our path had been broken by various indigenous civilizations, not just outside conquerors.

We arrived after dusk at the *agriturismo*, or farm-stay, in Villanova Monteleone, just on the edge of the town. It reminded me of northern Mexico in some ways, more arid than lush, the sparse forest of oaks and cork trees, and the clear terrain of horses and rail fences meeting us down the dirt road. The village, in fact, was known for its annual horse shows, especially the unique Sardinian Anglo-Arab horse, bred from the indigenous mares and Arabian and thoroughbred stallions for racing and stamina.

The farmhouse was modest, perched on the hillside, with a terrace of outdoor tables. Our hosts greeted us with the rural aplomb shared by many Sardinians. With darkness falling, they encouraged us to head into the village for a local festival.

As we ventured into Villanova Monteleone that night, the lights and sounds of the dance in the village clearing drew us like a bonfire of activity. I was not sure if it was a piazza or an empty lot, the crowd was so immense. Huddles of other dancers in their costumes swirled around the stage and along the side streets. Makeshift tables had been assembled, where food and drink were handed out. The smell of roasting meat, lamb and pork, never strayed far from a Sardinian festival, tinged with the flavorful smoke of myrtle and juniper wood.

I wandered around the village, a few elders sitting outside their doorways in chairs. Everyone acknowledged my foreign presence with an amicable greeting. I stumbled up the *sa pigada de su cantaru* stairs,

stone houses on either side of the stepping stones, as if the steep street
had cascaded down from a flattened tower or even a fallen nuraghe.
The streets were dark for the most part. After losing my way in the
back alleys, I ended up in front of the same elders in the doorway, who
traded amused looks at my apparent lack of direction.

Without a prompt, they pointed down a street, in the direction
of the dancing. I probably reminded them of *S'Istranzu avventuradu*,
"The Foreigner's Adventure," a story by their local writer, Bastià Pirisi,
about a lost American soldier during World War II, who is rescued
and hidden by locals. Thanks to the kindness of the Sardinians, the
American soldier returns *sanu e liberu*—healthy and free—to the States,
to hug his *muzere e fizu*—wife and kids, while the fallout of political
machinations remain on the island. An anti-fascist leader and agitator
for Sardinian independence, Pirisi won the prestigious Ozieri Prize in
Sardinian literature in 1969 for his comedy written in Sardinian, not
Italian, as a political satire.

I found my family in the swell of the dancers. They were easy to
pick out, precisely because there were so few tourists. The array of
dance groups mingled in the crowd, their various costumes differ-
ing in style and color, as other groups took the stage. No one seemed
to be dressed in twenty-first century style, and yet the elaborate and
beautiful costumes were incredibly fashionable. The lights flickered
in the background; the music of the organetto, which had replaced
the traditional Sardinian instrument of the *launeddas*, or the *tenores*
quartet, kept a driving pace.

As per its name, the ballu tondu, round dance, brought the dancers
into the middle, hand-in-hand, in a circle, as the men and women each
took turns with their elegant and subtle dance steps. Couples would
occasionally veer off, and the twirls of swinging took place, but for the
most part the dance was fairly constant in the circle. It felt more ritual

than entertainment, though for the watchful crowd—a young woman next to me kept pointing at the costumes and steps of one of the dancers, in awe—it was clearly a competitive event.

The darkness kept me from seeing the intricate details of the embroidery, the jewelry, the buttons, even the varying shades in the costumes that had taken years to devise in each village. Handmade, the soft *orbace* wool, linen, and velvet. The years of meticulous embroidery. Like the variants of the Sardinian language in each village and area, the costumes followed local traditions of colors, designs, and styles. At the bottom of the women's skirts, though, I did notice a sort of cubic design, as if taken from carvings of an ancient bas-relief.

All the figures on stage, however, were striking. Their black and red jackets hemmed their straight postures; in a cascade of colors, the women posed naturally in their corsets and jackets, their faces framed by the scarves, or shawls, a pose that nineteenth-century clergy observer and folk expert Jesuit Antonio Bresciani saw as a form of defiance to centuries of church calls to blanket themselves. Even Dante, in his prudish medieval vision, seemed obsessed with the dress of Sardinian women, deriding their modesty (or lack thereof for the Florentine) in his *Purgatory.* You understood the obsession by other observers over the centuries with the Sardinian dress; some referred to the costumes as a "symphony" or "riot" of colors, while others, such as a story in *The Atlantic Monthly* in the 1950s, found Sardinian women to be simply beautiful, lovely, and regal.

In 1926, *National Geographic* magazine dedicated an entire section to Sardinian dress, though it assumed the attire was soon destined "to be seen only in the museums."

The excitement around us, even for a festival, dispelled that notion a century later, of course. While traditional dresses in daily life gave way to modern attire, the spirit of celebration and resistance behind the costumes continued to thrive. (One famous photo we would see in Desulo, a village in the mountains, showed a woman pumping gas at her gas station, all decked out in her traditional dress, in the 1970s.) In turn, it had also influenced some modern designers. By 1917, artist and illustrator Edina Altara, from Sassari, who upturned the fashion and design circles in Milan with the panache of a Sardinian Frida Kahlo, would place traditional costumes on the cover of Italian arts and fashion magazines in Milan with an enigmatic flair.

A century later, Milan's hallowed fashion week in 2021 featured internationally celebrated designer Antonio Marras, from Alghero. Having spent decades presenting designs inspired by traditional customs, he created an original film mixing theatre and fantasy with the theme *De Innui Ses*, "where do you come from," in Sardinian. His fashion models shifted their runway to the massive ruins of the Su Nuraxi Nuraghe in Barumini, the UNESCO World Heritage site dating back to 1600 B.C., evoking what *Vogue* called "the ancient and eternal through Marras's authentically rooted and finely calibrated mixology."

While most observers tended to classify the Sardinian dancers and their costumes as a throwback to medieval Spain or Italy, Bresciani considered them much older, part of a "very ancient" tradition. In fact, some observers traced the style of the long skirts and head garments to various *bronzetti* (the little bronze figurines and statues from the Nuragic civilization in the Bronze Age), as well as artifacts with Minoan and Etruscan styles.

Either way, you felt the modern dancers carried on a tradition on the stages of their times, not as a relic of the past. Those stages had taken different shape. In the nearby caves of Sa Ucca de su Tintirriolu, dancing figures etched on to pottery dated back to 4100 B.C. At least four or five female dance figures, hand-in-hand, sashayed across the remains of a bowl at the Monte d'Accoddi pyramid in the same region, sometime around 3500 B.C. It didn't take much to imagine dancers in a circle outside the clearings of a nuraghe tower.

A more modern twist came in the medieval period. At the Church of San Pietro di Zuri in Ghilarza, for example, dancing figures ringed the outer shelf of a column from 1293 A.D. Three centuries later, Sardinia's first historian, Sigismondo Arquer from Cagliari, wrote about the endless dances in the *Cosmographia* book for a German cartographer.

"Singing, playing, dancing, cultivating, gathering, milking, carving, smelting, killing, dying, singing, playing, dancing was our life," says Antonio Setzu, the storytelling guardian of Sardinian standard time, in Atzeni's masterpiece of a novel, *Passavamo sulla terra leggeri*, which remains untranslated in English. Setzu adds: "We were happy, apart from the folly of killing each other for irrelevant reasons."

4 | AGRITURISMO

O sardu, si ses sardu e si ses bonu,
Semper sa limba tua apas presente:
No sias che isciau ubbidiente
Faeddende sa limba 'e su padronu.

O Sardinian, if you are Sardinian and you are good,
always have your language in mind:
do not be like an obedient slave
speaking the master's language.

—Remundu Piras, "su 29 de Santu Aine de su," 1977

American celebrity chef and traveler Anthony Bourdain, who had been married to a Sardinian, once did a *No Reservations* TV program on the island's foodways. He exclaimed with a fork of food and an honest delight that the concept of the agriturismo was the "greatest invention."

The rustic veneer of staying on a farm was irresistible, of course. Here in Sardinia, nature was always a character in any story; to bring the cork trays laden with food into that picture made it feel bountiful, almost festive, in that same joyous way that Bourdain always made food something to savor.

We woke our first morning in Sardinia to the sounds of a farm, a rooster doing its deed, and the braying of a donkey somewhere in the valley—all the makings of the stereotypical rural adventure our friends warned us about. The smell of coffee was a universal call to life, at least for me. While the late summer invited us outside to eat on the terrace, I had peeked inside the main house, the walls covered in rustic treasures from the farm. Equipment hung on hooks, alongside paintings of rural scenes, and a framed photo of a patriarch in his black berrita, his black jacket atop his white shirt, the thick grey beard flowing.

A character in Giulio Angioni's novel, *Assandira*, questioned the whole agriturismo, a completely "new word" for a shepherd whose son has returned from working in Denmark with a Danish wife intent on making tourism a new part of farm life. Selecting a Dane as the foreign foil had a slight precedence for Angioni, an eminent anthropologist as well as a novelist. In 1913, Danish travel writer and artist Marie Gamél Holten published an endearing, if not romantic, account of her journeys, titled *The Unknown Island*, which she felt could be called the "happy island, because the inhabitants of it are intelligent, strong, beautiful and healthy" and a traveler could not find "a more refined civilization." One of the island's pioneering voices in the Sardinian Literary Spring revival, Maria Giacobbe actually moved to Denmark in the late 1950s on the heels of the publication of her book as a teacher, *Diario de una maestria*.

"An ancient rural town, which suddenly becomes a place for tourists," Angioni's shepherd laments. "Either he gives himself to the farm, that is, he does or pretends to do what he has always done." For Angioni's characters, "there is no escape" from tourism, "the ball is already in play and the world is watching."

The word "Assandira" came from a Sardinian expression for greeting the morning sun, or so it seemed in various songs to a daughter-in-law character from Denmark, who sees the commercial value in cashing in on dirt-floor folk cultures. The novel, as a prophetic work written in 2004 on the sweep of tourism across the pastoral communities, was made into a riveting film by Sardinian filmmaker Salvatore Mereu. Poignantly, Mereu preserved the Sardinian language dialogue of the characters, as the clash between false and authentic forms of traditional cultures came into play in the form of a family tragedy.

The risk of agriturismo, of course, was not just the commodification of folk and rural cultures to meet stereotypical expectations. It also tidied up the contradictions and complexities of an agro-pastoral experience into a single image, to explain thousands of years of cultural shifts and traditions. One agriturismo even advertised a meeting with "a bandit."

Villanova Monteleone dispelled this fear of fake folklore to me. The dance did little to cater to tourism from the outside; it was clearly focused on the local participants. The delicious food spoke for itself. We were not served the notorious *casu marzu*, a maggot-infested cheese featured on CNN. Instead, our breakfast included *gioddu* yogurt from fermented sheep's milk, firmer than most types, with a platter of pecorino cheese, salami, and some figs. Our hosts came and went with few words.

But the chatter in the kitchen, and outbursts of laughter, spoke more to me than food or art or folkways in that moment. It rooted the agriturismo in something intangible, but stronger. A trio of people—I never did meet them—spoke in Sardinian, an official language outside of Italian that shares a certain lexicon from Latin but otherwise has its own indigenous roots, including pre-Indo-European migrations, borrowings from other languages, and rich terminologies.

Among four (or five, some insist) main variants of the language divided regionally, linguists have noted more than seventy-five dialects

across the island, if not more. Every village, of course, would claim it
has its own language, and there are languages that came with colonizers,
including Alghero's Catalan and San Pietro's Tabarchino or Genovese.

While some estimates put native Sardinian speakers at 68 percent
of the population, the dwindling role of the language in daily use on
the island, including school, had placed it in the "endangered" category on the UNESCO list of European languages.

I don't know why it moved me so much. I have spent much of my
life among indigenous language speakers in various countries, including
other parts of Italy. But starting the first morning with the Sardinian
language, instead of Italian, seemed to set the parameters of our journey,
as if the map would read now in a Sardinian way—*sa Sardigna*.

The issue of language for poet Remundu Piras from Villanova
Monteleone, one of the venerated champions in the oral poetry contests, was paramount to the authenticity of the Sardinian culture. His
legacy echoed the crusade by Alghero political leader Antonio Simon
Mossa, who warned in 1969 that if the Sardinians didn't save their
languages, and their traditional customs, they risked being "absorbed"
into Italian culture and would "no longer exist as the Sardinian people."

It wasn't until 1997 that the Sardinian language was officially
recognized by the regional government as a language with the same
"dignity" as Italian. This terminology seemed rather jarring, given the
fact that written records in Sardinian, including the pioneering *Carta
de Logu* charter that served as the law of the land for centuries—from
the 1390s until 1827—had been on the books for one thousand years.
(Ancient inscriptions on stones dated back to the Nuragic period, but
that's another discussion.) In fact, it was a reminder of Dante's mock-
ing back in the Middle Ages: "As far as the Sardinians," he wrote, "who
are not Italians," and whose Sardinian language was "imitating grammar, as monkeys do men."

In the 1590s, Sardinian poet Hieronimu (Gerolamo) Araolla, who had already written works to "exalt and enrich" the Sardinian language, wrote his own defense of poetry, declaring Sardinian was as dignified as any language and needed more writers; *tengiat cognitione de sa limba Sarda comente tenet de sas de pius.*

Sardinian, in essence, did not need any defense; it needed more defenders, and speakers. That the Sardinian language, oral and written, had withstood the iron fist of colonizers and their censors over thousands of years spoke to its inexorable rootedness. In 1848, government officials sought to "eradicate the Sardinian dialect" and "remove one of the biggest differences between Sardinia and the mainland." The same report also identified songs in Sardinian about the "saints" that were not "decent." Despite the cavalcade of official languages over centuries from Spain, Catalan of the Aragonese, and the Italian variants from Pisa, Genova, and Piedmont Savoyards to Mussolini's fascists and their policies for a unified "Italian" language, the island continued to churn out a treasury of literature and songs in the various Sardinian languages. This did not simply indicate the thriving function of the native languages; it was a powerful testimony to their foundational role in shaping society.

As the cooks in the kitchen chatted, and then sang, as I would soon learn, the ancient role of poetry and song on the island was still vibrant. It also dated back to the Bronze Age period of the Nuragic civilization. One of the three-thousand-year-old bronzetti statues wore an ornate cape, with intricate designs, a speaking stick gripped in one hand, a drum or head piece, bells on his ankles, as if he was *sa cantonàlzu*, the storyteller or poet. *Giama su cantonàlzu*: Call the storyteller, in Sardinia tradition.

In fact, Tigellius the Sardinian was such a famous lyric poet in the time of Julius Caesar, during the first century B.C. in Rome, that

his songs and proximity to power irked Cicero, the Roman statesman who detested all things Sardinian. Cicero complained that the
Sardinian's satirical poems were as pestilent as his malaria-ridden
island. The Sardinian proverb—*Ci bolit un annu a ddu fai cantai e
dexi annus a ddu fai xittiri* (It takes a year to get him to sing, and ten
years to get him to stop)—is attributed to his legacy. A final riposte
to Cicero could be found in Cagliari today; the "Villa of Tigellius," a
Roman house with an ornate mosaic, serves as an encore of adoration
as a tourist attraction.

The theme of the loquacious Sardinian, contrary to the stereotype of stoicism, continued for a thousand years. Dante even mused
the same in the medieval period, declaring in *The Divine Comedy*
that the Sardinians "don't weary" in speaking of Sardinia. He placed
them in Purgatory.

In truth, the powerful tradition of poetry and song, not simply
Dante's aside to gossip, had always permeated Sardinia like myrtle; it
laced through every village like a sacred bond, as if the lyrical word, as
much as the written text, maintained the natural order of all things.
For centuries, every traveler noticed the deep-rooted place of poetry
and song in the daily ways of the island, as if Sardinia was a floating
island of narration.

In 1787, Jesuit priest Matteo Madao wrote a book on the "ancient
and new ways" of making poetry in the Sardinian language, detailing
the various harmonic cadences, rhymes, and meters, and the role of
improvisation, all drawing from pastoral ways. The Sards were "enthusiastic" for poetry, wrote British traveler writer William Smyth in
1828, and improvising poets were in great demand. They "cheer the
poets," Goffredo Casalis added in 1833, like any other festive event.
The clergyman Giovanni Spano wrote that poets were "heroes" in
the villages in the nineteenth century. In 1869, pioneering anthropologist Paolo Mantegazza made his obligatory fact-finding trip to

Sardinia, astonished by the "sublime" role of the improvising poets in society. The founder of the first museum of anthropology in Florence, Mantegazza was particularly taken aback by the role of shepherds, who he had viewed as illiterate and therefore bereft of any cultural progress. In a near breathless note, Mantegezza exclaimed that they excelled in the arts of erotic and love poems.

But to hear the shepherds "with such grace, vivacity, wit and copy of sentences and poetic flashes to make you exclaim, here we are in the land of the Muses," Bresciani had added about the thriving literary traditions in the 1850s.

Even with the unification of Italy in 1861, those traditions continued to flourish and define much of the times in Sardinia. "My grandfather was a poet," one of the characters exclaims in the novel *Cenere* at the turn of the twentieth century, by Nobel Laureate Grazia Deledda. "And as soon as a storyteller repeated them in the street, all the people learned them and repeated them with enthusiasm." Sardinian journalist and Communist leader Antonio Gramsci wrote his sister from prison in 1927, asking her to "send me some of the Sardinian songs they sing in the streets, by the descendants of Pirisi Pirino," the legendary wandering poet on the island in the early nineteenth century.

Just as Goethe reminded us that one must walk around the poet's country in order to understand the poet, Piras drew from his "school of poetry" in the fields of Villanova Monteleone, and among other poets. *S'umile musa mia dirit / a cuddos bellos saltos ue s'ama / su pastore guidat e currigit,* he declared: "My humble muse / once again goes / to those pleasant fields where the flock / is led and formed by the shepherd." The poet was organic to his village, Paolo Pillonca wrote in a tribute to Piras's work in print, *Bonas Noas*, and in the process, the poet elevated Villanova Monteleone as a kind of Parnassus of oral poetry on the island.

As a teenager, Piras appeared at his first *gara*, or poetry competition, a sort of poetry slam circuit across Sardinia that formally took shape in the late nineteenth century. Piras became an imposing figure on the stage. As part of the *a bolu* tradition, which featured women as well as men, poets would face off against each other in town piazzas, or fields or festivals, following set formats of rhyme and meters, responding to select themes. The forms of poetry altered slightly in every area, each with their own set of rules and metrical forms, and names—the *Mutetus* in the southern Campidano, the *Repintina* in the west, the *Mutos* in the central Barbagia, and the *Otada* in the north. There were amateur divisions, and then there were those considered to be professional.

British traveler John William Warre Tyndale, in the 1840s, found the women poets and singers at wool-plucking sessions to be more compelling than the male suitors. Female *cantadores* like Chiarina Porqueddu and Maria Farina took part in the competitions in the 1920s and 30s, drawing huge crowds. Backed up by the tenore quartets, the poets sang their extemporaneous works, displaying instant composition of poems to overrule their rival on stage. They dealt with issues of class, politics, love, and war, or whatever theme was agreed on by the judges. Crowds packed the events; bootleg recordings were made and circulated in modern times.

Touring the country in the 1920s, Piras was the "essential link," according to one critic, "in the passage of the entire Sardinian poetic culture from orality to writing." That role halted in 1932, when fascist and church authorities joined to ban the oral poetry contests. Even when they were relaunched in 1937, with censorship rules on politics, Piras refused to participate, citing the incongruous constraints on his freedom of speech. The great poet was silenced for nearly fifteen years. He didn't return to the circuit until after World War II, and then he dominated the garas for the next quarter century.

In 1977, he issued a poetic manifesto to his followers to maintain their Sardinian language, or risk disappearing. He warned the schools that failure to teach Sardinian was effectively a process of *dissardizzando* or "de-Sardinating" a child's identity.

As the spokesperson for his people, "spokesperson of their daily affairs," Villanova Monteleone resident Maria Leonarda Correddu wrote, Piras fashioned the Sardinian language into a language of resistance.

A half century after Piras's admonition, the gara poetica continued to be a popular event in villages across the island, and at festivals, including the *Time in Jazz* in Berchidda. One ad in the newspaper, during our sojourn, advertised a gara in Silanus that set out the themes and rules of a bolu. The Ozieri Prize, founded in the town where famed oral poet Antonio Cubeddu had organized the first official poetry tournaments in 1896, as well as being the birthplace of eighteenth-century writer Madao, had become a prestigious and competitive award for works in the Sardinian language. The prize, in fact, launched in the 1950s to counter the influx of postwar Italian language and cultural trends, had sought to raise the quality of Sardinian writing in the fields of poetry, prose, and song.

"Elaborate or simple," the French writer Auguste Boullier wrote in 1864, after several sojourns on the island, "all these songs are necessary to understand the intimate life of Sardinia; since they are the soul of the pains and pleasures, the different expression of one's genius."

The traditions of oral poetry in the Sardinian language continued in other ways today. The rappers Sa Razza, based out of Iglesias and Cagliari and quite popular in the 1990s, openly invoked their country's ancient poetry traditions, as they adopted an urban hip-hop look and style and rapped in their own Sardinian language. The rapper Micio P called himself *deu seu cantadori deis gaggius* in one song, identifying himself as the storyteller or poet of the dispossessed. In his songs "In Sa Ia" and "Stiamo Giu," he dealt with the hardships of emigration, the collapse of the mining industry, racism in Italy, and even the loss of the language; Sa Razza's song "Grandu Festa" took on the NATO military bases, which still dominated nearly a third of the land and sea territory on the island.

In 2019 and in 2022, the singer Mahmood won the coveted San Remo Music Festival in Italy, drawing the ire of right-wing politician Matteo Salvini, who mocked the name of the Egyptian-Italian. But Salvini missed a larger cultural dynamic. *"Ja te la credias cras,"* Mahmood told his mother from Orosei, in Sardinian—his native language at home—after winning his prize, as his message went viral on social media. (The loose translation: "You wouldn't have expected it.") The pop singer soon released a single dedicated to her and his island, singing the classic love song in Sardinian, "No potho reposare."

"Ajò," I heard one of my sons call, back at the agriturismo. Let's go, in Sardinian.

5 | L'ALGUER

Voglio andare ad Alghero,
In compagnia di uno straniero.

I want to go to Alghero,
In the company of a foreigner.

—"Alghero," Italian pop song by Giuni Russo, 1986

Alghero is the most beautiful coastal town on the Mediterranean Sea.

This is what I thought as I joined our new friend Sardonicus along the cobblestoned backstreets in the old town center, following a labyrinth of outdoor cafés and restaurants and flowery piazzas. We had left our car on a side street—Via Antonio Lo Frasso—as Sardonicus pointed at various landmarks of his childhood with the nonchalance of a local, tossing out aphorisms like little morsels of bottarga in a mix of Italian, Sardinian, and Algherese (also called Alguerese or Alguerés), a variant of Catalan from northern Spain. *Cada arjola te' la sua porguera.* (I think the metaphor is about a farm or barn, but the gist is that every place has its flaws.) While I hurried to keep up with his comments, I started to realize the street names were in Algherese as well as Italian—*Carrer de les Arjoles* or Via Simon, *Carrer del Quarter* or Via Gilbert Ferret—not Sardinian.

We were fifteen miles and a few centuries of history away from Villanova Monteleone, or so it seemed. (*S'Alighera* was the proper name in Sardinian, though I would rarely hear that name. Most assume the origins of the town name come from the root word of "algae" found on the beach.)

The layers of history, of course, were complex, and forever bending; "Sardinians and people from Alghero are the same," declared Antonio Simon Mossa, one of the leading thinkers of Sardinian nationalism, in the 1960s—about his hometown. Mossa, as an architect, had also left behind a trail of innovations. Sardonicus pointed at the colorful dome of the Baroque-style Church of San Michele. Mossa's polychrome tiles, installed in 1950, fanned out with the octagonal design of a tapestry, overseeing the historic center like a lighthouse with a sense of *alegría*, not some sort of medieval darkness.

Alghero—or *L'Alguer* as in Alguerés—was the perfect city for walking, or more like sauntering. Sardonicus was our perfect guide. As a former diplomat who had lived on numerous continents—often chastised by his colleagues as an ambassador to Sardinia, as much as Italy—he had maintained his grandparents' home in the historic center, while tending to a permaculture farm a few minutes outside of the city. Our connection was a mutual friend in Bologna, who had volunteered on his farm.

Even though Alghero's population numbered a little over forty-five thousand today, King Ferdinand of Spain granted it Royal City status in 1501. In that imperial vein, King Charles V, who ruled over an empire that stretched from the Americas to the Holy Roman Empire of southern Italy, Spain, and parts of Germany to Hungary, declared the city to be *bonita* and *bien asentada* in 1541—"well established," at least, during his visit, as a fortress wedge between his enemies in France and the Ottoman Empire.

Vine amb a mi, mia bella vine-hi tu també, que passetjant mirem qui bella que és l'Alguer, popular folk singer Pino Piras (no relation to

Remundu Piras) had sung in Alguerés in the 1970s: "Come with me, my beauty, come too, let's walk and see how beautiful Alghero is."

The white-haired Sardonicus showed us the way, meandering down the narrow streets that rose in sandstone blocks that had been quarried nearby, as if the city had mounted itself on the edge of the coast like an ancient acropolis. Some blocks came from the same quarries of the Neolithic burial sites. The most beautiful side of the cathedral, he showed us, featured its bell tower on the back side from the alley.

The sandstone was called *massacà* in Alguerés, from the Catalan for an excavated foundation, casting a synchronicity across the three- and four-story buildings. Those foundations, of course, long predated the Spanish invasion in the 1350s, which had "put to the sword all the Algherese, without sparing either women or small children," leaving the city deserted and soon to be repopulated by the mainly Catalan colonizers. This rather graphically poetic interpretation of the "black legend" of the evil Spanish came from French travel writer Gaston Vuillier in his important magazine dispatches, which became the travel book *The Forgotten Isles* in 1896. Vuillier, who had left his "darkened" life in search of "luminous peace" through traveling, couldn't quite shake an enduring air of sadness in his journeys in Sardinia, a land he declared to have been "avoided" by other travelers. In the end, he picked up an illness, sending him home.

His casting of darkness over Alghero, of course, was not without some merit. Not that Alghero or the Spanish had conquered the market on incivility in the medieval age, or modern times, for that matter. (We'll discuss the destruction of the city during the bombings in World War II by Allied forces a little later.) Nor did rebellions simmer in Alghero, which continued to be a city of resistance into the nineteenth century under the Savoy government, and into the twentieth century after the war.

The lively Alghero streets were not deserted now, but demure in that natural way, a blend of sandstone white and yellow, light grey and hazelnut that Genovese colonizers had started to build in the twelfth century A.D. The occasional splash of color on the doorways—and the ornate facades—recalled the historical divisions of the neighborhoods, between farmers, fishermen, artisans, and the lords, including Genovese, Pisan, and then the Catalans of Aragon, the Spanish and the Savoyards. The Palazzo d'Albis, where the Spanish king had stared outside the Aragonese windows, was now fronted with cafés in the Piazza Civica, filled with the echoes of drinkers, children playing, competing strands of music, and endless shops that catered to locals and tourists alike—and virtually no cars.

Perhaps history retains its guise best in a town without cars, or as few as possible.

Via Antonio Lo Frasso, where we had left our car, had its own story, however. The street was named after an adventurer from Alghero, who had fled the city after a love affair turned murderous, and then participated in the epic Battle of Lepanto in Greece, one of the storied naval battles between the Catholic states and the Ottoman Empire in 1571. Lo Frasso, however, earned that street sign for a different reason. A prolific writer, his chivalrous novel in verse, *Los Diez Libros De Fortuna De Amor*, was rediscovered and published in London in 1740, as one of the great masterpieces of Spanish literature. A well-meaning publisher noted that the famous Miguel de Cervantes had singled out the Algherese poet for his romantic verses in one of the dialogues of *Don Quixote*—except the Spanish author was likely writing in jest. The barber in *Don Quixote* refers to Lo Frasso's *Ten Books*, which included poems in the "Sardinian mountain language," as "the best and most singular" of absurd romances.

In Cervantes's lesser known work, *Journey to Parnassus*, he continued his obsession with the Algherese poet, threatening to throw him off the ship. There was certainly a lot of water under the bridge for the two authors, both of whom served in the navy battles in the Mediterranean in that period. Cervantes couldn't have hated Lo Frasso too much. He likely borrowed the name of his Dulcinea del Toboso, the queen in the delusional mind of Don Quixote, from Lo Frasso's own characters.

When we reached the bastion walls, which encircled the city like a shield from the sea, we stared in awe at *la rada di Alghero*, the bay or gulf of Alghero. It was a natural harbor, and one of the few on the island. The open sea, framed by the coast on that blue day, seemed boundless. The bastion walls, meanwhile, dropped at least fifty feet or so to the side, as we followed the promenade. Massive trees with trunks like elephant feet provided shade; medieval towers cornered each section with their sentinel role. Sardonicus pointed out the corners of the walls, where kids would scale the metal bars and clamor down the bastion stones, gripping on to the ashlar bricks in a harrowing display of either youth or madness, and then plunge into the sea for a swim. (There were injuries, he admitted.)

Across the open sea, the green-topped cliffs of the Capo Caccia promontory to the north looked back at the medieval city with its own forbidding fortress of stone. The front line of houses on the bastion, in their blue and green and colorful doors and shutters, stood in the light, as the sea whipped waves below. Farther down the bastion, each section named after an explorer, we passed rows of restaurants, sidestepping the cannons and medieval catapults set up along the walls, as if still awaiting invaders. Then, we looked over the walls at the bobbing sailboats lined row by row at the lattice of docks, at least two dozen of them in white and blue, hoisting their masts like a phalanx of pikes, ready to embark on some adventure. Toward the outer edge of the port rested the fishing boats, small with wooden helms, with clumps of colorful nets piled along the docks. Jutting off from the city walls, palm trees lined the main coastal road.

El meu viatge ha començat en una alba de molts anys enrere. Amb una ullada he creuat tots els espais que em separen de la nostra primera trobada vora la mar, Algherese chaunteuse Franca Masu sang in her song, "El meu viatge." "My journey began at dawn many years ago. With one glance I crossed all the spaces that separate me from our first encounter by the sea."

The sea, of course, hid the defining element of the city and its bay, perched on its medieval coat of arms and flag, and found in so many jewelry shops in the historic center: the beautiful red coral from the *Costera del Coral* in Alguerés, or *Riviera del Corallo* in Italian. The memory of the Sardinians itself, wrote Nereide Rudas in her fascinating book *L'isola dei coralli*, was like a precious coral reef, "tenacious and labyrinthine." Rudas, the first woman to found and direct a psychiatry institute in Italy, considered her book an "itinerary into identities" on the island.

A lot of identities and memories were hidden in that sea, we would soon learn, and that included the city's ancient history. Masu cited Sardinian writer Francesco Masala as an exemplar: "Describe your garden and you will become universal," he once said in an interview. Raised in Alghero, acclaimed for her jazz singing in various languages, including her work with American jazz bands, Masu made an intentional decision to reclaim her Algherese roots. Her songs we would soon enjoy, bumping into her at various festivals and town events. "By choosing Alguerès," she said, "I have become a world reference."

And it was beautiful, but beautiful, as the jazz world would say.

6 | SARDIGNA

Sardinia, to exist, must invent itself wild but clean, archaic but
with Wi-Fi, silent but a patient listener, welcoming but not flashy,
made of stone and wind but carefree. In short, a nice movie set
without protagonists.

—Alfonso Stiglitz, "Fenomenologia dell'isola che non c'è,"
Il Manifesto Sardo, 2022

At one of our favorite cafés on the bastion, overlooking the sea and
Capo Caccia as if we were on the platform of some great ship, I ordered
an Ichnusa, a popular Sardinian beer in Italy. Owned by the Dutch
company Heineken since the 1980s, Ichnusa ran a prize-winning ad
about the "uniqueness of the Sardinian soul." The soul of those "who
rebel," the ad put in for good measure.

Sure enough, the founder of the delicious brew, back in 1912—I
was partial to the "non-filtered" type—was named after Ampsicora,
the Sardinian Punic leader who led the uprising against the Romans
in 215 B.C. An hour away from the company's brewery in Assemini,
oxalic acid residue on ceramics pieces at the Nuraghe Arrubiu dated
the presence of a possible brew back to 1500 B.C. Barley appears to be
the grain du jour in those days.

Ichnusa was the Greek name for Sardinia, not a Nuragic one. The origins of the name of Sardinia by its native inhabitants is less clear.

"What the ancient name given to it by the natives may have been, I know not," Greek writer Pausanias wrote in the second century A.D., "but the Greeks who made trading voyages thither called it Ichnusa, because the shape of the island is very much like a man's footstep (*ichnos*)." The Sardinians responded in turn, according to the great traveler and geographer, sending to Delphi, the sacred temple complex of the oracles and center of the world, "a bronze statue of the hero after whom they are named. In size and wealth, Sardinia is a match for the most celebrated islands." That hero was Sardus, of course—or more formally, Sardus Pater, the Sardinian father.

We do not know the Nuragic name for the island. The origin of the word *nuraghe* is disputed, as well. A little spelling detail: *nuraghe* is singular, also written as *nurache* or *nuraxi* [in the Sardinan language variants], and *nuraghe*s, *nuraxis* or *nuraghi* [in Italian] as plural. We tended to use *nuraghe* and *nuraghi*, since Italian was our common language, but for the English reader in this book, I have decided to stay with the Sardinian *nuraghe* and *nuraghes*.

Michelangelo Pira, an important Sardinian anthropologist, writer, and language expert, noted that "nur" or "nurra" referred to a "heap" or "chasm" in the Sardinian language. Arguments have been made for pre-Indo-European and Paleo-Sardinian roots of "nur," while others see Semitic connections. The word "nurac" was carved into stone above the entrance to Nuraghe Aidu Entos at Bortigali: *Ili(ensium) iur(ale) in / Nurac(-) Sessar*, which referred to the *Ilienses*, one of the indigenous populations identified by the Romans. It dated back to the first century A.D. Other non-Latin or Greek inscriptions in stone, much to the dismay of some Sardinians, are still contested, though some linguists have offered their interpretations.

Srdn—that was the word used by the Phoenicians, on a stone table found near Nora. Dating to the ninth century B.C., the "Nora stele" is considered the oldest inscription in that alphabet in Europe. It remains an extraordinary document—in stone—at the National Archaeological Museum in Cagliari, a three-thousand-year-old historical bookmark of the enigmatic Phoenician traders and their alphabet, which would influence the Greeks and Etruscans—and the Sardinians. Translations of the stele remain unresolved, however. Linguists and archaeologists tended to differ over whether the inscription celebrated a consecration of a temple or a military victory on Sardinian soil, including a recent interpretation referencing the destruction of a nearby nuraghe. But the name of Srdn or Sardinia, clearly, was written in stone three thousand years ago. The Phoenicians, having roamed from the Levant across the Mediterranean, soon establishing the powerful city-state of Carthage in North Africa, would continue to settle themselves on the island.

Shrdn or Shardana or or Sherdanu—that was also used by the Egyptian Ramesses II on a stele in the thirteenth century B.C., referring to the "Sea People" who arrived in their ships, swords and shields unfurled, at the collapse of the Bronze Age. "The ethnonym Shrdn, recorded for the first time at the time of Pharaoh Amenophi IV," according to Sardinian archaeologist Giovanni Ugas, was still attested in Egypt at the time of the Nora stele. "It cannot be a coincidence that to designate the Sardinians, the Phoenicians used the same word (Sherdanu) used at the time of Amenophi IV and their Canaanite ancestors of Byblos to indicate the warriors of the sea in the service of the Egyptians."

"*Sardinia ab oriente patens,*" Pliny the Roman elder wrote in Latin, around 60 A.D., about the island's geography, which had been wrestled from the Carthaginians by the Romans in 238 B.C. in the aftermath of the First Punic War. While the usage of the word *Sardinia* stays the norm in all Roman writings for a few centuries, Pliny noted that Timaeus still referred to the island as *Sandaliotimus*—the sandal.

The Greeks, too, shifted to *Sardinia*, noted Procopius, the historian of the Justinian reign in the Byzantine Empire. "Now this island of Sardinia was formerly called Sardo," he wrote around 560 A.D., adding a wonderful detail that had endured for centuries among the Greeks. "In that place there grows a certain herb such that, if men taste of it, a fatal convulsion immediately comes over them, and they die not long afterward, having the appearance of laughing, as it were, as a result of the convulsion, this laughter they call 'Sardonic' from the name of the place." That herb was most likely *ranunculus sceleratus*, better known as crowfoot, buttercup, or wild parsley. Pausanias described it as looking like celery.

In *Sardinia*, Pope Gregory lamented in letters to clergy in 590 A.D., the people on the island still worshipped *ligna autem et lapides* (wood and stones), an admission of the endurance of the post-Nuragic rituals and culture long after the fall of the Roman Empire and the Vandals and Goths had climbed back onto their sinking boats. The Pope appealed as well as to Ospitone, the *dux Barbaricinorum* or leader of the mountainous region, to bring the last Sardinians into the Christian fold.

Sardinia eventually fell under the auspices of the eastern Byzantine Empire, until it, too, lost effective control in the 800s.

Sardūs, Sardīniya, Sardāniya, and *Sartānyia* appeared in Arab chronicles, including the brief period in 1015, when Muǧāhid al-Āmirī, ruler of the Islamic kingdom of Dénia and the Balearic Islands off Spain occupied parts of southern Sardinia.

Sardigna emerged as the name of Sardinia in the Sardinian language and would remain on all official documents for centuries of relative independence on the island, including the Carta de Logu code of laws, written in Sardinian in the late 1300s. Divided into four judicates or *judicadus* ruled by judges, as a holdover from Byzantine times, the *Rennu de Sardigna*, the Kingdom of Sardinia, was guided more by territorial rivalry than unity.

In Sardinna was how the island appeared in the *Libellus iudicum Turritanorum*, the Sardinian chronicles in the thirteenth century A.D., which documented the great journeys of Gonario the Judge in 1147 and his return to the island to establish monasteries. In the north, however, those in Sassari preferred *Sardhigna,* while others in Gallura opted for *Saldigna.*

Sardigna was used also by Dante, Boccacio, and Petrarca in their foundational Italian works in the late medieval age, as well as the cartographer Porcacchi in Venice in the late 1500s, though he inadvertently used *Sardegna* on the same page, as well.

En Cerdeña or *Sardeña,* Cervantes would have interrupted in Spanish in *Don Quixote,* having lived there in 1573, as a soldier. Let's not forget the domination of the Aragonese from the late 1300s, and then the Spanish until it was handed over to the House of Savoy in Italy in the early 1700s, as a bargaining chip in the disputes between empires. The Catalans and Aragonese had actually written *en Sardenya,* as the poet Eduard Tola reminded his readers during the revival of Alguerés in the late 1880s.

It appears, therefore, that the Spanish and Catalan left their accent on the island's name. From Srdn to Sardinia to Sardigna, we ended up with the modern Italian, *Sardegna.*

In Sardegna, on August 4, 1720, the Spanish handed over the keys to the kingdom to Viceroy Filippo Guglielmo Pallavicino, the baron of Saint-Remy, who accepted it on behalf of Victor Amadeus II, the Duke of Savoy, who had obtained Sardinia in exchange for Sicily, as if trading cards with Austria in the aftermath of the War of the Quadruple Alliance (it's complicated)—but, more importantly, inheriting the title, *il re di Sardegna*, the King of Sardinia.

In 1759, Italian became the compulsory language in school and official business under the Savoyards, in the Kingdom of *Sardegna*, an inevitable splicing of the indigenous, Latin, Spanish, and now Italian.

Sardigna, of course, never disappeared among the Sardinians. In 1904, poet Pompeo Calvia from Sassari, exhorted his fellow writers to invoke their native language and reclaim its name: *Poeta, tu chi sai, parchì non giri in tondu / Tutta chista Sardigna, e in mezzu e drentu e fora? Poeta, la Sardigna / No, no è iscuberta ancora. Abà iscobbrila tu, chista Sardigna amadda, terra dimintiggadda.*

"Poet, you who are good, / why don't you go through / All this Sardinia, / of the interior and the coasts? / Poet, Sardinia / No, it has not yet been discovered. / Now you discover it, / this beloved Sardinia, / forgotten land."

In Sardigna.

Or Sardegna, as the Italians still insisted.

Of course, when foreigners have told tales, I tried to take them apart.

—Sergio Atzeni, *Raccontar fole*, 1999

Every morning I went to pick up the newspaper from an elder vendor at a kiosk on our street corner. Our apartment sat on the edge of the old town, our top-floor veranda overlooking the port and the sea, which shifted in colors, turning to silver, as Sardinian novelist Paola Soriga wrote about Alghero in *La stagione che verrá*, "where the clouds make you want to chase after them." I could see Capo Caccia from one end, and the bell tower of the cathedral from the other, the palms swaying with their own pace.

One morning, I toted a leaking bag of fish in one hand and a sack of spiny Sardinian artichokes and *carasau* flatbread in the other. There would be no Sardinia without carasau bread, I had been warned, and we soon took to its wondrous wood-burning stove flavor and crisp durum wheat texture as part of our daily diet. And our jaunts to the fish market at the port? While Stanley Tucci had sampled the Alghero delicacy of lobster on his CNN program, *Searching for Italy*, I had gone for the mussels, monkfish, and mullet.

I noticed the newspaper vendor behind the racks of magazines, clearly lost in a book. "Wait a moment," he told me after I asked him again for the newspaper, as his eyes moved across the page, and then he licked a finger and turned to the next one. A shelf of books sat above his head.

I had noticed that vending machines at the Alghero airport and public places in Sardinia sold books by local authors and historians. This would be monumental in any country, but for a writer, this was very monumental, as it seemed like Sardinia's statement of purpose at its port of entry.

Even the comic books, which lined the front row of the kiosk, had Sardinian themes. Of course, Tex Willer, one of the most famous adult comics in Italy, was illustrated by Aurelio Galleppini (known as "Galep"), the son of Sardinian parents, who had spent his formative years back on the island, and left behind several frescoes in churches in Cagliari. Galep's childhood world of Sardinia unfolded into Tex Willer's adventures in the Far West. By the 1960s, Italian spaghetti westerns would also be filmed in the dusty-road village of San Salvatore di Sinis in Sardinia, including the *Garter Colt* hit, referenced in Quentin Tarantino's *Kill Bill*.

There are a lot of books you'd never find in those vending machines, especially unwritten ones. And then there are books you stumble on in the most unlikely places, especially those handed over by avid readers.

My newspaper vendor, whose name was Antonio, had once recounted to me his misfortune of being railroaded out of years of a pension as a printer back on *il continente*, as Sardinians referred to the Italian mainland. Hence, his need to work in his late age. He was more interested in books than selling newspapers or snacks. He regularly ignored clients, including me, it seemed, this morning.

He disregarded my second request for the newspaper, so I hefted my bag of stinking fish, huffed as if I was ready to leave, and then I turned and asked, "What are you reading, anyway?"

He held up a red book with a gaudy cover: *La Storia di Sardegna*. "There's so much to learn," he said. The book, published by *La Nuova Sardegna* newspaper, was part of a series.

"Storia di Sardegna, not *della* Sardegna?" I asked, double-checking my grammar.

The historian, Francesco Cesare Casula, Antonio explained, titled his series of books as *La Storia di Sardegna* for a reason, stressing the history of Sardinia, not the history of the region of Sardinia. Between the lines and prepositions, he told me, laughing, is the story of the Sardinian *nation* in history.

"We Sardinians must put it in our heads, it is Sardinia that made Italy, not the other way around," Antonio read from the book.

Writing histories of Sardinia was a risky business. When the first Sardinian historian, Sigismondo Arquer from Cagliari, published his brief chronicle of the "dark" island in the *Cosmographia* in 1550, noting the excesses of the corrupt lords and churches, he ended up in Spain, his tongue locked into an iron clasp, where he was tortured and burned at the stake in Toledo in 1571. He wasn't even relieved of the pain by being strangled before his inquisitors lit the match. Arquer's defiance certainly outlived the Inquisition; his work was translated in numerous languages, the *Cosmographia* (edited by German writer Sebastian Münster) becoming one of the most successful and widely read books of the sixteenth century.

More importantly, Arquer placed Sardinia into the orbit of early modern Europe—not a distant outpost of terra incognita.

When I asked if I could buy a copy of the *Storia*, Antonio raised up the book and shook his head. "This is part three," he said. "You have to start at the beginning." As I stood there, the fish poking its slimy fin out of the plastic bag, he added, "but if you come tomorrow, I'll bring the first ones."

He finally handed me the daily newspaper, and then asked where I lived. Americans were not so common, though he remembered stories of the raucous film crew for the film *Boom!*, which nearly cost actor Elizabeth Taylor her life on the outskirts of Alghero, when her dressing trailer cascaded over the cliffs. Despite being written by American playwright Tennessee Williams and starring Richard Burton (as the Angel of Death), the movie flopped in 1968. Not that Sardinia played any role in the movie, other than providing the empty stage of the gorgeous Capo Caccia cliffs. In fact, the movie director set up massive Easter Island heads, for some odd reason, on the edge of the cliffs, as if Sardinia didn't have any prehistory of its own.

My friend Sardonicus wrote about a pair of monkeys that came with the film and ended up roving around the Alghero area for ages, startling tourists on the beach.

I pointed at my street corner, Via Alberto La Marmora. "That's a start," my vendor said, smiling, referring to the patrician soldier exiled to the island after being suspected of participating in an uprising on the continent in 1821, only to become one of its modern historians. La Marmora published his *Voyage en Sardaigne* in 1826—in French—as a reminder of his role as an interpreter of Sardinia. His brother would become one of the first prime ministers of modern Italy.

The news vendor wasn't terribly impressed with La Marmora, outside of the fact that he had spent nearly four decades of his life on the island. The highest peak in Sardinia was renamed in his memory. In 1918, Americans held a ceremony at the mountain, in celebration of the opening of a Red Cross center for children. "For the first time in the history of the world," the *New York Times* cheered, "the American flag has waved on the highest peak rising in the middle of the Mediterranean."

That detail probably would have irritated Antonio. It reminded me that Americans had been meddling in this "unknown" part of Italy for a long time.

La Marmora wrote his books in French due to his Piedmont up-
bringing and schooling at a French military academy. His personal
story was quite harrowing. As a young soldier in Napoleon's armies, he
fought in the brutal campaigns in Prussia, and as far as Russia in 1813–
14, surviving war and epidemics. Captured and then abandoned by the
defeated forces, he eventually made his way back to Turin on foot. His
family found him unrecognizable. He was clearly traumatized. His
eventual exile to Sardinia was providential. His formidable insights
on Sardinia, including his pioneering travels, probably did more than
any other European writer of his period to take the Sardinian stories
to a larger audience, though that audience like himself, as Sardinian
author Maria Bonaria Urban noted in her landmark book, *Sardinia on
Screen*, focused on the "island as a silent geographical entity, a resource
awaiting those who—like him, a typical spokesman of the conservative positivism then in vogue—will know how to make the best use
of it." It took years, however, before they were translated into Italian,
which underscored the mainland interest in the island in the nineteenth century.

We will encounter La Marmora later in the book. He produced one
of the first scientific maps of the island; he was one of the first people to
write about deforestation and the plunder of the forests. La Marmora
also did indispensable work on the bronzetti and archaeology, including the nuraghes, though he assumed they had come from Egyptian
hands. The former soldier didn't mind getting his hands dirty. In one
of his own excavations at the Nuraghe Lugheria near Oschiri, he uncovered a marvelous bronze of a miniature coffin or chest mounted on
a cart with four wheels attached to axels. With engravings on the side,
the lid decorated with the horns of a bighorn sheep or mouflon, the
Bronze Age cart was a reminder of the mechanics of the times.

"If the reader has been tempted to compare me to the imaginary
journey created by the famous [Daniel de] Foé," La Marmora declared,

wanting to get beyond the travel writers who had depicted Sardinia as barbarous or "a vast field open to satire," he promised a thorough inventory of the facts on the ground, as much as he interpreted them.

Beware of an imaginary journey or an imaginary Sardinia, La Marmora warned. That was largely the story by outside writers, Urban masterfully showed. Not all, of course.

But the more I read about travelers and travel writers in Sardinia, the more I was reminded of the story of a roving band of English crusaders, who landed in Sardinia in 1075 A.D.—or thereabouts. Having fled England after the conquest of William the Conqueror, embarking in a large fleet of a few thousand soldiers, they headed for the shores of the Byzantine empire to pledge their allegiance. They raided communities along the way. Arriving in Sardinia, according to the chronicles of an English monk in Laon, France, as well as the Játvarðar Saga from Iceland in the fourteenth century, the English plundered along the Sardinian coasts with Christian impunity, carting off the jewels and wealth from supposedly pagan settlements. When they were finally informed that the Sardinians were, in fact, Christians, the Crusaders halted their attacks. They even returned the items they had stolen, and asked for forgiveness, but their damage to Sardinia was already done. Nonetheless, the Byzantine emperor eventually bestowed "honor and gifts" for their service after they had left the island and ventured on to the Middle East.

In hearing that Italian poet Gabriele D'Annunzio, who had made a short jaunt to the island in 1892, was planning to return to write a book, Sardinian novelist Grazia Deledda declared, "Why do we need D'Annunzio? And besides, he could never know us well, especially if he stays for such a short period of time, he would just falsify everything about us."

Deledda, of course, had reasons to worry. In 1792, the Jesuit Matteo Madao let loose an invective of outrage, after reading the travel writings of Swedish writer Jacob Jorna Bjoernstaehl, which he deemed to be "sickly slanderous" and with "outlandish descriptions." Published in various languages, including German in the 1780s, the Swede had subtitled his Sardinian notes: "Ignorance, Barbarism, and the Dirty Costumes of the Inhabitants."

In the early 1600s, French geographer Pierre d'Avity asked why "historians have remarked that islanders in general are more uncultivated than men that live upon a continent." In a survey on islands including Sicily and Sardinia, d'Avity concluded that "travelers are to blame, for giving bad opinions or false information," especially the young who travel in a "partial light," and return home to make "erroneous and false reports of the places they have been in."

Island books were quite the rage at one point in the post-Renaissance period, and even had their own genre: *Isolari.*

A few years before d'Avity's work, whose writings would influence John Milton's *Paradise Lost*, the Spanish writer Martin Carrillo came to a similar conclusion in Sardinia, though he was more scandalized by his own country's colonial treatment of the island: "All these authors were deceived and have not seen *Sardeña* as I have, to give a true relationship." While dispelling the negative stereotypes, Carillo did fall into depictions of exotic travel, as if writing about the discovery of a new world—Sardinia, as in "discovering" the Americas.

I brought a handful of books with me to Sardinia—two of Deledda's novels, *Cosima* and *Cenere* (Ashes), Milena Agus's *Mal di pietre* and Michela Murgia's *Accabadora*, both award-winning novels that had been translated into several languages. I had already read Emilio Lussu's hair-raising memoir on resisting fascism, *Marcia su Roma*, which had been translated in English as *Road to Exile: The Story of a Sardinian Patriot*. After a gripping escape from prison, its ending riposte in 1935 had stayed with me: Is Fascism going to last forever? The answer: "The world is going neither to the right nor to the left. It is still continuing to revolve on its own axis, with periodic eclipses of the sun and the moon."

I'd also found a book on eBay, a first edition of *Sardinian Sideshow*, by another bon vivant, Swedish author Amelie Posse-Brázdová, who was interned in Alghero in 1915 during World War I. Her Czech husband, an artist in Rome, had unwittingly fallen on the wrong side of enemy lines. Their internment didn't sound too dreary. They had their own apartment overlooking the sea. They had a maid. Posse-Brázdová had also met with Deledda in Rome, picking up tips on how to live among the "primitive" Sardinians.

An evening among poets and singers in Alghero, though, had a profound impact on her life. While the Swede had often heard poets in the streets, or seen the dueling poets at local bars, the *improvisatori* considered "courageous" and "manly," she was spellbound by the groups of tenore singers and poets who would gather from the countryside and visit Alghero on the weekends. Detailing the four-part harmonies and improvised melodies, she found the music to be "overpowering" and of "incomparable beauty." Posse-Brázdová wrote about having a near mystical experience, "something new and inexpressible," from this ancient music.

And then there was the other book in my bag: D. H. Lawrence, and his *Sea and Sardinia*. David Herbert Lawrence, as the Sardinians referred to him. *Lawrence of Sardinia*.

"This land resembles no other place," Lawrence wrote in 1921.

If only he had stopped with that great line.

8 | MONT'E PRAMA

Sas paghes postas in sos nuraghes non s'iscontzan mai.
The peace agreements stipulated inside the nuraghes never dissolve.

—Logudoresu proverb,
Dizionario Universale Della Lingua Di Sardegna

The gathering packed into the back of the building. It was advertised as an *incontro* and a *dibattito*, as if the organizers in Alghero weren't sure if the discussion on prehistoric Sardinia would be a low-key meeting or a brawling argument. The topic: "The Giants of Mont'e Prama and a New Representation of Sardinia." Hosted by the *Camineras* magazine, the event included a panel of writers, historians, architects, and archaeologists. It brought out a multilingual crowd of locals that avidly sought to participate in the discussion.

While I had participated in many archaeological meetings, including notable findings about the Hohokam civilization in southern Arizona, I had never witnessed this kind of urgency and passion about ancient history among such a crowd in my life. The room was electrifying. In Italian, Alguerés, and Sardu.

The extraordinary findings of the "Giants of Mont'e Prama" in Cabras, on the western side of the island, had become the defining site of historical recognition, and the debate that would "rewrite the history" of the Mediterranean during our first sojourn. Such a claim, however, still unnerved some scholars and historians, including those who were wary of boosterism based on lore rather than facts. Others continued to pick at the scab of a nineteenth-century hoax in Sardinia over falsified historical documents, as if mythology rather than archaeology trumped Sardinia's fate.

When a farmer uncovered a head carved from limestone, and then another, in his fields in Cabras, not far from Oristano, in 1974, it effectively launched a potential shift and a disturbing delay in the global recognition of Sardinia's trailblazing role in Europe's ancient history. A phalanx of nearly forty massive stone giants, reconstructed out of more than five thousand pieces, faced in the direction of the nearby sea and its invaders in an array of intricately sculpted archers, soldiers, boxers, and other outsized figures in a monumental funeral complex from the tenth and ninth centuries B.C. They had stood six to eight feet tall. They had once been surrounded by dwarf palm trees. Platforms and tombs completed the stunning necropolis. There were also carved models of the nuraghe towers, as if placing the memory of the island's architectural symbol in an eternal role.

Beyond any "rediscovery" or even "rewriting of history," the shattered artifacts of Mont'e Prama stood on display like survivors; that another force, a greater force from the outside, had sought to crush their existence back into dust, as if they had never existed; and yet, a resistance, a greater resistance to that force, had somehow kept the seeds of their stories alive, buried under twenty-five centuries or more of historical sediment, including Roman ruins and modern-day agriculture, only to flourish again.

To suggest Mont'e Prama was a scene of a crime would miss the point. Its destruction, still unknown for the motive, was not just a case of historicide; that was obvious, as with any act of organized violence against a civilization's sacred places. The giants of Mont'e Prama were not mere works of art; they had defended the sanctity of a necropolis, where 170 tombs had been discovered, dating back to the twelfth century B.C. To raze such sculptures into oblivion was an intentional act of denial of thousands of years of civilization.

Therefore, viewing the site today as one of mystery, and not as documented historicide of an ancient civilization and its architectural and artistic achievements, perpetuated the "dominant narrative," as Sardinian writer Omar Onnis wrote, "that Sardinia is a peripheral and insignificant portion of something else." The control over the narrative and its reflection of Sardinian history, ultimately, had become as important as the discovery itself on the island.

The stone pieces were collected and carted off to storage—for three decades. (For comparison, the discovery of the illustrious terracotta warriors in Xi'an, China, took place in the same year, and were put on display in 1982.) Whether it was over a lack of funding or forbearance, it took a citizen's movement to jump-start governmental support. By 2012, Peter Rockwell, an American sculptor and expert in the history and techniques of stone carving (and the son of the famous artist Norman Rockwell) concluded the sculptures of Mont'e Prama were "truly singular and unique" and indicated "a remarkable skill in the sculptural technique."

In unveiling plans for a new museum to display the sculptures in 2021, archaeologists and art experts recognized the Mont'e Prama giant anthropomorphic stone sculptures as the oldest in the Mediterranean, and as "one of the most remarkable discoveries made anywhere on Italian soil in the twentieth century." Exhibits of the giants, like ambassadors, began to journey to museums across Italy, Germany, France, Russia, and the United States. Columbia University in New York City, for example, ran an extensive online exhibition on "a lost culture in the heart of the Mediterranean."

The Italian newspapers, such as the *Corriere della Sera*, hailed Mont'e Prama as the "Pompei of Sardinia." The kicker: Mont'e Prama was "rewriting" the history of the Mediterranean. That line of a historical shift in the narrative carried its own importance into the corridors of debate—and the hope for more exhaustive excavations.

Not long after the panel discussion, we made our first of many journeys to Cabras and its Giovanni Marongiu Civic Archaeological Museum, and to nearby Oristano, one of the more enigmatic cities on the island. Oristano required patience, and the generosity of a local guide, to find the keys to its marvels in architecture, cuisine, and literature. Home of *Sa Sartiglia*, a series of extraordinary horse races and chivalrous jousting during the Carnival season of Lent that dated back to the medieval period, the inland city of Oristano had gained prominence by 1070 A.D., when it became the seat of the bishop and capital of the judicadu of Arborea.

While the city maintained the spirit of Eleonora of Arborea, the beloved judge who had ushered in an updated era of laws under the Carta da Logu in the 1390s, the task of sorting history from myth and its fraudulent versions, had been in the modern hands of native writers like Peppetto Pau, *il cantore di Sinis*, and Michela Murgia, a novelist, essayist, and "L'Antitaliana" columnist for the national *L'Espresso* magazine, who served as a truth-teller for our modern times.

The entire area of the Gulf of Oristano, and farther north along the Sinis Peninsula, stretched like an ancient map of Mediterranean ventures over thousands of years. For starters, the endless platters of fish varieties, including the golden *bottarga di muggine*, at several restaurants along the lagoon of Cabras deserved their own monument.

As noted in 1861 by the clergyman archaeologist Spano, the coastal city of Tharros, which had originally been the regional capital, "dominated" the entire Gulf of Oristano to the east, and the Sardinian

Sea to the west, with piers and harbors built from "cyclopean boulders" that allowed for great ships to anchor. Tharros, with its excavated ruins from the Phoenician (eighth century B.C.) and later Roman periods, jutted off the hill of a peninsula like a fabulous amphitheatre. It was an incredible place to visit, sit back on the stone walls and simply contemplate the coasts with its possibilities. In fact, the city had evolved into one of the important trading centers of the Mediterranean in the Bronze and Iron Ages, especially in the markets of ceramics, and gold, silver and other precious metals, until it was abandoned in the tenth century A.D., due to outside attacks. The Phoenicians, as well as the Romans, left behind the impressive infrastructure of urban life and paved streets, and its jewels and ornate expressions, as well as burial tombs, that tended to frame the archaeology of the region.

Yet, as with virtually every corner of Sardinia, Tharros had emerged from the foundations of a Nuragic settlement. Along with establishing the port of Tharros, the nearby S'Uraki (or S'Urachi) Nuraghe of San Vero Milis, according to archaeologist Raimondo Zucca, had been "a catalyst for trade." In the same area of the Mont'e Prama statues, he added in a report, was "an important Nuragic road" between Tharros and Nurachi. Excavations at a nuraghe in the nearby Murru Mannu area had even turned up Mycenaean pottery from 1400 B.C., "demonstrating wide-ranging trade" with Greece and beyond, prior to the Phoenicians.

The complexity of this ancient story, though, was just beginning to be revealed in Cabras, and on the entire island.

Using pioneering geo-radar technology in a larger area around the stone sculptures, geophysicist Gaetano Ranieri from the University of Cagliari identified more anomalies in 2014 that corresponded to roads, walls, tombs, and even other statues in the Mont'e Prama area. He called it "the greatest archaeological discovery in the western Mediterranean in the last fifty years," still waiting to be excavated.

Below the soil, Ranieri concluded, the next chapters of history were asking to be recovered in order to be rewritten, as well. Given the extraordinary importance of the site, and its significance for Sardinia—and Italy, and Europe—as well as tourist potential, the delay in following up Ranieri's assessment certainly confounded most observers.

At the Civic Archaeological Museum in Cabras, the giants on displayed demanded some sort of explanation. The concentric circles for eyes on the sculptures were not haunting, but inquisitive. Some sported long plaits for hair. The precision on the grips of the archer was impressive. The immensity of their size, of course, especially within the context of their numbers having once stretched along a necropolis as representative figures of the island's rituals and ways, did not suggest a mystery to be solved, but a story to be told.

In the spring of 2022, in fact, two more giant heads emerged at new excavations at the Mont'e Prama site, once again drawing international media coverage. In Rome, government officials scrambled to hail the two "new jewels." Local groups, including the Mont'e Prama Foundation, the town of Cabras, and the superintendent's office for archaeology in Cagliari, continued to ramp up plans for future projects. Could there be a Natural Archaeological Park of Sinis, from Mont'e Prama to Tharros and the wider area, for example? In the meantime, much to the chagrin of advocates, a farmer had been allowed by authorities to continue his vineyard on the edge of the official site, which was only a small portion of what had been surveyed as part of a larger complex.

Archaeology in Sardinia, like a dream deferred, was a heavy load.

PART TWO

SOS MANNOS
THE ANCESTORS

Frailariu 'e cantones friscas
camino a tempus de luche
pudande sos mezus frores
in custa paca die chie m'abbarrat
prontu a intrare
in su nurache 'e s'umbra.

Blacksmith of fresh poems
I walk in the time of light
picking the best flowers
in the remains of the day,
ready to enter
the nuraghe of shade.

—Pedru Mura, "Fippo operaiu 'e luche soliana," 1963

9 | POSTCARD FROM SANT'ANTIOCO: THE ARCHER

Mir was the first to make the little bronze men with horns, many eyes and many arms. He put them in the landings and on the boulders along the paths.

—Sergio Atzeni, *Passavamo sulla terra leggeri*

We packed up the car one weekend, skirting down the dramatic road along the coast south of Alghero, trying not to stop every thirty seconds to take a photo of the endless coastline of cliffs and crashing waves, until we reached the colorful hill town of Bosa. The climb up the narrow alleys of Bosa seemed like blocks out of a painting, each building and house taking turns with the color. A stone carver, sitting outside his home, greeted us as if we were neighbors. We stopped and chatted. We ended up sharing a glass of wine with his brother, who joined us as if we had made an appointment. A little plaque on one wall for *mutuo soccorso*, mutual aid, began to make sense in Bosa.

From the top of the medieval fortress, we looked down on the Temo River as it snaked through the valley, slicing the town in half with a shade of dark blue, until it arrived at the sea. Uncovered during renovations a half century ago, the frescos at the Chiesa di Nostra

Signora di Regnos Altos, inside the fortress, had revealed the haunting story of the "three living and the three dead." Dating back to an
anonymous painter in the 1300s, the ghosts on the wall admonished
the rich travelers of the time that they could not take their wealth to
paradise with them. We departed Bosa with that admonition.

Heading inland, we connected to the main highway south, and
then crossed the Campidano valley, aiming for the southwestern coast.
It might have seemed like a long journey, but we were in search of a
nuraghe—and its famed defender. This trip, in fact, was about a crime,
and a tomb raider who had made this same journey a half century before us. A rare artifact from a Nuragic site had been stolen, placed on
the world market, displayed in a famous museum, only to be rescued
and brought back to the island in a bizarre twist of intrigue.

We finally made it to Sant'Antioco, an island off an island that
jutted out into the Mediterranean Sea as the southern entry gate to
Sardinia, the polar opposite of La Maddalena. Pink flamingos, standing in the lower water, had watched us cross over the land bar and
bridge, which made me wonder if they had done the same with the
Phoenicians and Romans.

The history of Sardinia is written in the stacks of stones, we had
been told. That becomes real when you see the remains of a nuraghe,
and then another, and even more, until you realize there are more than
seven thousand of these Bronze Age monuments across the island. Or
rather, seven thousand that have survived. Nearly two centuries before
our journey, French travel writer Antoine-Claude Pasquin—known as
Valéry—bemoaned the "indifference" to the Nuragic towers that had
been "demolished" for fences and by "hidden treasure seekers."

We spent the night in a unique agriturismo, the breathtaking Erbe
Matte campsite at the saddle of a bluff, where we watched from our
hammock and platform bed as the moon descended into the sea off the
southwestern tip of the island. We rose early the next morning. Our

destination was nearby. We took a dirt side road, no one in sight, as if following a winding route from the past. Then we saw the pyramid slope of the hill from a distance, where the boulders seemed to have been swallowed by the windswept forest of Mediterranean scrub.

We left our car by the remains of a stone house, which had a collapsed roof slumped like a lean-to for the last shepherd who had claimed this space for his sheep, and then moved on. We followed the trail along the rock walls, past an unmarked sign, the dwarf palm trees and their fans, the myrtle branches gone wild, and more rock walls that had been cribbed from even more ancient rock settlements.

Built from ashlar masonry and cut stones, the nuraghe towers included internal staircases and corbelled domes. Archaeologists used the term "cyclopean," in reference to the huge blocks moved by the mythical three-eyed cyclops in Mycenaean Greece. This particular complex of four massive stone towers straddled a hill with the imposition of a fortress, with a nearby sacred water temple that had been built a thousand years before the Roman Empire. Some nuraghe towers were huge—as tall as eighty to one hundred feet. The corbelled domes (an early form of the arch), according to archaeologists, predated their Greek counterparts, on the heels of the ancient Egyptians. Whether they functioned as temples, fortresses, gathering places, or palaces for the elite remains unclear. But they were grand.

"A most remarkable country, this Sardinia!" *Scientific American* magazine had exclaimed in 1899. Placing the Bronze Age Sardinian artifacts within the context of the Mediterranean, the venerable magazine continued: "The natives were far superior to their neighbors, as is proved by the number of monuments which still exist, after the lapse of so many thousands of years, to excite the wonder of all who visit the island; we refer to the *nuraghi*."

The trail veered off through a green swath of high *macchia* shrub. We began to make the gentle climb through holm oaks, sage, spurge olive, and strawberry trees. It was thick. The trail was rocky. With each step I thought about how many people had tread these same rocks over three thousand years. The stone towers held fast from a cascade of rubble and boulders at the top of the hill, as if pushing through the overgrown canopy with one last thrust for recognition.

The immensity of the stones at the top of the hill stopped me first, as if I had to understand how an ancient people had quarried, cut, carved, and transported such blocks to the top of a ridge, and then assembled them with a precision to last for centuries, if not thousands of years. This nuraghe was not even a great example; its form had been reclaimed by nature.

Stopping at an overlook, I could see the jagged drop of the cliffs along the nearby coast; down by the water, the breathtaking natural arches emerged from the waves, and then the wild shores along the Porto Sciusciau, where boats had landed thousands of years ago. On a clear day, the settlement could have picked up the faint line of the coasts of North Africa, less than 150 nautical miles away. In the opposite direction, the hills sloped like a savannah, the oaks breaking up the once-fertile agricultural plain of Canai.

Our journey had actually begun back at the namesake town of the island, Sant'Antioco, but that was a modern name, and a religious one. Sant'Antioco had been the first Christian martyr in Sardinia, the saint that came from the sea, *damnatio ad metalla* or condemned to the Sardinian lead mines by the Romans as punishment for his religious fervor in his native North Africa. The Romans had renamed the island after its lead deposits—Plumbaria. But they were latecomers, too. The seafaring Phoenicians from the Levant, who had arrived at the island around the ninth or eighth century B.C., had established their own port of Sulki among the indigenous Nuragic people that would become Sant'Antioco.

Nearby was Cape Refuge, or *Maladroxia*, the Phoenician landing, as if they knew their good fortune to be on the island; as if they knew that all settlements on Sardinia would forever be stacked onto the foundational stones of the nuraghes like foreign offerings placed over the original sanctuaries of ancient gods. The high concentration of these elaborate nuraghe towers served as a sort of stone flag for Sardinia and eventually gave name to the Nuragic civilization in the Bronze and Iron Ages.

More than forty nuraghes abounded across this tiny island alone. Menhirs and other artifacts provided the foundations of a remarkable cycle of civilizations that dated back more than seven thousand years.

While an estimated 50 percent of Sardinia's toponyms or place names in some regions came from pre-Roman indigenous languages—compared to 2 percent in the rest of Europe—there was no record of the Nuragic name for the island.

There was a display of Sant'Antioco's bones under glass in the town Basilica, found in the catacombs in 1615. Some considered him the patron saint of Sardinia.

But we had come for an even older display, and a different figure.

It had seemed so small in the glass case at the museum, straddling the piece of stone, with these two long unwieldy horns thrusting up on his helmet, as if challenging anyone to a charge. Yet, this miniature figure in bronze, a little over eight inches tall, which was tall for the rest of the pieces in the Bronze Age collection, stood there with a gesture of confidence, his hand outstretched in an offering, as if willing to tell the story of his twisted journey.

A few centuries before Homer composed the *Odyssey*, the Sardinians cast miniature bronzes or bronzetti, including ships, among hundreds of other types of bronze pieces. They were vessels of stories. Found mainly in sacred water temples or a rare tomb, they served as exquisite votive offerings dating back to the twelfth or eleventh centuries B.C.

The bronze boats rarely journeyed with an empty cargo. With an oversized horned deer or bull on the prow, some carried oxen figures pulling wheeled carts; others had hunting dogs and boars, doves, and deer. Some included monkeys, as if the bronze boats had returned from the nearby shores of North Africa with an ark of nature, ideas, and more stories. Keep in mind: Sardinian traders of obsidian, the razor-sharp black volcanic glass procured at Monte Arci in the southwestern part of the island, had been distributing their wares around the Mediterranean since the sixth millennium B.C.

Bronzetti statuettes lined up with musicians and singers, shepherds, enchanters and enchantresses, archers, wrestlers, and soldiers and more archers, dancers, drinkers, mothers, and children, among a vast array of figures. They accompanied the boats at the water temples and shrines with offerings to the daily ghosts. In 1865, a shepherd uncovered a trove of bronzetti at the Nuragic sanctuary site of Abini in the heart of the central mountains, including an otherworldly figure with four arms and four eyes, with two long horns jutting from its helmet, holding the two round shields that some associated with the ancient Shardana or "People of the Sea" that arrived in Egypt, while others believed it referred to Plato's "Symposium" on the original four-eyed humans divided in half by Zeus.

These tiny artifacts, often no more than five to twelve inches, spread across sacred sites on the island, including the most remote uplands, and then crossed over the sea into Etruscan tombs, at numerous sites in Tuscany, Lazio, and Apuglia. They journeyed along the Italian boot of civilizations, entering the Greek Sanctuary of Hera Lacinia at the tip of Calabria, on the Ionian Sea, on the eastern coast of Italy.

One elongated figure of a woman who carried a water jug on her head had been found at the Nuraghe Cabu Abbas o Riu Mulinu near Orosei on the eastern coast, dating back to 900 B.C. She also carried the reminder of the influence of the Sardinian artisans on the Etruscans; Nuragic bronzetti had been found in numerous Etruscan sites. The Etruscans' own thin bronze figures would eventually shape the work of celebrated Swiss artist Alberto Giacometti, one of the giants of modern art. Giacometti's sculptures shifted after a visit to an Etruscan exhibit, seeing the "Shadow of the Evening" figure forged several centuries after the Nuragic water carrier.

Each one of these boats, like the hundreds that remained behind in Sardinia, observed archaeologist Fulvia Lo Schiavo, was "not only a work of refined artistic craftsmanship and a precious and sacred object," but it was also "in itself a story and a message," following its own cosmology and narrative.

The Cleveland Museum had hailed one bronzetti figure as an "exceptionally fine example" of bronze work in the lost-wax method, produced by "a rather mysterious group of people who lived in Sardinia in the first millennium B.C. and who left no written records." In the catalog of their notable acquisitions in 1991, the American museum dated the artifact back to the ninth century B.C. They called it "the warrior," and used it as the logo for a section in the museum.

Anyone in Sardinia would have called it "the archer," given the extraordinary longbow hanging off the shoulder of the figure, the distinctive arm guard on the left forearm, a quiver for the arrows on his back. At least, that's what Lieutenant Roberto Lai thought when he saw the Polaroid photo of the bronze figure for the first time. Serving with the heritage protection unit of the Carabiniere police, Lai (no relation to Maria Lai) had been placed in charge of sorting through a treasure trove of documents and artifacts traced to a notorious trafficker of art in Basel, Switzerland, in the mid-1990s. Thanks to two strange, fatal car crashes in Sardinia over a ten-year period, both of which left behind briefcases of cash, diaries with addresses of clandestine diggers and their contacts, and a chart of acquisitions, Lai was able to connect the dots with the infamous Swiss brigand and his warehouse.

Turning over the photo of the archer, Lai got the surprise of a lifetime. "Grutt'e Acqua" was scrawled across the back, tracing the piece to its origins at the 1500 B.C. Nuragic site on the smaller island of Sant'Antioco, where Lai had grown up. It was neither "mysterious," that fulsome code word often trotted out to cover a lack of historical inquiry, nor legally acquired, in Lai's view.

Lai knew the legacy of the nuraghe at Grutt'e Acqua or *Grutti 'e Acqua*, variously translated as "the grottoes of water," or "the grottoes and water," was not just a pile of rocks, but an intricate architectural wonder of waterways and millennial planning. But he wasn't alone.

The tomb raider also knew, like any shepherd in Sardinia, that the ornate water temples or sacred wells nearby housed the bronze sculptures that had been left as communal offerings. Trudging up our same path, the raider most likely bypassed the Nuragic reservoir that sat at the basin of the hill, a green pool encased by small boulders with the mystic air of a lake in the woods. I couldn't help wonder: How many bronze pieces, daggers, necklaces, and pots rested under the water in the mud?

"Electrified" by the discovery of the photo and its connection to his island, Lai followed the trail left by the trafficker, his Polaroid in hand, only to come up empty-handed with its match to any institution or collector. Where had the archer gone? No final receipts of his transactions were to be found.

The cultural heritage detective didn't give up. Over the next few years, he obsessively dug through any announcements or catalogs or listings at museums, auctions, and private collections with artifacts from Sardinia and Italy. The collections were endless. They still are today.

An entire book on ancient Sardinian artifacts behind lock and key at the British Museum dated back to "boatloads" of "very remarkable" items that had been plundered at thirty-six tombs in the 1850s. Much of it came from the Tharros and Mont'e Prama areas. The British Museum had its own Sardinian archer, too, though he dramatically drew back his arrow, as if to protect himself. The Getty Museum in Los Angeles featured its Nuragic archer, though it differed in the details. In 1990, the *New York Times* featured a show at the Merrin Gallery in New York City: "Bronzes Conjure Up Images of a Fabled Past." It included the "raw power" of a Nuragic priest from the ninth century B.C. (The Merrin Gallery would be embroiled in fraud and the acquisition of "questionable antiquities" for years.)

In fact, hardly any major archaeological museum didn't have artifacts from the Bronze Age in Sardinia. While Christie's famous auction house once called off a million-dollar auction for a four thousand-year-old stone carving from the island in 2014, after the Italian police objected to the "robbery of the heritage and civilization of Sardinia," it still continues to peddle Sardinian bronzes. One five-inch Nuragic figure from the Bronze Age went for $125,000 during our sojourn in 2017. It came from a private dealer in Switzerland.

The trafficking of these prized pieces, among other riches, was an old tradition, of course, dating back to the Roman period. In 1365, the governor of Cagliari brought ancient jewels dug up from a prehistoric site to the Court of Spain, as an elaborate offering from the island. The honeycombing of ruins was so bad that a law was passed in 1481 to stop the digging for treasure, especially among the clergy. Not just for jewels. By the mid-sixteenth century, a common proverb recounted how the stone walls of the Nuragic, Phoenician, and Roman city of Tharros were "transported away in cartloads." In 1851, the pioneering archeologist and clergyman Giovanni Spano called on government officials to protect the prehistoric sites, which he feared had fallen into the hands of "other people who will not know how to appreciate them."

In 1923, *National Geographic* magazine lamented the national pastime of tomb raiders and archaeological thieves in Sardinia, as if the craze hadn't let up.

Even the Nazis craved Sardinian artifacts. During a visit to the island in the late 1930s, Adolf Hitler's deputy Hermann Göering attempted to take a priceless glass-beaded necklace that had been recently excavated at a Punic necropolis dating to 300 B.C. Jewish archaeologist Doro Levi, who had led several important excavations in Sardinia, managed to hide the artifact. When the Racial Laws dramatically changed the lives of Jews in Italy in 1938, Levi ended up in the United States.

So did the Nuragic archer, as Lai finally discovered. One evening, scrolling online, doing his usual regimen of going museum by museum, the Sardinian detective landed on the Cleveland Museum of Art site. He was stunned by the match. It was the archer in his Polaroid.

It took eighteen months of high-level negotiations, including the involvement of the attorney general in Ohio, but the Sardinians managed to convince the American museum to return the stolen artifact. In exchange, in fact, the Italian government had to agree to two conditions: that the archer, among other stolen goods, would be returned to its native place, and that Italy would loan thirteen exhibits of similar value for the next twenty-five years.

"If anyone ever landed, evading surveillance, finding them, he would have known that he had come across the land of horned men dancing on the cliffs," Atzeni wrote in his inventive novel of the Sardinian origin story, *Passavamo sulla terra leggeri*.

When the archer finally arrived at the Ferruccio Barreca Archaeological Museum in Sant'Antioco in 2009, Lai stood by for its installation. The archer's placement in that little glass case was deceiving with its significance. The detective would eventually write a book, as well as a graphic novel, on the true crime adventure, as well as other histories of Sant'Antioco. Lai declared the Nuragic archer had returned to "where history had placed it."

Or recovered it, perhaps.

The history of Sardinia, especially the extraordinary findings from its Nuragic civilization in the Bronze Age, seemed to be in a state of eternal recovery.

Online, and in person, a fierce citizens' movement lamented that the Grutti 'e Acqua ruins, like most of the Nuragic era monuments from the Bronze Age, had yet to be fully excavated. We left them that day, as they were, swallowed up by nature. Before we climbed down the hill, I felt the warm brush of the *sirocco* winds that had crossed over from the North African deserts, as they had for thousands of years. Our journey felt more like the marking of a burial ground than a place of discovery. As we pulled onto the dirt road, I looked back at the hill and its hidden nuraghe with a feeling of regret. It made me imagine what the tomb raider had thought, climbing into his own vehicle, the priceless artifacts loaded into his trunk. For he, in truth, had made the amazing discovery.

"I am an ancient, patient goldsmith," wrote the poet Stefano Susini from Sant'Antioco in 1928. "Always a treasure shines in front of me . . . and the other stones laugh in the embroidery of the sonnet."

One final note: a Nuragic warrior and bull, while only three inches tall, remained behind in Cleveland.

10 | RE-STORYING HISTORY

History does not belong only to its narrators, professional or amateur. While some of us debate what history is or was, others take it into their own hands.

—Michel-Rolph Trouillot, *Silencing the Past*

Crossing back over to the mainland, we wound through the mining country of the southwest to reach a crossroads near Gonnesa. We had already passed through the town of Iglesias, which had kept its medieval charm of churches and narrow streets; the town, in fact, had been the first royal city to be recognized in the new Kingdom of Sardinia in 1327. Yet, the mines had always defined Iglesias, dating back to pre-Nuragic settlements. At one point, an estimated twenty thousand miners toiled underground in the area. The town had also sent out its own acclaimed artists, including the miner poet Salvatore Poddighe, who we will discuss later in the book, and the enchanting singer-songwriter Marisa Sannia, the first Sardinian female performer at the national San Remo music festival, who took second place in 1968, and continued to write and perform in three languages on the national television stage.

The rugged coast was in view. The flares of light in the Sulcis-

Iglesiente region illuminated the turn off for a dirt road, a Bronze Age roadside attraction, winding up a rocky hill, and then to a clearing from one of our memorable journeys.

We arrived at the Nuraghe Seruci. Cars spread out in every direction like a secret gathering. A large crowd had already assembled. It almost felt like the village around the nuraghe had come alive. And in the middle of a circle of onlookers, as if taking part in a ritual, two figures emerged around the flames of a fire.

The muscles bulged on Andrea Loddo's arms as he stoked a cauldron, sparks flying into the air like spirits taken aflame. The fire lunged, the shadows danced in the background, and then the evening breeze carried the trails of smoke to the nearby base of the nuraghe. The flickers on the ashlar walls were dancing, too, as if we were sitting in front of the stage of a Bronze Age theatre, the walls stacked behind us like an immovable *scaenae frons*, Andrea and his assistant, both dressed in sleeveless tunics frayed at the bottom, clustered around the fire with gloves and stokers.

Andrea called himself an experimental archaeologist. The Nurnet crowd, the *appassionati* or passionate ones in the field of archaeology, clearly saw him as a mix of labors—part archaeologist, part artisan, and part performance artist. In truth, he saw himself as an advocate for the revitalization of the Nuragic civilization ever since he left behind a career as a surveyor and dedicated himself to the ancient arts. Growing up in the eastern Ogliastra region, Andrea had been beguiled by his visits as a child to the Nuragic sites near his town, many of which had retreated into the undergrowth.

Working with clay, leather, and now bronze, he moved around the fire with the expertise of a blacksmith, as he lowered the mold into the flames. The fire changed colors. Tools and leather sacks of instruments, as well as stones, surrounded him. Waiting in this communal gathering place, we watched the fire as it reached a certain temperature.

Andrea, meanwhile, explained how he had also taught himself the tanning trade well enough to fashion the Bronze Age outfits so fittingly designed in the bronze pieces. Those traditional outfits had also been used in films and festivals. He had spent years perfecting the process of forging bronzetti figurines. In the summer of 2020, joined by world champion sailboat skipper Andrea Mura, he also launched his first Nuragic boat into the sea, modeling it on the bronzetti figures.

The Nuraghe Seruci perched on the hill in the background, one of the largest on the island, with a center tower as high as sixty feet, surrounded by five other towers. A bulwark or outer wall was still visible; hundreds of stone huts had been part of the settlement. The burial tombs, as communal sites, were farther down the hill. The view from the nuraghe towers would have spanned out to the grey night expanse along the southwestern seacoast, serving as a key weigh station in the heart of the mining areas.

Discovered in 1897, the nuraghe dated to the fourteenth century B.C. Even though an Italian archaeological magazine in 1911 hailed the massive site for shining a new light on the Nuragic civilization on the island, it wasn't fully excavated for another century.

From the great sea, foreign sailors dating back to the Bronze Age had witnessed the mastery of the nuraghe towers, thousands upon thousands of single and multiple tower complexes that thrust off the cliffs and coves like sentinels, dotted the hills and valleys with an undulating chain of thriving communities, and eventually shifted into water temples and sanctuaries that drew legions of pilgrims. The nuraghes did not go unnoticed in the ancient chronicles. The works of Pseudo-Aristotle, written in Greek in the third century B.C., noted the "beautiful buildings and *tholos* [circular domes] finished in excellent proportions" on this island of towers.

Two thousand years later, *The Nation* magazine came to the same conclusions, sending off a correspondent to do a feature on the nuraghe towers in 1900. He was astounded by their presence—and the sheer numbers. "The clearest impression of the vast numbers of these towers are in some places so close together as to remind one of the 'Temperance Map' of London, in which each red spot stands for a tavern."

All one had to do now was download an app by the Nurnet archaeological organization on their iPhone for the map, and begin their journey back in time.

Walking with the microphone around the fire, Andrea explained the process of working with wax, melting copper to create the alloy, as he returned to the fire. He withdrew the gloves to show where he had been severely burned in his first attempts. He had collected herbs to heal himself like the Old Ones.

There was a powerful anticipation about Andrea's work, and his intensity. The crowd gathered closely when he and his assistant withdrew the molds from the fire, sparks flying on cue, and watched with awe as the bronzetti figures were revealed and cooled. I wondered if the Nuragic people did the same around their artisans. Within a short time, Andrea passed around the exact replica of a famous mother and child artifact that had been forged the same way, three thousand years ago.

The art of creating archaeology and making it anew, as opposed to locking it in a case, was riveting. Regrettably, it was too late to stave off the tomb raiders and museum collections. (In Arizona, I recalled how indigenous artists started producing replicas of petroglyphs on ceramic pieces, with the intent of persuading people to stop destroying and stealing the original ones on the desert stones.) Everyone held on to the bronzetti figures, flashing photos on their phones, as if they had become part of the discovery. I imagine those photos soon circulated on social media, in a leapfrog of technology, albeit along the continuum of the Nuragic ways.

The bronzes expanded the archives, so to speak, on this island of stories and storytellers. Similar bronzetti traditions took place in Cyprus, and among the Minoans in Crete, of course, and ideas likely exchanged like wine. Such an exchange of libraries, in many respects, opened with the sea, as the many bronzetti boats reminded us. "I remember my father, a great sailor," wrote Nicola Porcu in his book *Hi-Nu-Ra*, about his research as the "honorary inspector" of underwater archaeology in Sardinia. "To be able to narrate and write about the history of Sardinia you must first go to sea," his father told him.

There were also bronze figurines of orators, singers, and musicians, including the launeddas, the three-piped instrument made from reeds that still led dancers and singers and processions today. The most well-known launeddas bronzetti emerged in the northern town of Ittiri, the ithyphallic player, whose large phallic symbol suggested some fertility ritual of regenerating life.

Regeneration, in fact, drove Andrea's work. His concern that the Nuragic civilization had been "erased from history and memory," propelled these efforts to recreate their arts, including the lost-wax molds to shape the intricate bronzetti.

Erasure was a harsh term, but a clear one. I have called it "historicide" in other books: the conscious act of decimating a culture's presence in whatever present we inhabit, not merely the destruction of one's past or landscapes. The Romans even codified it into law, the edict of *damnatio memoriae* ensuring the literal destruction of monuments, documents, and evidence of someone's existence that had been condemned.

That any Nuragic ruins still survived, nearly four thousand years after their construction, would be a testament to the genius of any engineer and craftsman; that any Nuragic cultural ways still breathed fire into a cauldron of ore, and put art and stories into the hands of an artisan, honored more than a civilization's resilience. It testified to the deep roots of that culture and its foundations that still existed in Sardinia—thousands of years after the Phoenicians had permeated the island during a period of major upheaval and shift in the Late Bronze Age of the Nuragic civilization, and introduced vastly different social and cultural ways.

The presence of the nuraghes, and such rituals, also spoke of a form of passive resistance over thousands of years. Imagine a militaristic Carthaginian empire that had brutally seized most of the island around 500–480 B.C., instituted its regime's feudal ways and control over the agricultural fields and pastures, including slavery, and dismantled thousands of years of what archaeologist Emma Blake called a tradition of an acephalous cohesion or decentralized forms of governing across the island.

And then imagine a Roman empire overturning a collapsing Carthaginian system, without any provocation or "justice" according to the historian Polybius, and letting loose the hounds of war in their conquest of most of the island. The death toll among the Roman campaigns became so immense that by 174 B.C., Tiberius Sempronius Gracchus had installed a tablet in the shape of the island in the Temple Mater Matuta in Rome, with a memorial that his army had slain or captured eighty thousand Sardinians. There were so many enslaved Sardinians dumped into the market in Rome that they coined the term *Sardi venales*, "cheap and worthless as Sardinians."

The destruction of cities—and the disappearance of entire civilizations—was an old story, of course. The Etruscan civilization emerged long after the Nuragic; by 280 B.C., one of the last holdouts to the Romans fell in Vulci. Within two hundred years, the Etruscan world had assimilated into the Roman one. The great city of Sybaris on the Gulf of Taranto in Italy, for example (which gave us the word *sybaritic*, meaning extravagant or full of sensuous pleasure), was hailed by

Herodotus and others as one of the richest in the Mediterranean. It lasted only a few hundred years, vanishing in conflict below the sediment of a river and ruin by 400 B.C.

The remains of the Nuragic civilization still held their ground, in abundance. The thousands of nuraghe towers framed the borders of every region, and almost every village or town, with the exception of the Campidano valley, where the Carthaginians, Romans, and modern agriculture had intensified the cultivation of the land. You simply couldn't ignore the architectural role of the nuraghe in defining the foundations of Sardinian placemaking.

While historicide would include monuments and temples, of course, and works of art and literature, perhaps the more elusive but powerful roles of language, rituals, songs, and indigenous cultural ways were most terrifying to colonizers. This also included the narrative of memory, and the process of obliterating and replacing the narrative of one's ancestors in the continuum of our own lives. In this case: the recognition of the Nuragic civilization.

For example, take the case of the Roman narration of the Sardinian uprising in 215 B.C. in the coastal city of Cornus, not far from the decimated Mont'e Prama. The Roman poet Silius hailed the role of Ennius, a centurion soldier and the father of Latin poetry, in his heroic role in defeating the Sardinian-Punic rebellion—except Ennius was never there. The scene is fashioned as one of betrayal to Rome; a Sardinian-Punic leader has joined forces with the Punics—the city-state founded by the Phoenicians in Carthage, present-day Tunisia, in 800 B.C.—who had occupied and plundered Sardinia for centuries. In truth, Ennius served as a soldier in Sardinia ten years later, attracting the attention of Cato the Elder for his language abilities, who took him back to Rome.

In Sillius's rendering, Ennius appears in the crucial battle with the Sardinians and their Punic allies as though he has descended from

the ancient kings. Ennius's "hand's passion increased by the slaugh-
ter." When the Sardinian leader's son Hiostus charges Ennius, Sillius
declares that Apollo, sitting on a cloud, "laughed at the undertaking's
futile effort and let the spear go away into the air." How dare the
Sardinian even consider taking on Ennius, anointed by the gods. And
then Sillius adds, in Apollo's godly voice: Ennius is sacred, "a poet
worthy of Apollo, and he will sing his famous verses of the Italian wars
and will raise the generals to the sky." So, a spear rams through the
Sardinian Hiostus's head and he dies, his father Hampsicora commit-
ting suicide with him, going to the underworld where the Sardinians
and Punics belong—out of sight.

Still today, students in Sardinia follow a national curriculum on ancient history in Italy where the Nuragic civilization "practically doesn't
exist," according to anthropologist and author Fiorenzo Caterini. Our
kids, in fact, heard nothing at their school—outside of a few comments by fellow students, as if embarrassed of the "stack of rocks."
Or, if a Nuragic reference makes it into class, it is a footnote or *ramo
secco*, a kind of encased dry wood of no real value. Students rarely read
about the "constant Sardinian resistance" on the island, in the words
of pioneering archaeologist Giovanni Lilliu, and the clash of occupation and colonization over two thousand years—by the Phoenicians,
Carthaginians, Romans, Vandals, Goths, Byzantines, Muslims in
Dénia, Aghlabids and various North African reigns, pirates of every
persuasion, Spaniards, Aragons and Catalans, the Pisans, Genovese,
Savoyards and the fledging Italian republic, as well as the presence of
American and NATO military bases for half a century.

"None of our Sardinians," lamented the writer Proto Arca Sardo,
somewhere between the 1580s and 1590, "had done enough to celebrate the history of the island." While the background on this author
remains elusive, his criticism of the historiography of the island already
by the medieval period signaled the continuum of historical denial,

as much as recognition in the prevailing chronicles. "All of the deeds accomplished in the kingdom of Sardinia are dead and buried in perpetual oblivion," he concluded. His manuscript, *De bello et interitu marchionis Oristanei*, was a rousing defense of the last reign of the independent judicadus or kingdoms.

Nearly five hundred years later, modern writers and interpreters like Andrea were still forced to address a "constant exclusion" from history, as Caterini deemed it in his provocative 2018 book, *La Mano Destra Della Storia*: *La demolizione della memoria e il problema storiografico in Sardegna*. The subtitle didn't really need translating.

"How many times have we wished that the books of the compulsory classes would speak, with due prudence, of the ancient history of Sardinia," Nurnet Vice President Giorgio Valdès wrote on the group's blog in 2018. "However, if the events of our more remote past rarely appear in textbooks, sometimes this guilty absence has been remedied by school directors and above all passionate teachers aware of the fact that history cannot be gagged, even when the lack of bibliography and the presumed absence of writing makes it difficult to outline."

"The day that the student of Paris, or of London, of Berlin, of Madrid, of Bilbao, of Dublin, of Belfast, of Rome or of Milan, should understand that civilization does not continue only by contagion, but that it expresses itself at its best in the comparison between peoples," Caterini concluded in *La Mano Destra Della Storia* [The Right Hand of History], "as it would be clearer and more evident by studying the Nuragic history, it would mean that something on the planet is changing."

But, according to the research, that moment should have already arrived.

"Everything has changed," an archaeological report concluded in 2009, after examining discoveries of Bronze Age Sardinian ceramic and wares in southern Spain, prior to the advent of the Phoenician trading networks in the Mediterranean. Such a claim countered the long-held belief that the Nuragic people had only been a recipient, not a conduit, of exchange and navigation. The "old paradigms" needed to be carefully archived, according to the report, "in order to turn the page and start with new explanations that will undoubtedly give the necessary coherence" to the ancient history in Sardinia.

The key point had already been made back in the 1990s: "Sardinia was not a sitting duck waiting to be taken by Phoenicians," according to a Danish study on "urban Nuragic Sardinia," but "a very active partner in a large trading system."

Thanks to recent findings and breakthroughs in isotope analyses of metals, some archaeologists were now proposing that Bronze Age Sardinia had been a base of maritime "enterprises" that managed to "dominate sea-borne routes, and gained a prominent and independent international position." With the discovery of Nuragic tableware at the harbor site of Hala Sultan Tekke in Cyprus, in the winter of 2019, for example, archaeologists Fulvia Lo Schiavo and Serena Sabatini again raised the "question of the reasons behind this presence."

By the Late Bronze Age, Sardinian navigators had become a nexus in the "corrupting sea" routes of commerce, connecting with trading navies of the Phoenicians and Cypriots in the Eastern Mediterranean, exchanging their vast deposits of ore, ceramics, food and wine, weaponry, and notably their craftsmanship in bronze, beyond Spain and the Atlantic. The silver of Sardinia, among other resources, inlaid King Solomon's fabled city in the Eastern Mediterranean, according to the lead isotopes examined by archaeologists in the Hacksilber Project. In return, amber at Nuragic sites had arrived from the Baltics; loads of Cypriot ingots were scattered across the island; axes from Ireland were found in necropolis burial grounds in Sardinia that dated back to 2200 B.C.

A shipwreck off the coast of Canaan, according to tests by Israeli archaeologists, revealed lead ingots from southwestern mines in Sardinia dating back to the thirteenth century B.C.

Recent excavations at the Nuragic site of Conca 'e Sa Cresia, provided evidence of glassmaking in Sardinia in 1700 B.C., rivaling ancient Egypt. (Most archaeologists place the first glassmaking operations in Mesopotamia in the second millennium B.C.) "Materials that we thought had been imported to Sardinia," suggested American archaeologist Emily Holt, based at the University of Cardiff, "could instead have been produced first by local populations."

The island's soldiers and their horned helmets and round shields, according to archaeologists like longtime Sardinian expert Giovanni Ugas, who had spent a half century uncovering prehistoric sites, were immortalized on the stone steles of the Egyptian Ramesses II as the "Shardana" among the "People of the Sea." The Shardana's participation in the siege of Eastern Mediterranean cities in the final days of the Bronze Age, one of the most critical junctures in ancient history for Europe, Africa, Eurasia, and the Near East, still raged as an open question in a fierce debate among scholars.

In 1942, a peat bog cutter unearthed a horned bronze helmet in Denmark. Dating to 900 B.C., fifteen hundred years before the Vikings, the helmet was eventually tested and traced back to Sardinia. Sword pommels and daggers in Bronze Age Sweden were traced to Sardinian deposits as well.

Still, Sardinia remained on the periphery of that Mediterranean map of empires for most writers. Up until the late 1990s, as archaeologists Stephen Dyson and Robert Rowland noted, the most recent archaeological works on Italy "hardly" mentioned Sardinia. Writing in the *Journal of American Archaeology* in 1992, one venerable expert on ancient Sardinia flat out noted that there was little interest in the island because "there are no Greek remains," and partly due to a lack of translated material into English. Into the 2000s, according to American archaeologist Emma Blake, Sardinia was largely "ignored" by the broader academic community.

"Sardinia is not just the sea," Francesca Cossu, the president of Nurnet, wrote on Facebook one summer, as she sat on the outer walls of a nuraghe near the coast during a conference with other advocates. "And we Sardinians first and foremost have to tell the whole world about it."

Groups like Nurnet, and many other civic and education organizations, held gatherings, field trips, festivals, mapped out new sites, and continued a debate on social media and in the public square, calling on the government to expedite plans for greater enhancement of archaeology on the island.

Putting aside various differences over interpretation, a broad campaign across the island finally came together under the banner of "Sardinia Toward UNESCO" in 2020, petitioning the international cultural body to recognize the Nuragic monuments, as well as ancient art and architecture, as World Heritage Sites. (Only one nuraghe out of thousands—Su Nuraxi di Barumini—had been designated a UNESCO site in 1997.) The latest campaign included hundreds of communities, the regional assembly and the Autonomous Regional authorities, among corporate sponsors. The petitioners called it a "historic moment" to acknowledge the "importance that the Nuragic monuments have taken on in recent decades for Sardinians, as essential signs of their identity."

As part of its UNESCO campaign, a "Junior Master" initiative for schools and youth had been launched to study a new "interpretation of the Nuragic civilization" and its connection to "possible models of sustainable economic development," raising the looming question over how to pursue cultural tourism in Sardinia and all of Italy.

A collection of activists, historians, and writers also launched the *Comitato Civiltà Sarda*, calling for a campaign to rewrite the history books used by Sardinian schools, in order to update and broaden the texts, and make Sardinian cultures and languages compulsory subjects.

This historic movement didn't happen by chance, but by years, decades, even centuries of advocacy by Sardinian archaeology and cultural enthusiasts. The first archaeological museum in Cagliari dated back to 1802; Giovanni Spano put out his first issue of his *Bullettino archeologico sardo* in 1855, vigorously documenting prehistoric sites. In 2005, officials with the Autonomous Region of Sardinia, the Italian architecture magazine *Domus*, among others, launched a major campaign to establish a *Museo Mediterraneo dell'Arte Nuragica e dell'Arte Contemporanea*. The *Bètile*, as it was named (after the prehistoric stone monuments), sought to galvanize an awareness among Sardinians for the "value of their history and their culture," while making them interact with contemporary artistic research. Political disputes eventually derailed the funding for the project.

With the enormity of research revelations in the last two decades, renewed interest had jump-started campaigns for more development of Nuragic sites and education initiatives across the island. But the government caravans still moved at a glacial pace for some advocates, who often raised the ire of bureaucrats and academic institutions with their prompts. In his book, *Un Nuraghe per Tutti*, A Nuraghe for Everyone, Nurnet cofounder Antonello Gregorini set out his views for public participation; how the nuraghe "could be considered a tendential right, a symbol of citizenship, of belonging to a land and a nation in which everything was necessarily inseparable, whose inhabitants were aware of how wealth and well-being for the greatest number derived from social cohesion of individuals."

A century after that *Scientific American* article in 1899 recognized Sardinia's monumental past, a stunning acknowledgment of archaeology deferred on the island remained. An assessment by British archaeologist Robert Leighton in 2022 concluded that out of the more than seven thousand nuraghes that had been documented and survived modern-day destruction, "not more than one or two percent have been excavated."

If true, that statistic floored me with its outcome. Between memory and oblivion, Sardinian's ancient history remained aloof. Like some buried vault of archives, the historical treasury in Sardinia was locked underground. Pompei may have been covered in ash; in effect, 98 percent of Sardinia's Nuragic civilization had stayed concealed by the Mediterranean scrub and mounds of dirt.

"Perhaps, in some old nuraghe," Lilliu, the pioneering archaeologist, had written in a special edition of *Il Ponte* magazine in 1951, "is still a little secret of young Sardinia and its futuristic hopes."

Raising the bronzetti to the crowd, Andrea spoke of ethnogenesis now: the rebirth of the Nuragic culture, in some way, as if his indigenous ancestors still had a story to tell in an age of iPhones.

11 | LAWRENCE OF SARDINIA

What many assert is incorrect: that Sardinia has no history.
History it has, but it is either ignored or it was not written. There
is no people without history; and the stories are all similar, since
in the end they only summarize a series of struggles, more or less
fortunate, between the oppressed and the oppressors, between the
weak and the arrogant!

—Enrico Costa, *Racconto storico sassarese del secolo XV*, 1897

I enjoyed walking my youngest son Massimo to school in the early
mornings. The middle school was named after Grazia Deledda. We
would pass the café run by Annalisa and Walter, the parents of his
school friend Ivan, who took us under their wings for all things
Alghero. Massimo seemed to fit in with the Algherese kids, joining
their jaunts after school in the old town center. They would stop and
grab a piece of pizza with french fries on top at the corner joint, Pata
Pizza, and then continue their procession around the bastion. I'd stop
by the local bakery, pick up some bread, and use my status as a visiting
foreigner to try different sweets. The delicious *tabaccheras* "snuffbox"
cakes, filled with *menjar blanc* crème, for example.

Heading to my kiosk news vendor, I crossed the Giuseppe Manno

Gardens, where a towering sculpture of the esteemed Algherese historian and politician greeted passersby. Manno had led a storied life for a kid from Alghero, albeit a noble one born in the late 1700s. He certainly had the knack for being at the momentous places in history, starting with his role as the private secretary to the Viceroy of Sardinia, Charles Felix in Cagliari, who would eventually become the King of Sardinia, based in Turin, in 1821.

A quick word on the Kingdom of Sardinia. Dating back to the ninth century or even earlier, Sardinia had been divided into four kingdoms, judgeships or judicadus (*giudicati* in Italian), a term most historians date back to the Byzantine Empire under Justinian in the sixth century. If you looked at the map, the judicadus were largely defined by geography, with Gallura in the northeast, Cagliari in the south, Arborea in the west, and Torres or Logudoro in the northwest. By the eleventh century, as historian Laura Galoppini observed, the four judicadus were "a true kingdom, with the *giudice* (*Donnu*) exercising sovereignty over his subjects in his own territory." Succession to the throne was hereditary, she noted, including women.

Let's now jump to 1720, when the Kingdom of Sardinia was handed over to the House of Savoy in Turin, as part of a postwar shake-up of Europe, and began with King Vittorio Amedeo II and continued under Charles Emanuele III, who "terrorized the whole of Sardinia, with a brutal repression, under the pretext of fighting banditry," according to the indefatigable historian Francesco Casula. His book, *Carlo Felice e i tiranni sabaudi*, Charles Felix and the Savoyard Tyrants, presented a searing "counter story" to the largely whitewashed accounts from nineteenth-century and early-twentieth-century Savoyard historians, as well as the unvarnished statues and names that watched over streets and piazzas and schools today.

King Charles Emanuele IV became the first Savoyard to actually live in Sardinia, taking refuge in Cagliari in 1798, after the invasion of Napoleon in the Piedmont. (The Sardinians rescued the Kingdom of Sardinia and its pretenders, just as they had provided refuge for fleeing Romans during the siege of the Vandals more than a thousand years earlier.) In 1802, King Vittorio Emanuele I took power, Casula continued, "a king of little intelligence, of no culture, of little personality, presumptuous and warmongering." Thomas Jefferson agreed, referring to Vittorio Emanuele as a "fool" in 1810, based on his own experiences in Europe.

Taking the throne in 1821, King Charles Felix was "cruel, ferocious and bloodthirsty, to put it in the Sardinian language, *incainadu*," added historian Girolamo Sotgiu. With their return to Turin in the 1820s, the absentee reign of Savoyards continued under King Charles Alberto, who abolished feudalism but engineered the "Great Fusion" of the island with the Piedmont monarchy, turning Sardinia into "a Piedmont farm, miserable and starving for a heartless and brainless government," lamented Sardinian journalist Giovanni Battista Tuveri.

King Vittorio Emanuele II of Savoy became the last king of Sardinia in 1849 and the first king of Italy in 1861. It didn't get better, according to most Sardinian writers. "Impoverished and riotous Sardinians had nothing to do with Florence, Venice, Milan," novelist Dessì wrote, "which considered the island an overseas colony, or a land of confinement."

In the shadow of this rather stark colonization, the Algherese writer Manno worked his way up the conservative Savoyard ladder to eventually become the president of the senate (in Nice and the Piedmont), and even president of the Supreme Court of Cassation for the Kingdom of Sardinia in the mid-nineteenth century on the Italian mainland.

Manno had always wanted to be a travel writer. In fact, his first literary effort was a travel diary in *Italy*, not Sardinia, humorously titled *Lettere di un sardo in Italia, 1816–1817*, Letters of a Sardinian in Italy, 1816–1817, addressed to imaginary friends about his observations. In

1825, King Charles Felix handed him a manuscript of a German travel writer in Sardinia, which dramatically changed Manno's life. "Oh, the horror," Manno wrote. The German caricatures of the island outraged him. The Algherese felt a need to refute the "ancient shame of having been mocked" and to "purge our homeland from the unjust accusation of barbarism that was often made to it by foreigners."

Considered by many as the first modern historian of Sardinia, three centuries after Arquer's work, Manno wrote many books on the history of the island, starting with the multivolume *Storia di Sardegna* in 1825. Manno's allegiance to his King—on the Italian mainland—led him to downplay his Algherese roots and tread softly on the Sardinian histories of rebellion, including his father's own apparent role in the anti-Savoy uprisings. In fact, Manno issued a warning to his fellow islanders to not succumb "to the lure of the imagination," and employ "more diligence than discernment in gathering together what antiquity leaves us."

For most scholars, Manno ushered in a "new era" of history writing on the island, spawning contrasting narratives by other writers seeking to place Sardinia and its ancient history within the context of the greater Italian story that was taking shape in the mid-nineteenth century with the unfolding unification of the country.

One hundred years after Manno's history book reproached the foreign observer's misperceptions of his beloved island, the scandalous English writer David Herbert Lawrence and his German wife Frieda, the "Queen B," arrived in a steamer in Cagliari to discover Sardinia, "outside the circuit of civilization." *Let it be Sardinia.*

The impressive rollout of travel writers from Germany, France, Great Britain, Spain, Sweden, Denmark, Ireland, Italy, and my own United States had certainly tramped around on that circuit of civilization in Sardinia for centuries, of course. "Sardinia is a very narrated place," Murgia wrote in the travelogue of her own island, *Viaggio in Sardegna*. "More narrated than visited," she added for emphasis. "Sardinia exists in the stories told by others."

After reading the Roman narrative of Tacitus from 19 A.D., about silver in Sardinia, French author Honoré de Balzac made a calamitous journey in 1838, with a secret operation to cull the gold and silver from lead deposits. He ended up empty-handed, dismissing Sardinia as a "desert kingdom" with "real savages," though the villagers did impress him with their rich costumes.

German writers had been touring the island since the 1700s. All of their books, strangely enough, were published in one city, Leipzig. Even the Baedeker guide was published there. Heinrich von Maltzan ended up in Sardinia after missing his ferry to Tunisia. The city of Cagliari beguiled him so much that he stayed for months, writing a book. While there were a hundred books on Sicily, he noted, "we hardly see" Sardinia. He questioned how "our German literature, and even the Italian, French and English works" had become so obsolete, especially given all of the archaeological discoveries in the nineteenth century.

Despite his intent to find an "uncaptured Sardinia," Lawrence's fellow Brits had already covered every back trail and remote destination a century before his arrival. In 1828, William Smyth published his major work, *Sketch of the Present State of the Island of Sardinia, Based on Several Journeys across the Island on Horseback*. "If the traveller should meet with the same kindness I experienced," English writer Tyndale wrote in his multivolume series of books, *The Island of Sardinia*, twenty years after Smyth, "he will in no wise regret a deviation from the general routine of tourists."

By 1858, English author Thomas Forester complained about the *embarras de richesses* of literature on the island, remarking that it had been saturated by fellow travel writers. In his travelogue, *Rambles in the Islands of Corsica and Sardinia*, Forester sought to be a rambler more than a writer, though he recognized the political machinations of the day between England, France, and the Savoyards, giving Sardinia "an importance far beyond any estimate that may be formed of the value of her material wealth." Only a few years before Lawrence stepped off the steamer, English historian Edmund Spenser Bouchier published his short history, *Sardinia in Ancient Times*, laying the groundwork for Lawrence's view that the "old populations never made any mark in historic times."

That didn't include the adventurous *Badminton Magazine* in 1901, which put out a large feature on hunting in the back country of this "lovely country," where the "historical and even prehistorical monuments" made it worth a visit to this "remarkable" island. The *Badminton* correspondent encouraged all travelers to "acquire some little information about the island itself."

Lawrence didn't need no stinking little information. In 1921, his fame preceded him in certain circles, especially for the obscenity charges against his novels *Sons and Lovers* and *Women in Love*, which had just been released in the United States, not England. *Sea and Sardinia*, too, would first be published in the United States.

With his *Baedeker* guide in hand—the equivalent of today's *Lonely Planet* guide—which actually discouraged against visiting Sardinia due to fleas and malaria but encouraged travelers to check out the fascinating nuraghes, Lawrence never mentioned a single nuraghe or prehistoric site, which would be like failing to note a barn in the American Midwest. (Even an architecture magazine in London, *The Builder*, ran a feature on nuraghe towers in 1907, as part of the island's "very important and conspicuous prehistoric remains.") Instead, Lawrence went in search of a place for his envisioned utopia of "Rananim." In Sardinia, he sought out so-called exotic and fossil-ized folk cultures that had spurned the dreaded Industrial Revolution, all the while toting his own modern conveniences. The Sards were fascinated by the vapors sifting from his thermos for his beloved tea, still a novelty invention.

A decade before Lawrence's trip, Scottish archaeologist and writer Duncan Mackenzie, who would also take part in some key digs among the Bronze Age Minoans in Crete, warned travelers in a special paper presented to the British School in Rome that they would "miss much of the strange beauty" of the island if they only depended on the lim-ited rails. "If the traveler is wise," he added, "he would see the nuraghe first of all," and then depart for the distant Gennargentu mountains to see the grandeur and "lovely" island.

Lawrence and the Queen B spent less than a week in Sardinia. Lawrence took no notes, he famously declared. From their arrival in Cagliari, a "naked town rising steep," they took buses and trains, first to Mandas, "where there is nothing to do," and then to Sorgono, full of "degenerate aborigines, the dirty-breasted host" and "sordid villag-ers," crossed the mountains until they arrived at Nuoro, the home of Deledda, where "there is nothing to see," to Orosei on the eastern coast, "a dilapidated, sun-smitten, god-forsaken little town," until they reached Siniscola, where a "young hussy" full of the "barbaric *mefiance*" served them roughly at a café.

After returning to his home in Sicily, where he claimed he found himself without anything to do, Lawrence wrote *Sea and Sardinia*, which he had originally titled *Sardinian Films* or *Sketches in Sardinia*, in a few weeks. *Only one draft.* But Lawrence injected his novelist skills into the journey, conjuring some beautiful scenes of nature, especially in the train ride through the Gennargentu mountains, and praised the Sardinians for being "downright" and "manly." In many respects, *Sea and Sardinia* served as a stage for some funny but downright obnoxious character sketches, as if Lawrence were more intent in drawing up characters for a novel.

Lawrence's book was first excerpted in *Dial* magazine in the United States. The *New York Times* started its review in grand style: Anyone wishing to travel to Sardinia "would find no better guidebook." Then, the reviewer faltered in trying to describe what exactly Lawrence wrote, feeling as if the book reminded him of an incomplete notebook that had been handed over to a typist by a writer who "told her" to copy it. But it *was* full of color, the reviewer confessed.

On its one hundredth anniversary, *Sea and Sardinia* remained the best known work on Sardinia in the English language, and celebrated in Sardinia at various festivals. Several choice lines are found in brochures and banners: "Sardinia is something else. Enchanting spaces and distances to travel—nothing finished, nothing definitive. It is like freedom itself." The restaurant Risveglio in Sorgono, which Lawrence had excoriated as filthy, even put out a special Mandrolisai wine in his name. *The Best American Travel Writing* anthology in 2020 selected *Sea and Sardinia* as one of the landmark travel books, recognizing its early role in narrative travel writing.

The English author, admittedly, had bushwhacked around the world, from Europe to the American Southwest to Mexico and back to Italy, and even Australia. I didn't read his work in school, like many Americans; I discovered him in Mexico, where I once lived and journeyed across the border into Guatemala, first reading his political novel, *The Plumed Serpent*, and his travel essays, *Morning in Mexico*, which I found to be heavy-handed in their depictions of characters. But they *were* colorful.

Of course, coming from a coal mining family, I also shared Lawrence's intense dislike for coal, *il carbone*, which even haunted him on the steamer crossing over to Sardinia. "No escape. You become—if you are English—*l'Inghilterra, il carbone,* and *il cambio*." When we visited the town of Carbonia (Coaltown), which Mussolini had founded in the 1930s as a fascist experiment in shaping a "modern center for industrial life," I took Lawrence with me into the bowels of the mine. The extraordinary museum with its multimedia displays in that huge mine would have shattered Lawrence's illusions of the primitive island. At its height in 1938, over seventeen thousand miners worked in Carbonia alone as one of the drivers of Italy's national energy plan.

Some people, though, had taken a closer look at Lawrence's Italian work. *Under the Tuscan Sun* author Frances Mayes, in an interview with the *New York Times Book Review,* picked *Sea and Sardinia* as the most overrated book on her list. The headline cut through one hundred years of misinformation: "Frances Mayes Admires Travel Writers, with One Big Exception." Mayes added: "So brilliant in flashes. He had a genius for sense of place, but his travel narratives are marred by petty narcissism. Must have been a dreary travel companion."

While initially praising the book as insightful in understanding the Sardinian ways of silence and passive resistance, Sardinian writer Dessì reconsidered the travel book on a second reading in the 1960s. "Disappointment following the rereading of *Sea and Sardinia.* But is my disappointment justified?" he wrote a fellow writer. "The squalor of this image of *Sardegna* now seems disconcerting to me, and I understand how that fellow wrote, at one point: 'Enough with Lawrence.' Yes, that's right, enough with Lawrence. But there is also a voice inside that tells me: 'Enough with *Sardegna.*'"

Dessì's comment made me think of a different scenario, flipping the narrative, like Manno's original travel writings on a Sardinian in Italy. In 1877, in Lawrence's England, near York, a man noticed that a water trough for the horses outside an inn had an inscription. It was a stone sarcophagus from the ancient Roman period. It read: *In memory of Julia Fortunata, from Sardinia.* Perhaps the Sardinian had left her mark in England, two thousand years ago, as a harbinger of travel writings to come.

12 | PORTO CONTE

"What makes the desert beautiful," said the little prince, "is that somewhere it hides a well."

—Antoine de Saint-Exupéry, *The Little Prince*, 1943

One of the hardest choices in Alghero was selecting the beach for the day. There were too many nearby. Not to mention the vast stretches farther up the northern coast, including my beloved outpost of Porto Ferro, where the cliffs and sea met along the rugged and mostly secluded beaches.

Spiraling along the gulf like mini republics, each beach community had its own swagger, all of them unfolding into the clear sea, with the green stretch of hilly uprisings around Capo Caccia as a backdrop. Emerging from the maritime pine forests; the sand dunes of the urban Maria Pia beach stretched with action; the wonderful Bombarde and Lazzaretto competed in their lovely coves; and while little inlets made for secret hideouts along the coast, if you continued in the direction of Capo Caccia, you arrived at the breathtaking Mugoni beach, with its expanse of white sand, and the protective bay of Porto Conte.

I swam in the bay until the first week of November—along with the rest of the Nordic folks.

But our first swims in the late summer, still taking in the clear water unencumbered by ships or industry, with slopes of the green hills in the background and the ever-present promontory of Capo Caccia, gave us this impression of eternal newness, or even a stroke away from wilderness, as if the shores had remained untarnished by invasion. The sand was like a satin bed.

Of course, the truth was something else.

In the distance in the bay, I could see the Torre di Porto Conte, one of the many Aragonese lookout towers from the sixteenth century that hugged the coasts in anticipation of an invasion of pirates or whatever enemy of the period. The stone towers, beautiful in their limestone bases, seemed like condemned relics; a rope ladder led to the doors, which perched at fifteen feet high from the floor. It would be hard to imagine the fate of the solitary soldier sealed inside, as boatloads of invaders crashed the shores.

While the history of invasions began before the medieval Spanish, obviously, the array of World War II bunkers along the coasts of Sardinia still sat along the beaches with the aplomb of beachcombers. There were hundreds of them, neatly positioned as concrete "pillboxes," with just enough room for a machine gunner to swivel at any advance. The shores of Sardinia often felt like a continuum of historic forts.

One of my favorite walks in the nearby Parco Regionale di Porto Conte, which scaled up the hills and overlooks from the cliffs, was the hike to Punta Giglio. The aqua-blue waters below fanned out in shades that seemed to turn Sardinia into an outpost of the Caribbean. Large tracks of agave and prickly pear cacti jutted from the trails. The views toward Capo Caccia to the northwest, and back toward the Gulf of Alghero to the east, including the dramatic cliffs of Cape Galera, made you feel like you were on an island, inside an island.

The ruins from World War II, however, brought you back to reality. The *caserma* or barracks on Punta Giglio, with their breathtaking views, were a reminder of the anticipation of invasion by Allied forces—that never happened. In fact, one of the great tricks by the Allies was Operation Mincemeat, when they sent the body of a dead Welshman ashore in Spain with fake papers about a planned invasion of Sardinia. Instead, as General George Patton made famous as the blood and guts leader, the Allies launched an assault on Sicily.

I don't know if the Sardinian forces at the caserma at Punta Giglio could appreciate their view amid the tension of war, but the residual of graffiti on the ruins shored up their fascist beliefs. The walls were stained in historical commands: *Credere, Obbedire, Combattere* (Believe, Obey, Fight) and *Cuando Tuona il Cannone e Veramente la Voce della Patria Che Chiama* (When the Cannon Thunders, Truly the Voice of the Fatherland Calls).

The Italian soldiers certainly had reason to be on alert. Historian Giuseppe Manno's ancestral home in Alghero was destroyed in May 1943, during the brutal bombing of the city by Allied forces during World War II. Guided by the moonlight, British Wellington bombers pounded the historic center, strafing as low as two hundred feet. *La Nit de Sant Pasqual*, as it is called in Algherese, resulted in 150 deaths, and the destruction of hundreds of homes. Food riots of desperate citizens erupted in the aftermath.

The Torre di Porto Conte now featured the life of another soldier, French writer Antoine de Saint-Exupéry, better known as the author of *The Little Prince*, one of the bestselling books on the planet. "It's not clear if Saint-Exupéry flew to write or wrote to fly," as Italian author Umberto Eco once said, but his treasury of books as a pilot had traced his journeys across Europe, the Americas, and Africa. The French writer won the National Book Award for his memoir *Wind, Sand and Stars* in 1941. But living in exile from the war, having fled the Nazi invasion of his country, Saint-Exupéry anxiously sought to return to the front lines as a pilot. Despite his age and erratic career, including an epic crash in the Libyan desert during a Paris to Vietnam race, he managed to join the Free French Air Force in North Africa in 1943. He had just published *The Little Prince* in the United States.

Transferred to Alghero in the spring of 1944, the French author lived in a house at Porto Conte. *Life Magazine* photographer John Philips accompanied Saint-Exupéry, and eventually nudged him into writing a "Letter to an American." Exclaiming that he had made it past his forty-third birthday, the French author appealed to the American readers: "Friends in America, you see it seems that something new is emerging on our planet. It is true that technical progress in modern times has linked men together like a complex nervous system. The means of travel are numerous and communication is instantaneous. We are joined together materially like the cells of a single body, but this body has as yet no soul."

Disappearing on an unarmed P-38 flight in July, Saint-Exupéry's body was never found. In 1998, a fisherman south of Marseille, however, found a bracelet with the author's name. Parts of his plane were eventually identified in the same area.

The letter from Alghero was one of the last—if not the last—piece of writing by the famous author. "All tenderness, all memories, all reasons for living are spread out thirty-five thousand feet below, illuminated by sunlight, and nevertheless more inaccessible than any Egyptian treasures locked away in the glass cases of a museum."

13 | EMPORIUM

No ddu scit ca ses mori chi si pendit
tra pitzioleddas e lutzinas
in is orus cuaus
de un'andera antiga
ancà t'incraras timarosu.
In su tempus aresti
fust nasciu che spiga
po obrescidroxus de arrosa.
E imoi ses dònnia cosa
chi mi ndi torrat una stòria arrèscia
de ancà si spannat
un'àlidu 'e memòria.

He does not know that you are the path
that inclines between towering peaks and puddles
in the hidden shores of an ancient way
where, fearful, you show yourself.
In untamed times
you were born
as an ear of wheat
for rose-colored dawns.
Now you are everything
that brings me back to an entangled history
that opens like
a breath of memory.

—Anna Cristina Serra, "Tempus Nostru"

The restaurant at the beach had a view of *la torre*, this time on the Lazzaretto beach on the northern end of the Gulf of Alghero. There's always a view of a tower. It also served *fregula*, the Sardinian beads of pasta often considered one of its traditional dishes. Best served with saffron, we were told, that thrived on the island. But I enjoyed mine with *arselle*, the shiny little local clams. The robust flavor of fregula set it apart from other Italian pastas for me. Mixed from semolina and water, it had been cut by hand into little pearls and then roasted over a wood-fired oven, prior to cooking it in a sauce.

Appearing like large couscous, some believed fregula—also referred to as *fregola* in Italian—arrived with Ligurian immigrants displaced in Tunisia, who settled on the island of San Pietro, off the southwest coast of the main island. By the fourteenth century, however, fregula was already listed in official statutes in Tempio Pausania in the northern Gallura region, regulating its milling and use of water on Monday through Friday. Recent archaeobotanical research at various nuraghes, including Nuraghe S'Urachi, also showed that naked wheat as well as barley were common elements in the Nuragic diet, including widespread evidence for festivals and feasts across the island. Milling stones for grain abounded. The island's role as a granary for its colonizers from Carthage and Rome attested in the vibrant exchange of foodways, including early forms of pasta.

The Carthaginians and Romans, of course, were latecomers to the Sardinian navigators of the Strait of Bonifacio and its access to the various seas. (James Bond, with Russian agent Triple X in *The Spy Who Loved Me*, emerged onto the island from the sea in his amphibious Lotus Esprit sports car near Porto Conte, but this is an entirely different story.)

Just ask the ancient mariners in Homer's *Odyssey*, wary of the "sardonic" smile and island cannibals, or earlier still, read the first writings in western Europe left on the southern tip of the island by the

Phoenician sailors on Sardinian stone tables in the ninth century B.C. Even more remarkable, thousands of years before the Phoenicians or Romans or even Homer's Ulysses fable or actor Roger Moore, obsidian traders from Monte Arci in the interior of Sardinia traversed the waterways, peddling their precious stones as far as France and northern Italy, as well as North Africa. The Museum of Obsidian in Pau, as part of Europe's first ever Historical and Environmental Geomining Park, mapped out that incredible trading route to the sixth millennium B.C.

A few miles outside the northern city of Sassari, not far from where the Romans established one of their first ports and left behind a stone bridge, the six-thousand-year-old step pyramid of Monte d'Accoddi unfolded down a rock staircase as the only ziggurat-like structure in Europe, hailed by some archaeologists as "the most singular cultic monument in the early Western Mediterranean."

A sperm whale's tooth was found at the shrine, as a reminder of the ritual importance of the sea in Neolithic days.

A little less than three thousand years before Saint-Exupéry stood on the beach at Porto Conte, long wooden ships pulled into the calm bay, with their large sails stretching across the masts. There was most likely a bull or deer protome on the bow. The flat deck would have been piled with ingots of copper or lead or silver. Other ships laden with rows of amphorae, carrying oil and wine, and fish products, trundled close behind. Ceramics were stacked like bricks.

Less than a hundred yards from the beach, a Nuragic community gathered around its single tower, including a wide square that served as a marketplace. This was the Nuraghe Sant'Imbenia, as it is called today, built around 1400 B.C. In the last decade, new excavations had uncovered the key role of Sant'Imbenia as an "emporium" for the Mediterranean, dating back to the rise of the Nuragic civilization, and the eventual settlement of the Phoenician traders.

Ancient Sardinia was far from any outpost of isolation. Recent findings in Spain, Cyprus, and along the former Phoenician coast in the Levant, demonstrated that Nuragic goods, including silver hoards and exquisite pottery, had been exchanged from the farthest stretches of the western to eastern Mediterranean since the 1300 B.C.—long before the Phoenicians entered the Porto Conte waters and established their own networks, working alongside Nuragic artisans, miners, farmers and traders in the ninth or eighth century B.C.

There would have been other ships, too, in that harbor—from Greece, the Iberian shores of Spain, Cyprus, and North Africa.

While Alghero is often considered a modern city, in historic terms, the truth is that it rose in the shadows of Nuragic, Phoenician, and Roman settlements in nearby bays and harbors. The Roman city of Carbia, for example, left behind a stone bridge in today's Fertilia, not far from the Maria Pia beach. Carbia was mentioned on the Antonine Itinerary, the register of Roman roads across the empire in the third century A.D. The Nuraghe Palmavera, just down the road, had been established nearly two thousand years earlier.

With a protective bay, Porto Conte did not expose itself like the Gulf of Alghero, allowing for the natural development of a coastal community. But that community was not simply relegated to fishing or nearby agricultural ventures; recent analysis of lead isotopes found at Sant'Imbenia demonstrated that the bay served as a weigh station for mining materials, including lead, copper, and silver, that also arrived in boats from the southwestern Sardinian coast and as far as the Iberian peninsula and North Africa. From the ninth century onward, according to an archaeological report, Sant'Imbenia became a hub for the silver mines of Argentiera to the north (where Balzac had trotted off for a failed mining venture), iron in Canaglia in the interior areas, and copper from mines south of Alghero in Calabona. It also received shipments of oxide ingots of copper from Cyprus, found all over the island.

The bay, according to archaeologists, was a traveler's hotspot. Numerous Nuragic settlements, including the huge Nuraghe Palmavera nearby, clearly patronized the emporium at the bay for incoming goods.

The marketplace spread out with shops and artisan workshops. Silversmiths pounded axes, swords, daggers; jewelry makers forged the silver, copper, and bronze pieces, even gold. Pottery kilns fashioned pitchers, plates, and food wares; pieces of lead, including lamina clamps for repairs, were found. The ceramic pieces included large amphora containers for transporting goods like wine and oil. Other parts of the market were set aside for meat, cheeses, cereals, grains, breads, and other food produced in the interior areas. Items made from wool, of course, would have been in demand.

Medicine, too, could be found in the market. Archaeologists found hoards of milk thistle seeds, which Pliny the Elder, the Roman author of a natural history in 77 A.D., identified in his writings as valuable plants to treat the intestinal problems of sailors.

The exchange brought in goods from other islands and cultures. The oldest *skyphos* on the island—the two-handed Greek vase for drinking wine—was found at Sant'Imbenia, dating back to the eighth century B.C. Meanwhile, the Nuragic *askoid* jug, with its unique long neck bent slightly as if to facilitate drinking and pouring, was popular in Bronze Age parts of Spain and North Africa, as well as Crete. The remains from a shipwreck off Malta contained wine amphorae dating from the eleventh century B.C. from Sardinia.

The biblical story about Jonah and the whale, and Jonah fleeing for Tarshish begins to take shape here, though, still as a story befitting our Little Prince. According to archaeologist William Foxwell Albright, "tarshish" was most likely a Phoenician word for "mines," not necessarily a destination. "Tarshish" appears numerous times in the

Old Testament of the Bible as the source of silver and King Solomon's wealth, his "Tarshish fleets" of ships. Other ancient documents, including the Akkadian inscriptions from the Assyrian Empire in 660 B.C., refer to Tarshish as an island, as well.

The link to Sardinia, however, gets more intriguing. On the Nora stele in southern Sardinia, which inscribed the word "Srdn" or Sardinia into stone for the first time in the ninth century B.C., someone also carved the word "tarshish" in the same dedication, according to several interpretations. While the actual meaning of the stele is still in debate, researchers traced silver isotopes found in the historic Phoenicia area to Sardinia and Iberian sources in the tenth century B.C.—the time of King Solomon's fabled wealth. More importantly, recent evidence showed that the Nuragic people had developed the technology to carry out the cupellation refining process to separate the metals, like silver, prior to the settlement of the Phoenicians.

In fact, the ancient Greeks occasionally referred to Sardinia as *Argyròphleps nésos*—the island of silver veins.

The Nuragic village and eventual Phoenician settlement, in a seeming integration of cultures, would endure for a thousand years until the fifth century B.C. at Porto Conte. The nuraghe tower, however, would lose its point of reference soon after the arrival of the Phoenicians. The bay itself would take on a different role by the first century A.D., when the Romans took control and established an extravagant estate and villa that included marble walls, frescoes, and a remarkable mosaic with a gorgon Medusa's head depicted within "a shield of peltae."

The villa prompted Ptolemy to refer to Porto Conte as the *Nymphaeus Portus*, or "Bay of Nymphs" in his *Geography* in the second century A.D. The Roman Villa apparently served as more of a vacation home for whatever Roman elite, as the island's first tourism center.

That made our swimming a little more crowded, but still pleasurable.

14 | TRAVELING WRITERS

Often authors come to Sardinia in a hurry, hire a motor car, run through the country at a speed of 30 miles per hour, and after a few days go back to the Continent, and write a book about what they have seen . . . Misstatements about Sardinia are therefore so numerous they would, and do, fill many a book.

—Guido Costa, *National Geographic*, 1923

I couldn't really get D. H. Lawrence out of my mind, for a long time.

Strolling down the backstreets of Alghero one day, I spent a little time chatting with Rosa, a vivacious young coral jewelry maker, who sat in the back of her shop threading an earring from the red coral beads. Rosa's passion in understanding the history behind the coral jewelry, as well as her own beautiful designs, made her art come alive. It hung on the walls in drapes of coral necklaces, as if it had just sprouted from the sea. She had attended the University of Bologna, wrote her thesis on the philosophies of social critic Ivan Illich in Mexico, and to her own amazement, jumped at the opportunity to return to Alghero and take over the coral jewelry work of an elderly artist. "The desire to return," as Cambosu reminded us about Sardinians, in *Miele Amaro*.

"How could a small island like Sardinia express so many creative

talents in the various fields of thought and art?" the renowned psychia-
trist Nereide Rudas had asked in her analysis of Sardinian culture, on
this "island of corals." It was all the more revealing to her since Sardinia
was not limited to being home to "a single great creative personality."
She noted that at least four major literary figures had emerged out of
the island in the twentieth century and "enriched culture and history
beyond the border of their land." Deledda and Gramsci were obvious candidates, of course. As a revered political and cultural theorist,
Gramsci's *Prison Notebooks* were first published in 1947, winning the
Viareggio Prize in Italy, and went on to be translated in more than
forty languages. His concepts of civil society, cultural hegemony, organic intellectuals, and wars of maneuver and position, notable in his
Prison Notebooks, would eventually place him in the pantheon of political philosophers. His works remain a vibrant part of political theory
and cultural studies in universities around the world today.

Rudas was also referring to two lesser-known authors: anti-fascist
leader and writer Emilio Lussu and the intellectual jurist and novelist Salvatore Satta, whose books would reach international audiences.
(More on both of those authors later, when we arrive at their towns.)
Rudas could have easily added other internationally famous Sardinians
who had left their mark in Italy and abroad, including jazz leader Fresu,
bestselling novelist Gavino Ledda, beloved singer Maria Carta, opera singer Mario de Candia, the most celebrated tenor in Europe in
the mid-nineteenth century, a bevy of sculptors like Francesco Ciusa,
Costantino Nivola, Albino Manca and Pinuccio Sciola, or Giuseppe
Anedda, the "Paganini of the mandolin," who brought that instrument
into classical music alongside Igor Stravinky and other world-famous
composers and performers.

There were also inventors like Augusto Bissiri, from the village of
Seui, whose pioneering experiments and patents transmitted photos
from one room to another in 1906 and laid the groundwork for the

cathode ray tube and development of the television, and Francesco Antonio Broccu, who built the first percussion-cup revolver in 1833, three years before Samuel Colt's famous patent and mass production. In 1915, author Italo Calvino's mother, Eva Mameli Calvino from Sassari, became the first Italian woman to obtain a teaching certification in botany. In the 1950s and '60s, Sardinian actress Pier Angeli managed to break both James Dean's and Kirk Douglas's hearts as a star in Hollywood. (Her mom didn't like Dean because he wasn't Catholic.). As Mr. Olympia and the "World's Strongest Man," bodybuilder Franco Columbu went from being a shepherd to Arnold Schwarzenegger's training partner in California, as well. Indeed, the list of famous Sardinians was long—not to mention so many sports figures.

Just down the street from Rosa's coral jewelry, one could find Antonio Marras, the internationally celebrated fashion designer and Alghero native, who had worked "quietly in a poet's corner," as the *New York Times* once wrote, to become one of the most innovative designers in Italy. Since his first collection in 1987, his work in fashion, as well as in ceramics and textiles, had taken the *ligazzio rubio* or red threads of Sardinia's traditions and even historical events into some incredibly original designs for the global market.

Sardinia was not simply a place, or a background, but the protagonist and subject of their work, according to Rudas, who questioned what she called an obsession. But the greater question for the islanders was how "to cultivate and put to good use the hidden corals," as she wrote, with this powerful creativity, amid such economic difficulties, isolation, and upheavals. Still, it always seemed notable that the reams of historical documents on the endless discussions about the "Plan of Rebirth" of Sardinia after World War II invariably overlooked the island's legacy of creativity for input, as if only outsiders from the mainland had the wherewithal to determine Sardinia's fate.

This theme of isolation was a common thread with a lot of travel

writers on Sardinia, as well as Sardinians. And yet, literary endeavors themselves, dating back to the sixteenth century, had been fer-
vent efforts to bridge the supposed divide between the island and its
Mediterranean neighbors and the rest of Europe. Libraries and even
street book vendors thrived in Alghero in the late 1500s; Stefano
Moretti, a bookseller and printer in Cagliari, first sold copies of the
Carta de Logu in Sardinian, among other books in Spanish, in the
1550s. Five hundred years later, we attended numerous readings hosted
by the Libreria Il Labirinto Mondadori in Alghero, including authors
in Catalan, Sardinian, and Italian, usually to large crowds, and found
ourselves often thumbing through the shelves at the crowded Cyrano
bookstore in town.

On Via Gilbert Ferret, there was a popular library in the fifteenth
century. Nowadays, on that same street, I stumbled onto the Libreria
Vademecum bookstore, whose historic wooden doors opened into a
grotta of used books, stacked and piled so high that Beppe Ferrari, the
literary shopkeeper, always seemed buried behind the counter from an
avalanche of publications. He warned that a mysterious warehouse in
an undisclosed location contained any book I might be seeking.

In the mid-twentieth century, novelist Dessì asked the world to
listen to "the silent odyssey of the Sardinian people," and was soon
greeted by the Sardinian Literary Spring revival that would reshape
the role of new writers on the island—and Italy.

Not that Americans and other foreigners were entirely aware of this
literary explosion. So little of Sardinian literature had been translated
into Italian, and even less had been translated into English. Expecting
"a thousand years of solitude," *New Yorker* literary critic George Steiner
trod up the mountain to visit Deledda's city of Nuoro in 1979. He
attended a special panel to recognize what Steiner called "one of the
masterpieces of solitude in modern literature, perhaps in all literature,"
Salvatore Satta's novel, *The Day of Judgment*, based in Nuoro.

Steiner found that the Sardinian odyssey was no longer silent or solitary, if it ever was. Sardinian stories had long navigated in all directions at sea, on land, and in the mountains, on their own terms, for centuries, even millennia. Paolo Pillonca, the poem catcher and publisher and founder of the Sa Cantada museum for oral poetry in Silanus, had proclaimed: *O bella musa, ove sei tu?* Oh dear muse, where are you?

In 2017, as we arrived in Sardinia, the prestigious Venice Biennale exhibited the work of artist and poet Maria Lai, whose intricate fabric compositions drew on the island's tradition of weaving as writing; her series of "Libri" and "Geografie" embroidered imaginary maps and narratives in a tangle of threads in book form, as if the reader had to decipher the Sardinian stories for themselves. Her work presented a completely original and different history of Sardinia, and its histories and stories, by Sardinians. "We are for us what we can tell about ourselves," Sardinian writer Giulio Angioni wrote, in *Sulla faccia della terra*, "and for others, we are what they tell about us."

In writing about the life of Deledda in Nuoro, Angioni referred to the conjoined role of history and memoir in her stories, her "sort of sardography."

That "sardography," Sardinia seen through the stories of Sardinians, was the splendor awaiting discovery by outsiders like ourselves, in so many forms.

Thanks to several active publishing houses on the island, Sardinian writers were flourishing when we toured in villages, towns and cities. I rarely returned home to Alghero without a stack of books by local authors. There, at Beppe's bookstore in Alghero, my arms started to feel heavy, thanks to his suggestions, as we moved from shelf to shelf. Sardinian authors, mainly in Sardinian, Alguerés, and Italian, lined the front of the store like guardians. "You need this," he would say, handing me a book by Lilliu, the militant archaeologist, and then

Salvatore Mannuzzu, Atzeni, and Angioni from the great Sardinian Literary Spring in the 1980s, then more recent novelists like Milena Agus, Salvatore Niffoi, and Murgia. Take this one by Benevenuto Lobina, *Po cantu Biddanoa*. And this autobiography by Vincenzo Sulis, who was technically a local writer in Alghero; he had been imprisoned for over twenty years in the Tower of Sulis on the bastion for his role in the rebellions against the Savoyards in Cagliari in the 1790s. The creative memoir of his tragic life, in all its embellishments, would not be published until 1964, despite the fact that Sulis had handed over the manuscript to historian Pasquale Tola in 1832. And this other novel by Gavino Ledda, the genius shepherd, whose first novel had sold over a million copies in Italy alone. So many other authors, especially poets, looked back as if outraged at being left on the shelf.

And then there was D. H. Lawrence.

"For the rest, I am not a Baedeker," Lawrence had proudly exclaimed, as he skirted the cathedral in Cagliari, referring to the British travel guide. The Englishman made no bones about his refusal to provide the facts and figures of his journeys—though, he did find the children in Cagliari, unexpectedly, to dress more "chic" than those in Kensington Gardens.

I often thought about this moniker of "travel writers." I had never cared for the term. It seemed contrary to its mission, as if giving boundaries or even borders to the very narratives that sought to transcend them. I had always preferred "traveling writer."

La Marmora, that venerable chronicler of Sardinia, even mocked the title of his book, decades after its publication. With all the "steamships and later by telegraphy, electric submarine," he wrote in 1860, the island was so close to the "continent" that he couldn't stand his title of "Voyage," as if any true journey demanded some unfathomable distance into the unknown.

In 1959, at the age of eighteen, a precocious cataloguer at Sotheby's in London named Bruce Chatwin arrived in Alghero and a wrote a postcard from Porto Conte to his parents about his experience hopping a coral boat. Without a car, Chatwin decided to give up on Sardinia and head back to the convenience of mainland Italy. He also had a harrowing evening looking for accommodations in Orgosolo in the mountainous Barbagia region, terrified of bandits. (There was none, to be sure.)

In 1974, Chatwin famously quit his job—then at *The Sunday Times Magazine*—and headed to South America. His first book, *In Patagonia*, published in 1977, introduced an innovative style of literary travel writing, and yet, Chatwin had written his American publisher and asked that the book not be listed in the category of travel.

Instead of following a linear script of his journey across Argentina, Chatwin's work followed the literary digressions of a wanderer, reflecting the restlessness of his own curiosity and the lives of those he met, especially immigrants. "All the stories," he told his agent, illustrated some aspect of wandering or exile, "what happens when you get stuck." In a letter to a friend, Chatwin described it as somewhere between "the narrative of an actual journey and a symbolic one." The distance in between those narratives, of course, was the literary journey.

In a new introduction to the book, author Nicholas Shakespeare wrote that Chatwin did not seek to depict Patagonia as it really is, but to "create a landscape called Patagonia—a new way of looking, a new aspect of the world."

In that respect, Lawrence similarly didn't seem to worry much with capturing Sardinia as it really was in 1921. His theme resounds in the wonderful first line of the book: "Comes over one an absolute necessity to move." Sardinia was the corridor of his personal journey, not the destination. Lawrence, like many traveling writers, rarely got beyond the doorstep of Sardinian cultures; he preferred to imagine the hills "so untouched, dark-blue, virgin-wild . . . standing outside of life."

Geoff Dyer, who chronicled Lawrence's journeys in his own quest, *Out of Sheer Rage: Wrestling with D. H. Lawrence*, explained the format of *Sea and Sardinia* was like being drenched in a "spray of ideas." Dyer considered it one of Lawrence's best books; Anthony Burgess called it his "most charming." Writing in the *Washington Post* in 2021, on the hundredth anniversary, journalist Walter Nicklin argued *Sea and Sardinia* marked the birth of modern travel writing.

After reading it, the wealthy arts patron Mabel Dodge Luhan wrote Lawrence and invited him to Taos, New Mexico. Lawrence responded the same day; within a year, he and the Queen B took up residence at a Taos ranch, the only property he would own in his life, having swapped the manuscript of his famous *Son and Lovers* novel in exchange for the property with Dodge Luhan. The wanderlust never let up in Lawrence's life, of course. He continued to travel and write until 1930, where he died in the south of France, unable to shake the complications of tuberculosis. His ashes were returned to his ranch in Taos.

Dodge Luhan told Lawrence that *Sea and Sardinia* was the "most actual of travel books," and praised him for his ability to relive his journeys "more vividly than he was able to do at the time." The narrative of the novelist's trip and his views ultimately became the attraction.

That attraction, including Lawrence's self-conscious crankiness, often seemed like a ploy to perk up the ears of the readers, to make sure they were paying attention. But the ridicule often missed its target outside the window. In Sardinia, Lawrence could capture the emotions of an elderly man, roasting a goat kid over the fire, quietly bewildered by the loss of young villagers in World War I—a war over what, still unsure—and then, in an immediate shift in tone, express his outrage over a lack of milk and food, cursing the "degenerate aborigines" and their long stocking caps.

As Sardinian journalist Giovanni Fancello noted in an anthology of essays on the hundredth anniversary of the Englishman's arrival in Sardinia, Lawrence toured the island in a period of economic crisis following the war, including areas of famine.

In 1919, in a column for the *Avanti* newspaper, Antonio Gramsci asked his readers: "Why can't one recall that Sardinian miners are paid starvation wages, while the shareholders in Turin fatten their portfolios with dividends crystallized from the blood of Sardinian miners, who often are reduced to eating roots to avoid dying of hunger?"

One month before Lawrence arrived in Sardinia, miners in Iglesias (in the southwestern area) were celebrating a victory in salary increases and cost of living allowances, as well as some concessions to their union. But it didn't come easy. They had to withstand a brutal period of repression against their strikes, including a massacre in the summer of 1920 that had left seven miners dead. Meanwhile, the mine owners in Sardinia had begun laying the first tracks of fascist groups on the island. On a bus trip, Lawrence couldn't help himself from goading a bus driver who mocked Sardinians and their mining strikes.

In January 1921, in the same days Lawrence toured Sardinia, Gramsci and Palmiro Togliatti, who had attended high school in Sassari, founded the Communist Party of Italy in Livorno. Sorgono, where Lawrence spent a rough night of discomfort, had been a hotbed of socialism in the 1890s, when Gramsci was a little child there. Gramsci would go on to represent the Communist Party in parliament until his arrest and imprisonment by the fascist government in 1926.

Later that spring in 1921, led by Sardinian patriots Lussu and Camillo Bellieni, veterans from the Sassari Brigade founded the Sardinian Action Party—*Partidu Sardu* or *Partito Sardo d'Azione*—as the first political party in Italy to demand autonomy. Bursting onto the national scene, the party won 36 percent of the vote on the island and sent Lussu to parliament as one of the leading anti-fascist political figures in the country.

There in Rome, in 1921, *Germinale sardo* was published by the Palombi Graphic Arts of Rome, featuring the poetry of Sardinian writer Stefano Susini. Celebrated Sardinian artist Francesco Ciusa designed the cover work; one of his sculptures had already been recognized as one of the "most important revelations" by critics at the Biennale in Venice. Along with work by artist Melkiorre Melis from Bosa, musician and scholar Gavino Gabriel from Gallura, who would become one of the most important musicologists in Italy (and the first to record Mussolini's voice on wax cylinder), wrote the preface.

While Deledda published a novel in 1921 (three books, actually), five years away from winning the Nobel Prize, Italian diva Eleonora Duse had already appeared in her only silent film, *Cenere*, in 1916, based on Deledda's famous novel. Across the sea in Paris, London, and New York, Jazz Age dancers kicked up their heels to the tunes by Sardinian composer Lao Silesu, who had cut his teeth playing piano in the mining town of Iglesias.

And while numerous Sardinian authors published books and continued to draw crowds for oral poetry competitions—the most important stage for narrative in that period—the year of 1921 also saw the publication of *Das ländliche Leben Sardiniens* by Max Wagner (eventually translated as *Rustic Life in Sardinia*), marking the beginning of decades of cherished ethnographical research and books by the revered German linguist on the island.

"Travel is certainly not comfortable," Wagner wrote in 1921, almost in anticipation of Lawrence's visit. "But, it's worth it. I do not believe that there are many regions in Europe where ancient customs and traditions have been better preserved; here, moreover, men—a beautiful and free race—reward all hardships."

14 | UNEARTHING MEMORY

For the Sardinians, stone is the main symbolic place of memory, since the most evident signs of an ancient history that have not been left very visible are mainly in stone. This election of the stone to the bearer of memory is so deeply rooted that in Campidano, to favor the memory of something important, it was customary to put a small stone in a pocket—sa pedra de s'arregodu, the stone of memory—in the same way where elsewhere a knot was made in the handkerchief.

—Michela Murgia, *Viaggio in Sardegna*

While our youngest son, Massimo, joined the Alghero village band with his saxophone, taking part in numerous concerts and processions that marked the calendar like a soundtrack, our oldest son, Diego, took the train every morning to Sassari, where he attended the Liceo Azuni high school, with a specific focus on music. He played the trombone and piano; he would eventually become a jazz pianist. Sassari was about a half-hour train ride to the northeast. The Azuni officials were proud of their alumni, including two former Italian heads of state, two former leaders of the Communist Party in Italy, and acclaimed writers Sebastiano Satta, Salvatore Ruju, Salvatore Mannuzzu, and Gavino

Ledda, among many others. (The role of women on this list, obviously, required more research.)

Born in Sassari, Azuni had been an eighteenth-century jurist, largely serving Napoleon in France, who eventually returned to Sardinia as a judge in Cagliari and as director of the university library. In 1798, he published a book in French on the history of Sardinia, which the *British Critic* magazine praised modestly: Sardinia, which had been little known, would now be "sufficiently" less so "by those who read this work."

With the kids in school, we decided to make two trips to two separate villages—one nearby in the northern area of Gallura, and a longer day trip to the Campidano valley in the south—to be sufficiently more aware of the island. And yet, both villages were more alike than we expected. They were connected by stones.

Couched by the granite boulders and green range of Monte Limbara, the agricultural village of Berchidda numbered less than a few thousand souls on a typical day. In the summer, it opened its doors and squares and farms, and whatever venues it could invent, and it became the cultural laboratory for tens of thousands of travelers for one of the largest jazz festivals in Italy.

A shepherd from the village once told a newspaper that he let his cows listen to jazz, because it "produced more milk."

At the other end of the island, less than fifteen miles north of Cagliari in the corridor that traversed the great valley toward Oristano, the village of San Sperate emerged like a sudden series of backstreets, unassuming at first, the buildings no more than a story or two, until the array of murals on the walls began to tell the story of a *paese-museo* or village museum that had also served as a cultural laboratory or arts incubator for the past half century.

The murals opened like unending windows into another Sardinia, envisioned by artists. Three men in their berritas huddled behind a newspaper. Others took their drink in a tavern. An open market, cornered by prickly pear—called *Sa Figu Murisca* or *Morisca* in Sardinian—shows a woman selling potatoes.

In 1923, *National Geographic* magazine featured a photo of women and children collecting the fruit from a massive prickly pear, with a note that a company was opening a factory near Cagliari to make alcohol from the fruits. Prickly pears and potatoes, like tomatoes, were imports from the Americas, which dramatically altered the diet in Italy and Europe. As one of the first regions in Italy to embrace the tomato, Sassari writer Andrea Manca dell'Arca wrote in 1780 on the use of tomatoes in Sardinian cooking. The recipes were a "milestone" in the history of the tomato in Italy, according to historian David Gentilcore. While one recipe was crucial on the ways to preserve tomatoes, a second recipe mentioned sun-dried tomatoes for the first time in the country. In 1805, as a year of famine had ravaged the island, Giuseppe Cossu published a pamphlet in Sardinian on the uses of "patatas." The simplest way to cook them, he suggested, was "in embers like chestnuts."

Born in San Sperate in 1942 to a farm family, similar to jazz leader Paolo Fresu, Pinuccio Sciola had grown up working in the fields. He called San Sperate a village of mud—and in fact, a tragic flood in 1892 drew international news, when a sudden downpour swept through the village and tore away half of the buildings, taking two hundred lives with it. "The floods that pour into the Campidano carry treasures to the sea," wrote the revered Sardinian poet Peppino Mereu.

Interested in pursuing art, Sciola, like Fresu, attended school in Cagliari, and then university in Florence, Salzburg, and Madrid. After living in Paris, he returned to San Sperate in the late 1960s as a student of the "university of nature," intent on shaping his village into an arts laboratory, with an emphasis on public art. Sciola's first phase was called the "Years in Lime" as he began to transform the walls of the village. After visiting and training in Mexico with famed muralist David Alfaro Siqueiros in the 1970s, Sciola returned to the stones of his childhood and led a campaign to paint hundreds of murals on the village walls.

On the other end of the island, the "fantastic slab-formed granite rocks were my stone books," recounted Fresu, "each with a story I told myself while I was helping my father with the sheep." The great trumpet player, the son of a shepherd, had joined the village band at the age of eleven, after it passed his house with a tremendous roar. "I was the only one convinced that being Sardinian was a sign of distinction, that we had unique things," he told an interviewer. Once Fresu heard a recording of Miles Davis, and then Chet Baker, the trumpet player never looked back, but he never lost touch with his village or Sardinia. The island was "the umbilical cord with the world."

By the time the *New York Times* hailed him as "original and sophisticated as any top trumpeter," and the cool jazz heir to Davis and Baker (who had spent a lot of time in Italy in the early 1960s, including a stint in prison for drugs), Fresu had appeared on the main stages in the world of jazz.

In 1988, he founded the "Time in Jazz" festival in Berchidda, bringing well-known artists to the village to perform in the countryside, as well as other unusual venues for jazz. What set the festival apart, for many musicians, was the diversity of the music, drawing on Sardinian and Italian folk music, as well as Classical and Baroque music, and jazz—and its connection to nature.

The trees, the stones, the water—as well as the village—became vital parts of the musical collaboration. "It was Paolo's concept to present a band at the main stage, and then a special project the next day in a different part of the island," Cuban pianist Omar Sosa recounted in *Downbeat* magazine in 2012. "He invited me to play solo by a eucalyptus tree. In the middle of the concert, I heard a trumpet. I looked around. It was Paolo on top of the tree. I thought, 'Wow, my man is crazy.' I switched to play some real conceptual Latin thing, and he followed. I said, 'Hey, my man is in the tree, but he listened to what I do.' He's got the freedom to create a moment and a space and be himself, no matter what happens."

"Why not play over the tree?" Fresu asked rhetorically. "The tree is one of the elements of this concert. For me, place is very important in music."

In 1996, that profound sense of place prompted Fresu to invite Sciola to the festival. The celebrated sculptor had already exhibited work at the Biennale in Venice, and in installations in Germany and across Italy, as well as in Sardinia. His memorial to coal miners massacred during a strike in 1904 in Buggeru featured the trachyte figures of the fallen miners in agonizing poses in stone.

Sciola's main focus was to "free the voice and the sound" of the stones, and allow "already existing voices, trapped for millions of years, to be heard." In carving a "jazz stone," Sciola collaborated with world-renowned percussionist Pierre Favre, who had also arrived in Berchidda. As the first public event to demonstrate his *pietre sonore* or sound stones, Sciola had cut precise grooves and lines in blocks of basalt and trachyte, like a stone accordion, which Favre played with his mallets and sticks, along with cymbals and other pieces of percussion. The main concern was whether the heavy stones would collapse the stage.

Studying the ancient forms of the Neolithic menhirs, the tall sacred stones found throughout the island, as well as the nuraghes, Sciola sought to "unearth memory from the stones." Using a blow torch, bringing back the rock to its molten origins, he was able to slice through the limestone and basalt and make "seed sculptures." Sciola cut exact lines, as if carving bread. In the process, the vertical cut released a harmonic sound from the vibration of touching or caressing the stones. Sciola, in fact, did not want the rocks to be played as percussive.

After making our journey to San Sperate, following the coastal road from Bosa and then across the Campidano, we remained spellbound at Sciola's stone garden in San Sperate for hours. After his death in 2016, his work exhibited around the world, his orchard had become his open museum. Hundreds of large blocks of stone were positioned in rows or circles, interspersed with fruit trees, as if Sciola had arranged his sculptures as monuments—or a series of instruments to play for some sort of ritual. Sciola's work possessed the intricate cuts that allowed the stones to tell their own stories, with the eerie song of a glass harmonium. In some ways, they appeared like a series of monuments with grids carved into them like codes; and, looking closely, you could see the incredibly thin slabs of stone that wavered with the touch.

The universe is made up of stones, Sciola would say. "If you give me complete freedom, I can give you the blood of stones."

Back in Berchidda, Fresu and his team created a year-round cultural institution that included art, cinema, and books, as well as music. It annually hosted over thirty-five thousand visitors, many from abroad. It had helped to shape the village's transition from an agro-pastoral village to an international arts center. The former milk cooperative, the Berchiddese, where Fresu's father had worked, was in the process of transforming into a recording studio—the first jazz production center in the Mediterranean islands, producing shows year-round with Sardinian and global musicians.

For his fiftieth birthday in 2011, Fresu performed at fifty locations in fifty days on the island, in a celebration of the diversity and richness of Sardinia's cultures. This extraordinary journey included venues on farms, piazzas, churches, mines, wind turbines, prisons, and ports. Appearing in front of the Nuraghe Nolza, in the village of Meana Sardo, Fresu was joined by singer Elena Ledda, the "diva" of Sardinian music, and Luigi Lai, the famed player of the traditional launeddas reed instrument, which dated back to the Nuragic period, among other musicians. A film montage by Sardinian director Gianfranco Cabiddu cast the images of *Sonos 'E Memoria* in the background. Other nationally known Sardinian writers and musicians joined Fresu on his tour, including rising literary stars Murgia and Flavio Soriga, testifying to a burgeoning cultural movement on the island that had long spilled over into Italy.

There at the nuraghe, though, which he felt "scrutinized" the Sardinia of today, Fresu sought to "give new life to the images of a remote past" and shake up our modern senses of its meaning—to weave new paths, he later wrote, "between tradition and modernity, memory and future."

Meeting with Fresu again in 2011 for an interview in a jazz magazine, Sciola said his dream had been to create a "symphony" of stones, with a unique and infinite sound. He referenced a letter from a friend: "When I listened to the sound of your rocks, my life was overwhelmed. I cannot look at a mountain or a nuraghe or a rock now without thinking that inside there is a repressed sound."

"If you think of a stone, you think of Sardinia," Sciola would say. "And if you don't find one here or there, it's because God, when he created the world, kept it in his pocket."

Before I left the stone garden, I picked up a notebook in the gift shop—made of limestone.

16 | MONTE D'ACCODDI

Fiza-limba tràchitas a ghineperu.
Una tremita tua naschinde
Est ch'astula de livrina in mes'a isteddos

et sas nues, sas nues a sa thurpas fughint
iscanzellande dae chelu onzi zenìas.

Daughter-tongue: you creak as the juniper does.
Your shudder at birth's a shard chipped off
a storm among the planets

and the clouds, the clouds blindly race
obliterating from the skies
all trace of lineage.

—Antonella Anedda, "Limba," 2007

The ziggurat of Monte d'Accoddi was a place of the gods, somewhere between *chelu e mare*, as singer Maria Carta might have sung.

That very word seemed somewhat outlandish—a ziggurat in Europe, in Sardinia of all places. Ziggurats were the ancient platform mounds and step pyramids that took shape in Mesopotamia in the fifth millennium B.C. like some scene out of the Tower of Babel. After driving down the back country road to reach the site, not quite seven miles from Sassari, passing farms on either side, I parked my car at a grassy clearing. At first glance, it looked like a hill; in fact, Monte d'Accoddi means a "mountain of stones." Stationed in the middle of the empty field like an airstrip, a long ramp came into view, bordered by stones that reached a slight landing, and then it climbed a wide staircase of stone steps up to the top of a mound platform on the pyramid. Walking around to the bottom of the ramp, I stood with a mix of wonder and bewilderment.

From a distance, the pyramid had seemed eerily alone, stripped of any humanity or other signs of construction. It stretched about 120 feet by 120 feet at the base. A massive stone carved in the shape of an egg at the foot of the long ramp appeared as if someone had rolled it down the steps. The oval stone was similar to the omphalos at Delphi in ancient Greece, a sacred rock boulder indicating the center of the world. To one side stood a seven-foot-tall, thin menhir, like a stone totem symbol. Four other menhirs were stationed around the area. On the opposite side of the pyramid was a dolmen, a small stack of rocks similar to Stonehenge.

I walked up the dirt ramp until I reached a platform, and then I began to scale the stone steps. It did not have the sharp climb of the pyramids in central Mexico, for example; and yet, the final ascent carried the same weight of solemnity of hallowed ground. From the top of the platform, I could see the full view of the valley, the long ramp of stone steps now appearing like a sacred passage from earth to the sky. I felt the powerful role of an altar that sought to connect to the cosmos of the times.

Discovered in the 1950s, the original pyramid structure dated back to 4000–3500 B.C.—nearly six thousand years ago. One thing set it apart from other ziggurats or pyramids: Monte d'Accoddi was built on a carefully arranged stone foundation, brick by brick, including the corner foundations, as well as the ramp. The ziggurats in Mesopotamia, for example, used mud bricks, not stone. According to archaeologists, the pyramid developed over two stages. The second stage, around 3200 B.C., added an altar, where excavations have found the residue of sheep, pigs, and cattle, most likely used for sacrifices.

For all of its otherworldliness, there was something incredibly inviting about the pyramid, as if it had been built as a stepping stone to a singular moment of humanity in time. It beckoned one to scale it. I could imagine Monte d'Accoddi being a site of pilgrimage for those across the island. Standing at the top, on the platform where an altar had once been positioned to either petition the gods or defy them, I marveled at being all alone. There was no one else at the site, other than a couple of staff in a small office at the edge of the field.

While I had scaled the Tikal pyramids in Guatemala with a similar feeling of awe, this monument in Sardinia went back several more thousands of years on our timeline of existence, as a sacred landmark in Neolithic Europe. The antiquity, still preserved, signaled a hinge moment in history; it recognized an organization of civilization that literally took a step forward, and beyond what had been imagined in the past. It was truly one of the most incomparable scenes in Europe, at least in my experience.

I never would have expected such a place in Sardinia. A place where one stood on the foundations of "civilization" in Europe; a sacred space that had endured for thousands of years, I should add, drawing pilgrims from far-flung stretches of the island, and beyond.

"We are used to thinking of 'civilization' as something that originates in cities," David Graeber reminded us in his book, *The Dawn of Everything: A New History of Humanity*, "but, armed with new knowledge, it seems more realistic to put things the other way round and to imagine the first cities as one of those great regional confederacies, compressed into a small space."

This sentiment resounded with me often in Sardinia. The reality that architectural wonders, for example, had emerged out of the genius of small communities on a small island; and the more breathtaking reality that these massive artifacts, like the nuraghes and this ziggurat, still endured as a presence on the island. They were not simply legends or tales in a story, however ancient. They were not bits and pieces of stones in a museum, however enigmatic. The foundations of civilization on this island, as a nexus in the Mediterranean, and ultimately Europe, provided a glimpse into the very stepping stones of progress in an age that saw a shift from the first stone tools for organized farming to the first stone wheels that rolled into existence. In the process, these architectural marvels were assembled in Sardinia as a collective act of knowledge and ability, not as a mysterious phenomenon.

Archaeologists also found numerous tombs within the pyramid, including subterranean chambers similar to the Neolithic *domus de janas* burial grounds carved into rock chambers all across the island. Like many of the stone necropolis sites in Sardinia, the tombs included the carvings of bull horns, as symbols of status. As noted earlier, a whale's tooth, among other artifacts, had been discovered, linking the inland site to the sea.

Aerial photos of the site had captured the seemingly obvious, but hidden ruins in 1950. It was literally buried under mounds of dirt and overgrowth for thousands of years. Abandoned at the beginning of the Nuragic civilization, the site had been known for centuries. Most visitors, including archaeologists in the early 1900s, assumed it contained the ruins of another nuraghe. Like thousands of others, it was left to sit underground.

Imagine how many other Monte d'Accoddi sites are sitting under the seven thousand nuraghes that have never been excavated in Sardinia.

It wasn't until the 1950s, with the land owned by Antonio Segni, one of the alumni from Liceo Azuni, who would go on to become the president of Italy, that the first excavations were funded. Segni actually procured the initial funds.

A ceramic bowl with dancing figures, as noted during the ballu tondu, among other pottery pieces, was collected in the excavation. A small limestone stele with clear incisions, as if marking time or a name, appeared in one of the tombs. To be sure, it marked a lexicon on the island in ancient times. Other pieces of ceramics, as well as a male figure in red ochre, were found. In one section of the tombs, large amounts of obsidian, shells, and other materials covered the area. In fact, the limestone foundations for a village hut surrounded one side of the pyramid.

In the underworld of the tombs, archaeologists also uncovered a beautiful stone carving of a goddess. Her hands on her hips, with thin arms, and a triangular torso, the goddess had been interpreted as representing "mother earth"—*la Dea Madre*. The endearing figure, with her circular head and "globe" eyes, was not alone. Similar carvings of the dea madre had been found at Neolithic necropolis sites across Sardinia, from the smaller island of Sant'Antioco, to the western coasts near Cabras, to the Barbagia mountains near Orgosolo, to domus de janas sites near Alghero, Porto Torres, and Sassari. A carpenter in the 1940s near Macomer, who was digging near his orchards, found the oldest recorded female sculpture. He had reached into the ground and picked up the "Venus of Macomer," as it is called, fractured in certain areas, but with a clear face, trunk, and thighs carved from a volcanic or basalt rock. It was recently dated to the late Pleistocene age—at least fifteen thousand years old.

Such antiquity, mixed with art and ritual, did not feel extraneous to the island today, like some relic of another culture, but a fundamental part of the Sardinian experience.

As I made my way back to the car and then slowly eased through the farms in the flatlands, rows and rows of artichokes in season, I wondered how a forty-five-hundred-year-old dea madre statue ended up on the Christie's auction block in 2014, on sale for $1 million, only to be halted at the last minute by an uproar from Sardinian activists. Nurnet had launched similar campaigns to stop the auction of Nuragic bronzetti in London.

It was a question American archaeologist Gary Webster asked in his own analysis in 2019: How could Monte d'Accoddi, with its singular existence, be missing from most studies on Neolithic Europe, including the most recent *Oxford Handbook of Neolithic Europe*, which actually featured a dea madre sculpture from Sardinia on its cover? Classical archaeology and its bevy of scholars had certainly carved out a new role for Sardinia in their once narrow corridors of western civilization. The *Cambridge Prehistory of the Bronze and Iron Age Mediterranean* handbook even featured a Nuragic bronze ship on its cover, as well, as if its shipment still waited to be inspected.

"The Carthaginians drown any strangers who sail past, on their voyage to Sardinia," Strabo wrote in his *Geography* in Greek, sometime around 23 A.D., reminding us that a nation's odyssey was not necessarily silent, but silenced. In modern times, that silencing continued in other forms.

This made me think of Murgia's powerful novel, *Accabadora*, winner of the Premio Campiello, and its mother-daughter drama of adoption and historical denial—and historical revelation. "Maria had long ago stopped pondering the mysterious nocturnal expeditions of her elderly adoptive mother," Murgia wrote, "but now these suppressed memories came back to hit her like the elastic of a catapult, prompting the thought that Bonaria Urrai might have something serious to hide."

I was also curious what was hiding in the worship of a female goddess from the Paleolithic to the Neolithic that supposedly came to an end in the Bronze Age? The emphasis on dea madre artifacts eventually shifted to Nuragic bronze and other sculptures dominated by men, including archers and warriors, boxers and wrestlers, and priests and village headsmen. The pioneering Sardinian archaeologist Lilliu glibly remarked in 1963, perhaps as a reflection of his own times, that "in this society of men—body and soul—women bring a note of kindness and grace but also of dignity and severe composure, sometimes of a silent and solemn tragic nature: as she still is today, the Sardinian woman."

In assessing materials found in burial tombs, as well as the portraits in the bronzetti, such as Nuragic priestesses, archaeologist Fulvia Lo Schiavo observed that Nuragic women actually shared an "equal treatment" in life and death rituals at a level that was "almost unique in the ancient world." Decades after Lilliu's pioneering Nuragic research, Lo Schiavo's more updated analysis suggested that the "secret" of Nuragic welfare and equality for women ultimately faded into the upheaval from colonization of the Phoenicians and then the Carthaginians.

That "secret" continued to be in dispute in the 1390s, when Eleonora of Arborea became the judge or ruler of her judicadu, in defiance of the Aragon incursions onto the island. In updating and promulgating the Carta de Logu code of laws, written in Sardinian, which provided women rights for inheritance, compensation for adultery, and stricter laws for rape, Eleonora placed Sardinia ahead of most European nations in the medieval period.

"In the 'stranger's room' of the Porru house a woman sat crying," began Deledda's novel, *After the Divorce*, questioning that "secret" in Sardinian life for women, five hundred years after Eleonora's reign. It was one of the first novels to deal with the theme of divorce, published in 1902.

After Deledda won the Nobel Prize in 1926, an American news story noted that it was "strange" that she continued to write about Sardinia after she moved to Rome. "Sardinia holds very little interest for the world in general. It is not rich in artistic treasures as is most of Italy. Sardinia's charm, perhaps, is its isolation; civilization has not as yet dulled it or cut it down to the standardized pattern."

In the 1920s, Sardinian poet Marianna Bussalai, an ardent feminist voice and an anti-fascist and independence activist from the mountain village of Orani until her death in 1947, once wrote a note to poet Antioco "Montanaru" Casula, about "the Sardinian women, quiet and ignored poetesses of the shadows." As a performer and writer of poetry, in Sardinian, Bussalai saw her Sardinian identity inseparable with her role as a woman.

Hiding Sardinian patriot Emilio Lussu from fascist forces under the trapdoor of her cellar, after he had once fled Cagliari, she would later add: "My Sardism dates from before the Sardinian Action Party arose, that is, from when, on the benches of elementary schools, I humbled myself why in the history of Italy there was never any talk of Sardinia. I came to the point that Sardinia was not Italy and had to have a history of its own."

Its own history, like Monte d'Accoddi, you could add, like the dea madre—and all the women in Sardinia.

PART THREE

SA DIE DE SA SARDIGNA
THE DAY OF THE
SARDINIAN PEOPLE

E commo Deus de chelu, a chie canto cust'urtima cantone
    cana?
A bentanas apertas a su tempu nobu primissu a Sardigna,
barandilla de mare e de chelos? Su bentu ghettat boches.

And now, God of heaven, to whom do I sing this last,
    white-haired poem?
With windows wide open to the new time promised to
    Sardinia,
balcony of seas and skies? The wind whispers voices to me.

        —Pedru Mura, "Fippo operaiu 'e luche soliana," 1963

15 | SARDINIAN CONTADINA

After meeting Maria Carta, once again I affirm that the only great men in Sardinia are our women.

—Giuseppe Dessí, "Delirio," 1974

A decade or so before Saul Steinberg's iconic "View of the World from 9th Avenue" cover for *The New Yorker*, that wonderful portrait of Manhattan as the center of the world, the Romanian-American artist did a similar take on Paris and Sardinia. Steinberg, by the way, had studied in Italy, and did his first satirical cartoons for a magazine in Milan until he had to flee during the fascist Racial Laws. He and Sardinian artist Costantino Nivola were lifelong friends, having reunited in New York City in the 1940s, and exhibited their work together. Untitled, the cartoon featured a "sophisticated Paris *femme* and a Sardinian *contadina*, who compare their lives in the form of talk-balloon maps." The Parisian map covers a block of wide boulevards. The smaller Sardinian map has a few roads crossing the entire island. When the drawing made the cover of *The New Yorke*r in 1963, the Sardinian had been altered to a more urbane-looking woman, though with the same map.

Sardinian illustrator Edina Altara, who grew up in Sassari, also did several covers for art magazines in Italy based on images from her island, a generation or so before Steinberg. Her work, in fact, as a designer, was featured in the Brooklyn Museum of Art in the same years that Steinberg was establishing himself in New York. Edina would have had plenty of streets to chat about on that *New Yorker* cover; along with her two sisters, Iride and Lavinia, their work in ceramic, textiles, sculpture, painting and illustration, furniture design, and even toymaking, had appeared in numerous exhibits, books, and magazine stories. In a special edition of his *Domus* magazine, the famous Italian architect Giovanni "Gio" Ponti praised Edina for her works of art as the "painting storyteller," especially in her design of mirrors and chests, which fanned out with the illustrated stories from Athena and Bacchus myths.

Born in the 1890s, the Altara sisters had no formal training in Sassari. As children, they experimented with colored pencils and paper. Working first with collage, Edina was discovered by Sassari artist Giuseppe Biasi, who would go on to become known as the "Gauguin of Sardinia" for his extraordinary paintings of rural scenes and landscapes, and nude portraits from his journeys in North Africa. As part of an arts and cultural revival of a more romantic version of Sardinian pastoral life in the 1910s, driven by the success of novelist Grazia Deledda, Biasi became the leading painter to interpret "primitive" scenes of shepherds and villagers at work. He illustrated the covers for several of Deledda's novels.

Biasi, to be sure, was from the city—he went to Liceo Azuni, too. His impressions of rural life in Sardinia, especially as he traveled extensively one summer, brought its own set of judgments. But Biasi's impressionistic paintings were incredibly evocative, transcending the "ethnographic" curiosity of "primitive" Sardinia into a more "noble" representation of pastoral life. His work also countered the bandit narrative of the times

with colorful scenes of dances, women poets and singers, religious gatherings, and daily life. His Sardinians gathered in picturesque but dignified settings. Sardinia was no arcadian paradise, however. There was
beauty, but also heartbreak. His painting, *The Bride of Teulada*, for example, juxtaposed the ornate traditional dress of a young bride atop a
horse, in the foreground of a bleak landscape, an accordion player and
shawled nun looking away, as if the future of the young woman was unclear, even painful. His *Processione nella Barbagia di Fonni* in watercolor,
which beautifully captures a procession through a mountain village, appeared to raves at the Venice Biennale in 1909. Despite comparisons to
Matisse and Modigliani, and his continual appearance at shows in Rome,
Milan, and Venice, Biasi struggled, like many artists, to pay his bills.
His last solo show in Sassari was in 1939, though he returned in 1940 to
create a flowing mosaic on the central staircase of the Palace of Justice.

In 1945, accused of being a collaborator with the Nazis, Biasi was
killed in the aftermath of World War II, then living in northern Italy.

Biasi's support of Altara, however, allowed a teenage Edina to de-
velop and exhibit her collage work in paper, fabric, and thread. In his
footsteps, she moved to northern Italy, where her "cubo-futurist" collage work at an exhibition in Turin in 1917, *In the land of the intrepid
Sardinians*, was purchased by King Vittorio Emanuele III. It still re-
sides today in the Quirinale, the palace residence of the president of
the Italian Republic. With Edina still in her teens, the critics in Italy
hailed her "prodigious hands" and "stylistic synthesis, of truth, of a
local character, and even of psychological expression." Other critics
slammed Edina for her audacity as a young woman in the male-dominated art world. One critic questioned the "excessive" admiration for
the "gracefulness of her slender person and the brightness of her black
eyes." There is a photo of Edina that captures the flare of her artistic
attire in a flowing dress, her dark hair pulled back in a bun with a

flower, her dark eyebrows, and her turned bare shoulder rebuffing the photographer's gaze. As a woman, a Sardinian, and an artist, she defied the expectations of her times.

Married in the 1920s to a successful illustrator and artist, Edina turned their home into an arts laboratory in Milan, where she worked as a designer in various materials for magazines, furniture and toy production, and large-scale paintings and installations. In 1932, she illustrated the lavish thirty-six-page Art Deco booklet for the *SS Rex*, the Italian version of the *Titanic*, which sought to woo the aristocrats at the height of the fascist dictatorship. The *Rex* had a similar fate of the *Titanic*, though; it sank in the Adriatic Sea after being bombed by the British air force during World War II.

Separating from her husband in 1934, Edina continued to work with leading magazines and companies throughout the 1950s, including Ponti's *Domus*, and *Belleza*, a competitor of *Vogue*. Along with her illustrations for children's books, which she had done since the 1920s, she focused on reinterpreting furniture as art, adding a storytelling component. She wanted fine furniture to not be "embalmed" in museums but treated as living things.

Her career as a single businesswoman, however, would eventually fade. Edina returned to Sassari in the 1970s to reunite with her sisters. She died in 1983, in the town of Lanusei, not far from Maria Lai's artistic village in the Ogliastra hills near the southeastern coast. It would take another forty years before her once-famous work reappeared in Sassari, when two painted mirrors that had been commissioned and installed on a ship in the 1950s, titled *Neptune and Allegory of the Earth*, were exhibited at the Pinacoteca (the National Art Museum) in the city of her birth in 2022.

I thought about that *New Yorker* map, comparing the lives of women in Sardinia, when I departed Sassari one day, winding about its enigmatic roads, and then past the Gothic feel of the hillside Corso Vittorio Emanuele, where side streets of commerce and incidental piazzas appeared out of nowhere. The Parisian and Sardinian had more in common than we could imagine. The most famous cuisine of Sassari might have been the *ciogga* (*minuta* or *grossa*)—escargot, in French—these wonderous little snails that ended up in a broth of potatoes, garlic, and parsley or various sauces. The snail-sucking *Ciogghitta d'oro* festival in Sassari was one of the most popular events.

Sassari was a city of surprises. Home of the University of Sassari, founded in 1558 by a member of the imperial chancellery and led by the Jesuits in 1562, it had an unvarnished sophistication about it. While dating back to ancient times, the Fountain of Rosello—*funtana di Ruseddu*, in Sassarese—was a late Renaissance symbol of the city, which had weathered enough plagues, riots, and conflicts to stand as a monument to the city's resilience and eternal waterways. In August, the historic center was lined with thousands of people, who followed a procession of artisan guilds that carried a massive wooden candlestick to mark the end of a plague that dated back to the seventeenth century.

Not everything was on the map in Sassari, especially for women. At the G.A. Sanna National Archaeological Museum, built like a Roman temple on Via Roma, the treasures from Monte d'Accoddi were on display. The venerable dea madre from the historic site stretched her five-thousand-year-old arms in stone; the dancers from the ceramic appeared to move in a circle. A small bronzetti of a Nuragic woman in a long cloak awaited visitors, holding a bowl as an offering, her head wrapped by an apparent veil. She didn't look demure; she looked in charge.

Farther down the streets, the Piazza Castello opened into a large square that was a reminder that the namesake *castello* or castle, which had been built by the occupying forces of the Aragonese from Spain

in 1323, was demolished by the Savoyards in the late nineteenth century to smite that memory. Excavations by archaeologists in 2008
uncovered underground tunnels and limestone rooms that had been
used by the Inquisition in the sixteenth century as prisons, including the *carcel de las mujeres*, the women's prison. One of the most
famous trials was against Julia Carta, as a witch and heretic for using
traditional medicines. While Carta's life was spared, the Inquisitor
condemned her to wear the *sanbenito*, a garment of shame that included a special tunic or hooded robe, or even a hat that resembled
a dunce cap.

The heretic Julia Carta had come from the town of Siligo, which
was twenty miles south of the city, and where I was heading for another visit. But I was in search of another Carta—Maria Carta, the
celebrated folk singer, poet, and actress of Sardinia, who, incidentally,
as a "barefoot" village girl, ended up serving as a city councillor in
Rome in the bare-fisted politics of the 1970s as a representative of the
Communist Party.

Carta, who was born in 1934, emerged as an internationally known
folk singer in the 1960s, though her range drew on the extraordinary
diverse traditions in Sardinian song. She could bring a crowd to tears,
joy, or outrage with her renditions of traditional ballads to the polyphonic *gosos* of the tenores, Gregorian chants, religious music, and her
own original songs based on ethnographic research.

French music scholar François Regis Barbry declared in the 1970s:
"There are women whose talent, face or voice have the perfection of
symbols, the evidence of flags. Women who, on their own, represent
a country. France had Piaf, and Chile, Violeta Parra, Greece, Irene
Pappas, Portugal, Amalia Rodriguez. A certain America, Joan Baez.
Sardinia is Maria Carta."

"In Sardinia, singing was born female, together with poetry, in the
time of matriarchy," Carta told an interviewer once. When you collect

a song, she added, it was like opening an archive of women that had been closed, and then giving it "new life" by "putting something of your own pain and joy."

Losing her father at the age of eight placed the family in economic hardship. Maria recalled working in the fields of wheat and olives, spinning wool, and collecting wood with a grandmother who "stared at the timeless stones, felt the charm of nothingness." At an early age, Maria drew attention for her singing in the church, and among the women *cantadores* that performed the improvised poetry songs in the competitions in the piazzas and festivals. "In the street I always sang. When the shepherds heard me they said, today, there is Maria from the river." In 1957, she won the "Miss Sardinia" contest, though her real victory, in her own words, was to get a driver's license and leave for Rome.

While Rome opened the door for music schools and stages with other folk singers, Carta realized it was her Sardinian songs, sung in her Logudorese variant, that distinguished her. She continued to do more research, collect and write more songs. "At a certain point I announced *sa disisperada*," Carta wrote, "a song of the dawn, of the awakening that comes from the archaic Sardinian folk traditions." In a nice intersection of traditions among generations, she worked with pioneering ethnomusicologist and composer Gavino Gabriel, who had come from the northern area of Gallura and made the first gramophone recordings of *canti di Gallura, dell'Anglona, Marghine e della Barbagia* in 1922.

"Among the rare documents of the Logudorese language," novelist Dessì noted, "there are the songs that Maria makes known to the world." By 1971, Carta released her first album, soon joining Amalia Rodrigues, queen of Portuguese *fado* music, on tour. She headlined concerts and festival across Europe, the Soviet Union, and the States. She was a regular performer on national Italian TV programs. In 1974,

Carta published a collection of poetry, *Canto Rituale*, dealing with the social justice issues of the day, including the poor treatment of miners, the destruction of Sardinian forests, and the clash over tourism. "Ziu Grallinu saw on the news an industrialist dancing in Porto Cervo buying coasts in Sardinia. He shouted: they give him the contributions, we don't have anything to eat!"

With her national profile and social justice activities, Carta's entrance into politics on behalf of the Communist Party should not have been a surprise. The Communist Party, of course, had been founded by Gramsci and other Sardinians, among others. The leader of the Communist Party in Italy in the 1970s and early 1980s was Enrico Berlinguer, who had been a student at the Liceo Azuni in Sassari, and a popular Sardinian political leader since the 1940s. (Berlinguer's name underscored his family's Catalan origins; he was also distantly related to the two future presidents and prime ministers from Sassari, Antonio Segni and Francesco Cossiga. His grandfather had founded *La Nuova Sardegna* newspaper.)

Carta's four-year tenure on the Rome city council also corresponded with her growing role as an actress in the theatre and in film. She appeared in numerous films, including Franco Zeffirelli's *Jesus of Nazareth*, Francis Ford Coppola's *The Godfather II*, Giuseppe Tornatore's first film, *Il Camorrista*, and Sardinian filmmaker Gianfranco Cabiddu's *Disamistade*.

In one of her last visits to Siligo in 1993, Carta spoke with the community about her journey. "Going out into the world, entering a culture that is not ours and giving sound to our songs has not always been easy, because there was a great fear of not being understood," she said. In order to give life to the identity of Sardinians, she added, it was necessary to get the songs "out of the archives, to make them dance, to make them sing, because through singing we become women."

Meandering through the little hill town of Siligo, where modest two-story buildings framed the streets as if out of a song by Carta, unaffected by the crass facades of tourism, it felt like the singer's world-renowned legacy had finally come home at a museum dedicated in her memory. Her image hung on the side of a home. The rest of the world ambled by, as if she resided there like any local. She died in 1994, at the age of sixty, from cancer. Her songs, she would have reminded us, had long been freed from the closed doors of the archives.

A few miles down from Siligo was the little village of Borutta, where Ninetta Bartoli became the first woman mayor in all of Italy, elected on March 10, 1946. (Italian women only gained the right to vote in 1945. In 1947, Margherita Sanna was elected mayor in the Sardinian hill town of Orune, "wrapped in a peasant's shawl," Italian writer Carlo Levi wrote in his travel memoir on the island.) She won 332 out of 371 votes. At her inauguration, Bartoli wore her traditional dress. Over twelve years of service, she built the first schools, and sewage system, and established a milk cooperative for the shepherds.

The role of women in leadership positions in Sardinia, in defiance of a male-dominated politics, dated back hundreds of years, as we have learned, with Eleonora of Arborea, the judge who ruled over much of Sardinia in the late 1300s. As author Dessì said of Maria Carta, her voice filled the "deep spaces, where Sardinia at the edge of prehistory is relived."

18 | THE VALLEY OF THE NURAGHES

And it is in this way that—thanks to the brilliant bed of Mother
Earth—continually enriching herself with the virtues of the other
stars as well, she has made herself the star pillar of the sky and
will be able to erect Nuraghi ever closer to the galaxies.

—Gavino Ledda,

Un'ode alla mia Madre Terra: per lei farò parlare le pietre, 2011

South of Siligo, the road continued across rolling green hills into rolling green plains, where outcroppings of rocks and long stretches of
rugged fields cultivated the feeling of solitude. The abandoned rows of
almond trees always impressed me. Someone's dream, now gone with
the travails of the market, while the fruit nuts waited in anticipation.
By now, I knew better; so many of the "empty" fields and quiet narrow
roads that had more grazing animals than car traffic belied a history
of forced depopulation and displacement, rather than any arcadian
story of nature.

Every traveling writer—every tourist, for that matter, that ventured into the interior—noticed the seemingly lonely landscapes in
Sardinia. Having grown up in southern Illinois and Arizona, where
one could literally drive on back roads for long stints without a glimpse

of steel and concrete, such solitary wanders appeared normal to me. Not in the rest of Italy. Of course, Italy's urban design since the ancient Roman grid to the agropolis was more than urban planning or architecture; it was rare to be alone on the mainland, even if you sought it out. The Italians tended to congregate, as if the single reader in the café or piazza, immersed in a good novel, was a sad stranger to the local ways, an outlier to the norm. On the long stretches of a beach, it was more common to see a huddle of a group than the wider spacing of individuals.

Therefore, the "freedom" of Sardinia that Lawrence and everyone gushed over was real, and not just because of the predominance of natural beauty. To be sure, Sardinia's splendor of wilderness and forests, from the coasts to the Gennargentu mountain range, determined so much of its geography. Yet, the freedom of so many of those open corridors of "nature," instead, was a paradox; what we saw, as outsiders, was its forced abandonment over the years—the decades, the centuries, even the millennia. As American historian John Day noted in his essays on medieval history in Sardinia, "no region of Europe has been more cruelly tested than Sardinia by famines, epidemics and violence" in the Middle Ages. Day's groundbreaking work on censuses found that half of the Sardinian villages were "wiped from the map" in the medieval period. It didn't get better into the Renaissance or post-Renaissance period; the Thirty Years' War was not only contained in central Europe in the early to mid-1600s. An estimated twelve thousand Sardinian soldiers were sent off to die in battles alongside the Spanish, depleting nearly 5 percent of the population. The Spanish returned with a plague at midcentury that decimated rural communities for the rest of the century. Historians calculate that a third of the island perished in a famine in the 1680s. More plagues and famines continued into the 1700s and early 1800s, as the reign of the Savoyards controlled the economies of the island. And then we must address the devastation from two world wars and their fallout in the first half of the twentieth century.

How does a field or plain show the aftermath of plagues and climatic disruptions, of invasions, of colonial occupations and wars and deployment of its men in foreign wars? I wondered how we could understand the gross mismanagement by absentee lords and landlords that had plundered the land of its forests, and eventually altered thousands of years of tradition by partitioning the land with *tanca* walls that ended the open grazing and seasonal movement of shepherds to open pastures. In our lifetimes, we saw the remains of the upheaval of a pastoral market for products in a synthetic age and global economy.

Freedom in Sardinia was indeed embedded in the landscape and the DNA of its inhabitants. But that was a different freedom outside our purview as visitors—that freedom of transhumance, the seasonal shift of pastoral societies from summer to winter to summer, from the mountains to the valleys; it was the freedom of navigators along the sea; it was the freedom of traders, on an island, whose thousands of years of endurance had been predicated on exchange and cooperation of decentralized small communities, not the building of towering cities.

I stumbled onto a newspaper in the 1960s, the *Messaggero Sardo*, which had been created for Sardinians who had emigrated elsewhere. One of the headlines served as the street marker of my journey now, as I drove to the Nuraghe Santu Antine: "In the shadow of the great nuraghe is the struggle to live." The subtitle: "Immigration has emptied Torralba and destroyed hope."

The great Sardinian pastoral was forever in flux.

"To be a writer I had to come back here and become a shepherd of sounds, of music, just as I had been a shepherd of sheep," the extraordinary novelist and linguist Gavino Ledda once said. Several years younger than Maria Carta, Ledda had also grown up in Siligo, or just outside.

A hundred years earlier, the famed Italian anthropologist Paolo Mantegezza had strangely warned: "The errant herder, the perfect character for the anthropologist or the novelist, is the ruin of Sardinia."

With the publication of his autobiographical novel, *Padre Padrone* (My Father, My Master), Ledda's story became a global sensation, selling millions of copies in over forty languages. At the age of six, Ledda was dragged out of the school in Siligo by his authoritarian father, who divided the world between the lambs and the lion, and subjected his son and family to the brutal rigors of the pastoral life. Ledda herded sheep and tended to the dirt farm until the age of twenty. Like those in the pages of the *Messaggero Sardo*, he had planned on immigrating to northern Europe to work in the factories; instead, he did his military service on the mainland in Italy, which provided a new access to education. At the age of twenty-five, Ledda ended up back in Sassari, where he attended the Liceo Azuni high school and managed to gain his diploma. As one teacher said, "we didn't know Gavino Ledda would become Gavino Ledda." Within a few years, he earned a degree in linguistics at the University of Rome and became a professor and scholar of minority languages, including Sardinian.

Ledda's novel, which was published in 1975, and immediately sold 1.5 million copies in Italy alone, did more than any work since Deledda's novels to take the Sardinian pastoral story to an international audience. Its harshness, at the hands of the father, became a searing statement on the realities of life in rural Sardinia—and a young man's struggle to rebel and understand his rapport with the land. The film adaptation by celebrated Italian filmmakers Paolo and Vittorio Taviani in 1977 won the Palme d'Or at the Cannes film festival. The

New York Times hailed it as "stirringly affirmative." Ledda went on to publish other novels and essays, and appear in films and theatre as an actor, including the recent film on agriturismo, *Assandira*, where Ledda flipped the script and played the role of the shepherd father.

To his father's version of the lamb and the lion, Ledda would add: "I learned another language, that of the elephant. The elephant does not tear lambs to pieces, but no lion dares to touch the elephant, because it fears its trumpeting and the blows of its trunk." That seemed like an apt metaphor for many Sardinians. (Funnily enough, the remains of dwarf elephants from the late Pleistocene—twenty-five thousand to one hundred thousand years or so ago—were found near Alghero.)

I wasn't interested in going back that far in history, though. I ventured into this area known as the Valley of the Nuraghes or Nuraghi. In fact, my Nurnet app on the nuraghe map was blowing up on the drive. Ledda himself had been "adopted" as the island's "living nuraghe" by the southern town of Orroli, at the site of the massive Nuraghe Arrubiu in 2011, where he dedicated an ode to the earth, and on making the "stones speak."

I had chosen this particular nuraghe, Santu Antine, one of the largest in northern Sardinia, for a couple of reasons. Mainly, though, I wanted to see one of the earliest examples of the tholos nuraghe towers, which emerged in the Middle Bronze as "a historical turning point," according to Lilliu. The tholos were effectively a step up from the earlier, less-sophisticated protonuraghes rock structures that had been developed by the "Bonnanara phase" in the third and second millennium. Those stone structures were more like platforms.

While the natural progression of thousands of years of megalithic trial and error in Sardinia would seem obvious, most observers and archaeologists in the nineteenth and even mid-twentieth century assumed the technology to build the nuraghes and their corbelled vaults had been brought by outside civilizations, such as the Egyptians, the Minoans, the Phoenicians or Canaanites, the Iberians, or whatever mythical heroes and giant sons had been put into a classical story. Even Lilliu, the militant Sardinian archaeologist, held out until the 1960s that the Mycenaeans (ancient Greeks in the Bronze Age), with their cyclopean stone buildings, had assisted in the development of the Nuragic towers. With updated radiocarbon dating techniques, however, archaeologists learned that the nuraghe actually predated or corresponded with eastern Mediterranean structures, forcing them to "recalibrate" their theories on east-to-west technological exchange and the internal progression of Neolithic to Bronze Age cultural ways. To be sure, similar stone towers, though far less prevalent or expansive, could be found in the Balearic Islands off Spain, as well as Corsica.

In 1955, a delegation of well-known Italian writers visited Santu Antine, among other sites in Sardinia. The national RAI television network documented the journey of the writers, which included Nobel Laureate Giuseppe Ungaretti, all in their suits and ties and fedora hats. The cameras clearly sought to juxtapose the writers with rustic elements and characters, as if to showcase Italy's fascination with the "other world" of Sardinia in a postwar industrial economy.

Traveling the dirt roads in a bus from village to village and landmark to landmark, the writers did their part to uplift the "thousands-of-years-old civilization," as if the island was on the cusp of joining the modern world. The esteemed Italian poet Giorgio Caproni, as part of the crew, declared the stones of Sardinian were "talking stones," and the first language of the island. Keep in mind: In that same summer in 1955, the *New York Times* ran a travel piece on "pre-tourist Europe in Sardinia," where the island was still trying to get beyond the conviction that it was as "dangerous and disagreeable as the heart of the African jungle."

When I arrived at the parking lot of the nuraghe, I noticed a charming outside dining space and education center adjacent to a shop and bookstore. Its setting in this pleasant green valley, the rocky promontories and nearby plateaus perfectly aligned as lookout stations, reminded me of visiting a national park. I could envision *La Sardegna verso l'UNESCO* campaign rooted here. The movement to recognize the nuraghes and other Neolithic and Bronze Age monuments as World Heritage Sites, celebrating the "deep identity that comes from the historical roots of Sardinia and its ancient civilization, as well as representing a milestone of Sardinian culture," made sense out here. It was less than an hour's drive from either Sassari or Alghero, and an easy day trip from the Costa Smeralda tourist areas.

For comparison, more than a quarter million people annually visited the Cahokia Mounds State Park and its pyramid-like mound in my own southern Illinois, since it had been listed as a World Heritage Site. The peak of that indigenous civilization dated back to 1000 A.D. More than five million visitors took in the Chesapeake and Ohio Canal National Historical Park near Washington, DC, every year. That "historic" park was a lovely canal that operated from 1831 until 1924 along the Potomac River. In England, an estimated one million tourists journey to the prehistoric Stonehenge ring of standing stones every year.

The campaign to attract more visitors to Sardinia's nearly four-thousand-year-old nuraghe splendors and the surrounding communities, as cultural and historic tourist sites, seemed like a sensible economic venture that could have been launched back in the 1950s, with that busload of writers. Seven decades later, the abundance of archaeological sites on the island almost screamed for a more rigorous Nurnet-like promotion of Nuragic and prehistoric sites, as if following Sardinia's own native Appian way for cultural tourism development.

Whether it was named *Sa Domu de su Re* (the "house of the king")
or the Santu Antine, in honor of the Roman Emperor Constantine,
the nuraghe stood back from the road with a regal presence. I took
out a copy of Franceso Cetti's book, *I Quadrupedi di Sardegna*, which
he had published in 1774. The German-Italian Jesuit's drawing of the
towering nuraghe almost resembled a grain silo; in the picture, two
farmers stand aside chatting, fields and hills in the background, with
incidental tree branches dangling atop the single tower of the nuraghe, as if placed for shade. It took another 150 years before the first
archaeological dig was conducted at the site. The stone foundations
of circular walls for huts surrounded the bastion with the remains
of a village.

The use of archaeological ruins as sheepfolds or animal pens, of
course, was nothing new. Shepherds used the abandoned shell of the
Roman Colosseum into the eighteenth century. (Ancient shepherds
founded that city, too, but that's another story.) Scottish archaeologist
Duncan Mackenzie wrote about stumbling onto Sardinian shepherds
using a nuraghe for the same in 1909. Having worked on the first excavations of the famed Knossos palace site on Crete, Mackenzie's colorful
descriptions of his journeys in search of Neolithic and Bronze Age sites
in Sardinia complimented the "symmetry" and "unity of construction" of the nuraghes, which he associated with the progression of the
"sacred pillars" of dolmens and earlier Neolithic phases "handed down"
to the Nuragic civilization.

Dating back to the eighteenth to sixteenth centuries B.C., the Santu
Antine nuraghe, as Lilliu had suggested, brought to mind the presence
of a medieval castle. That would certainly make sense, as if an elite
dominated the stone structures and societal organization. But, within
this valley alone, at least seven nuraghes abounded, many within view
of each other, which raised doubts on whether such towers and walled
bastions served other purposes.

One central tower stood sixty feet high, stacked on two stories; a third story of the tower had fallen. Three single-story towers formed an outer triangle, along the thick bastion walls. Archaeologists concluded that these towers, as well, once had another story. There was a courtyard, with a well, between two of those single towers. This was connected to interlocking corridors to the other towers. A staircase within the walls from the courtyard led to a large room in the main tower, with a beehive ceiling of stones in the form of what the Greeks had called tholos or a false cupola. Remember: the Greeks had written about the marvels of architecture on the island of Sardinia in the third century B.C. But they could never allow themselves to attribute the nuraghe to indigenous builders. By the first century B.C., Greek historian Diodorus Siculus explained the "great works" in Sardinia had been carried out by Daedalus, the mythic architect and craftsman, and referred to the nuraghe as "Daedaleia."

The size of the boulders amazed me most. The huge basalt blocks on the outer wall, as well as the entrance, had been cut in precise measurements, not quite a yard deep and two yards long. By comparison, the millions of blocks of granite at the Great Pyramids in Giza, Egypt, were only a foot or two longer. The precision in stacking the blocks without mortar—almost four thousand years ago—established that the stones had been quarried and cut, not simply collected. The engineering required to assemble the corbelled ceilings, internal walls, and towers spoke of a complex social organization of labor, of the forging of metal tools, and the transportation of the stones, as well. In a study from 2002, archeoastronomists from Spain and England noted that the stacked chamber on the multiple floors of the central tower "undoubtedly makes this nuraghe the most sophisticated dry stone monument on the surface of the Earth."

I took a seat inside the courtyard of the nuraghe. Open air, it felt spacious enough for twenty, even thirty people to congregate and tend to whatever duty of the times. I couldn't help but laugh at our modern expectations. In the 1580s, Sardinian historian and clergyman Giovanni Fara lamented that the nearby Basilica di Saccargia, a stunning church and bell tower with its interlocking black basalt ashlars and white limestone, "now lies deserted and defaced." It had been built for the Camaldolese order of monks in 1116 A.D., who were expelled by the Aragonese in the 1300s. It took another century after Fara for the church to be restored, though the monastery had been abandoned. As one of the most beautiful Romanesque churches on the island, it continued to be a tourist destination today.

However, there was not a whole lot of space for even larger groups of habitation in any of the nuraghes. While the side corridors ran nearly one hundred feet long, with plenty of storage space and places to take refuge, the three corners provided only small rooms for habitation. The beehived quarters in the central tower would have been suitable for a handful of people.

Unless the elite families or supposed "chieftains" or "priests" had small families, it was hard to imagine any long-term court in these structures. As lookout towers, you could see for miles from the top walls. Perhaps the nuraghe had only served as a defensive post, in times of attack; and yet, there was no such evidence of widespread violence on the island in the Bronze Age. Most archaeologists agreed that "an egalitarian society of farmer-pastoralists" defined this period of the Nuragic civilization.

In truth, the absence of written mythology, such as that of the Greeks, still somehow penalized the Nuragic civilization for many historians and archaeologists. For some observers, Diodorus Siculus's belief that the nuraghes were built by the mythic father of Icarus, whose wings assembled by Daedalus melted when he flew too close to the sun, somehow provided a more authentic foundation than any Sardinian artifact or oral story today.

I was taken aback, for example, when I turned the page in one of the first books of *La Storia di Sardegna* series that Antonio had supplied me at the kiosk in Alghero. The historian Francesco Cesare Casula simply threw up his hands: "I skip the prehistoric period," he explained, "because otherwise I would touch a naive myth that we Sardinians have and that frankly I do not agree with. After all, the stones do not speak, and about that period everyone can say what they want." For Cesare Casula, the history of Sardinia began with the Phoenicians' landing, and their alphabet and inscribed steles.

All of the hypotheses about the function of the nuraghe fascinated me. I looked at the cyclopic size of the stones in awe. In his book, *L'isola Sacra* (The Sacred Island), archaeologist Augusto Mulas suggested more of an astronomical role of the nuraghe as a temple, in a Bronze Age that transformed its cosmology based on the stars into rituals on the land. Whatever their function, their assemblage underscored a sophisticated level of engineering and architecture that transcended the enduring assumptions of ancient Sardinia's dark past.

Yet, in 1909, one researcher published his study at a conference in Villacidro on the "Use of the Nuraghi," concluding that they served "as a place of refuge to murders and public criminals, which asylums were common among the peoples of antiquity." Half a century later, Italian author Carlo Levi, whose celebrated book *Christ Stopped at Eboli* became a classic on his internment among the impoverished communities in the southern region of Basilicata during fascism in Italy, had made a similar journey of inquiry into the "archaic" timelessness in Sardinian society. His travel memoir was called *Tutto il miele è finito* (All the Honey is Gone). Based on two trips, ten years apart in 1952 and 1962, Levi felt the "wild grandeur" of being inside a nuraghe. Its colossal walls reminded him of "indeterminate terrors, and the sense of the archaic cruelty of those archaic men, barricaded in the towers, in a cruel nature."

I had brought a little container of melons to snack on, as if to conjure the past. Recent excavations at the Nuragic site of Sa Osa, in Cabras, had uncovered forty-seven melon seeds that dated back to 1300 B.C. The archaeobotanical team led by Gianluigi Bacchetta at the Biodiversity Conservation Center at the University of Cagliari declared that the discovery "partially rewrites the history of crops on the island." While earlier research assumed the cultivation of melons had arrived with the Romans and Greeks, these seeds marked the cultivation of the oldest melon in the western Mediterranean.

Seed by seed, stone by stone, shepherd by shepherd, story by story, the "rewriting" of ancient history in Sardinia continued with archaeological research, as if the artifacts were slowly dislodging the two-thousand-year grip of disparagement by the Greeks, Romans, and modern writers on a bus ride. Even the naïve myths.

19 | GIRL WRITER FOUND DEAD IN MYSTERY CASE

Fin sos larghos chelos
su mannu libr'insoro, senza velos.
Cust'isola pro issos fit su mundu.

The vast heavens were their great book, without mysteries.
This island was the world for them.

—Antioco Casula (Montanaru), "Sa Lantia," 1950

In 1838, having sold his jewelry and borrowed money to finance his mining adventure—despite his successful novels, his *La Chronique de Paris* journal had just gone bankrupt—the illustrious Balzac arrived in Alghero in a coral fishing boat. Outraged that the "savages" in the port had required him to remain in quarantine with his crew for several days, Balzac mocked their concern over cholera. "Africa begins here," he wrote in a letter.

That letter came to mind as I passed the cemetery in Sassari after dropping my son off at a school engagement. A little over a decade after Balzac, cholera raged through Sassari, taking the lives of a third of the residents. Historian Giovanni Siotto Pintor put the numbers at eight thousand, though most considered that to be on the low end, given the lack of information on the lives of so many peasants. Most historians associated the rapid spread of cholera to the wretched conditions for the poor, the lack of doctors, and a failure to quarantine. "It presses the heart to enter those hovels," a report noted, "where iniquity and the most cruel selfishness have confined those who struggle most with life."

Novelist Salvatore Farina lost his mother in the cholera epidemic in Sassari. He recounted the agonizing scene of selecting a new mother in his novel, *From the Dawn to Noon*, in 1910. The *British Cornhill* Magazine compared Farina to Charles Dickens, proclaiming in a book review that Farina was one of the only known Italian authors in England. (Not sure how Deledda was left off that list.)

I pulled over the car at the cemetery and decided to look for another ghost. Again, D. H. Lawrence haunted my visit. The Englishman "reports nothing," author Georgiana King had once declared in one of the most insightful snapshots of the writer, stating it abruptly in her own book on ancient Sardinian painting. "His senses are attuned to the inner, not the visible."

While King's book came out on the heels of Lawrence's publication, she had already earned a stellar reputation as a pioneering religious art historian, with a particular focus on Spanish and medieval art. She was also a travel writer. American novelist Edith Wharton carried King's landmark book that came out in 1920, *The Way of Saint James*, on her own travels along the *Camino de Santiago* in Spain.

But King's journey across the sea to Sardinia was the result of more than curiosity or a fit of wanderlust. She made a pilgrimage in the wake of the tragedy of a fellow Byrn Mawr writer, Ellen Rose Giles, who had seen "just about everything there was" in Sardinia, until "death stepped in and took her" and her "great work" that she was "never to write."

Ellen Rose Giles already had a title for her book back in 1907: *Sard Folklore, Birth, Marriage and Death.*

She told a Sardinian journalist that publishers in New York City were awaiting the manuscript; proposals had been lined up for translation. *La Nuova Sardegna* newspaper reporter called it a precious collection of *folas e contados*, stories and songs; a future art researcher would refer to her work as the most "extensive collection of original data in Sardinia."

An extraordinary student in philosophy and languages at Byrn Mawr, Giles had come from an affluent family from Philadelphia, her father in finance. In an anthology of the college writers, Giles had written a short story titled "The Apostasy of Anita Fiske," about a young woman disinterested in high-society protocol, anxious to pursue another life in New York City.

So began Ellen's odyssey. She earned scholarships to study at the Sorbonne in Paris, and at the University of Berlin. She traveled the Middle East, becoming an expert on ancient languages, fluent in Greek, Latin, Italian, German, French, and Arabic.

On her return voyage back to the States from Italy, Giles had a near mystical experience when the ship pulled into Cagliari for a stop. In the gulf, she felt a sort of vision that she had been connected to Sardinia in some way, almost as if she had been born there. She made up her mind to return. With a year, she stepped onto the island with a new mission.

Featured in *La Donna* magazine in 1908, Giles cultivated the image of an adventurous explorer departing into a wintry night in the Barbagia mountains of Sardinia. She packed a camera, a palette, and a Browning revolver. She befriended bandits and met with rival clans. She became known as the American writer who had "visited every corner" of Sardinia, was conversant in Sardinian languages, and was fluent in Italian. The American writer met other writers on the island;

a copy of a novel inscribed to Ellen by the son of Enrico Costa, the celebrated historical novelist from Sassari, eventually made its way to the Byrn Mawr library.

In an earlier interview, Giles had declared her book would be a tribute to the friendly Sardinian hospitality, and a land "so beautiful and so great, as it is ignored and poorly discussed," and a land she "now feels so fatally linked."

Those last words proved fateful.

When her housekeeper found her body in the drawing room in the northern city of Sassari in the winter of 1914, Giles was clinging to the last minutes of her mysterious life. The acrid smell of the gun still lingered in the air. The Browning pistol was on the floor amid a scattered array of Italian money. A bottle of chloral hydrate and bromides was nearby. That was a fairly heavy but common cocktail in the "alkaloids era" for anxiety or sleep problems.

Finding Giles still alive, a bullet wound in her chest, the housekeeper ran for a nearby doctor, but his frantic last efforts to revive her did not succeed. He ruled her death a suicide, and then a murder—and then a suicide again. One strange detail confounded him; the bullet wound had not left a mark on her blouse, as if she had been covered up after the fact, and that detail quickly led to rumors of a mysterious lover who had escaped the scene of the crime.

In the winter of 1914, the American writer's death headlined all the major newspapers in the United States, Italy, and Europe. The wire services called it the "tremendous sensation" of the day.

The *New York Tribune* ran with the lead: "Artist Killed in Sardinia." That story evolved into various versions: "Byrn Mawr Girl is Murdered in Her Sardinian Home," *The Courier* in rural Pennsylvania screamed, running with the story of a nobleman suspected of foul play with the "noted artist and author," while a newspaper in rural Wisconsin went with "Girl Writer Found Dead in Mystery Case." The *Muskogee Daily Phoenix* added their own moral twist: "Girl Artist Who 'Was Different' Is Murdered Abroad."

The Italian newspapers dropped the murder intrigue but kept up the sensational headline: "*Impressionante Suicidio.*"

A *New York Times* story added more intrigue, noting that Giles had just changed her will, leaving behind $40,000 to her mother, even though they had fallen out over a disagreement. "An unhappy heart affair in Sardinia had resulted in a quarrel with the mother," the *New York Tribune* added, as if its readers were part of the family drama now. Strangely enough, Giles's mother Anne had recently moved to the rustic confines of a rural monastery in another part of Sardinia.

Ellen had been working on her book for years. In 1907, in that interview with *La Nuova Sardegna* newspaper, she had mentioned spending fifteen months in the most remote areas, listening to "the voices that arise from the Nuraghi and from the forgotten Phoenician and Roman necropolis and from the ruins of medieval castles." She had crossed the countryside and mountains on horseback, living among the "shepherds' hut."

The reports on her funeral noted a huge crowd of onlookers and mourners. *La Nuova Sardegna* described her as "blond" and in her forties. A Philadelphia newspaper told its readers she was a "spiritual girl, with dark eyes and dark curling hair."

The *Boston Globe* interviewed a former classmate, who remarked that she was "different" from the other students. "Not eccentric," she added, but Ellen's life seemed "apart" from the others. She brought to mind Elizabeth Barrett Browning, and a "cultivated circle" of Americans and Brits that lived in Florence in the Victorian Era.

Ellen's mother, as well, left behind an unfinished manuscript: *The Religious Drama in the Sard Language.* She lived alone for another twenty years in a remote part of the island. Her books and papers, according to a Byrn Mawr newsletter, had been donated to the library, under the auspices of author and professor Georgiana King. The incredible treasury of Ellen's notes, as well, ended up with King, though they were eventually lost over the years.

The body of Giles was buried in a "foreign grave," the *New York Sun* concluded.

There, in the Sassari cemetery, I looked at the grave with only her name—no date or place of birth or year of death, as if only a place marker of her journey in Sardinia. As if only her name would ever make it into print.

What is the point of going at length investigating the causes of so
much of our literary obscurity in ancient centuries?

—Giovanni S. Pintor, *Storia letteraria di Sardegna*, 1843

"It was called the Republic of Sassari," said Paolo, the father of one of
the students at our son Diego's Azuni school in Sassari. They had gra-
ciously invited us to a local restaurant in Sassari in order to try "fainè,"
a local specialty. Made with chickpea flour, water, and a tiny bit of
olive oil, the mixture was cooked in a pan inside a oven. It looked like
a cross between a pancake and focaccia. Sliced up like pizza, in Sassari
it came with heaps of onions or sausage, or even mushrooms. It was
delicious, though quite heavy, and required plenty of Ichnusa beer.

Paolo recounted how the fainè came with the Genovese in the
1290s, after the fall of the Pisan rule of the city earlier in the century.
Perhaps the most infamous person of that period was Michele Zanche,
a corrupt member of the ruling family, who ended up a character in
Dante's *Inferno*, chatting endlessly about Sardinia in the boiling waters of Tolomea, the third division of hell. The city-state didn't last
too long either. Within twenty-five years, the Genevese handed over
power to the Aragon kingdom, though it would go through several
more rebellions.

Our conversation shifted from medieval Sassari to *The Simpsons*, though, at one point. Groundskeeper Willie in *The Simpsons*, the angry Scottish janitor who lives in a shack, was dubbed in Italian with a Sardinian accent. He even loses his kilt in Sardinia in one episode. This ridiculous image probably made sense to the Italian producer. For Paolo, this was just another reminder of how those from the "continent" still viewed Sardinians. More than any disparaging stereotype, he objected to Sardinia being viewed through a singular lens, as if there weren't various cities, cultures, and languages with their own diverse backgrounds.

The language of Sassari, for example, spoken as commonly as Italian, was Sassarese, a mixture of Sardinian, Corsican, Tuscan, and a little Genovese. *"Lu sassaresu no, no era maccu, mastru i ra vigna, mastru i l'oitharizia,"* the great poet Salvatore Ruju wrote in *Sassari véccia e nóba*, in his native Sassarese: "Those from Sassari were not fools, but experts in the vineyards and in the fields of vegetable gardens." While most traced the language back to more ancient origins, German linguist Wagner pinpointed the devastating cholera epidemic as an important shift in language development, when a hybrid language emerged from the survivors.

The entanglement with American media appeared to have had long legs in Sardinia. In the 1950s, Disney filmmaker Ben Sharpsteen's crew parachuted into Sardinia to make a film for a series on unusual places on the planet. (The first film had focused on the "Eskimos" in Alaska.) Sharpsteen had enlivened the dread of wartime American audiences with his cartoon classics, including *Dumbo*, *Pinocchio*, and untold *Mickey Mouse* adventures. With a whimsical soundtrack out of his cartoons, Disney's "Sardinia" was about an island "lost in time," where foreign invaders had left behind "mysterious" towers across the island. Again, this took place in the 1950s, after Lilliu had published his major work on the nuraghes, and archaeological works on the Nuragic civilization had been in print for one hundred years.

The film focused on folk traditions and costumes as charming relics from the nineteenth century. While the crew spent most of their time in the mountain village of Desulo in the Barbagia, tracking down every little character, they failed to meet with Antioco Casula in the small village, the celebrated poet laureate of Sardinia, who had been working with Italian writer and filmmaker Pier Paolo Pasolini on an important anthology of poetry, including Sardinian poets, in that same period.

Disney also failed to mention that the prime minister of Italy in that period, Antonio Segni, was Sardinian, as well—and had attended Liceo Azuni in Sassari.

Celebrated American travel writer Paul Theroux touched down in Sardinia in the mid-1990s for his travel book through the Mediterranean, *The Pillars of Hercules*. Riding the rails, he found Sardinia to be "utterly boring," the inhabitants of the mountainous region of Barbagia were "toothless and skinny and undersized people," and Oristano was an "inbred town." The village of Oschiri, near Berchidda, had the "look of a penal colony." Chilivani was just an intersection of two railroad lines. "The only aspects of the outside world that had penetrated here were the extremely violent American videos and Disney comics," for Theroux.

The view outside a train's window, of course, can be deceiving, slouching around Sardinia. And unhappy travel writers in Sardinia had their own corner on the bookshelves. "We understand an oasis in a desert, but how to understand barbarism in civilization? How to explain Sardinia?" lamented Gustave Jourdan in 1861, in his French viewpoint, *L'Ile de Sardaigne*.

In truth, Oristano was a fascinating and multilayered city, where Eleonora of Arborea's charter of laws in the late 1300s did not only grant women certain rights that their American counterparts wouldn't enjoy for five hundred more years, but it banned the possession of weapons at public events—another right that would elude Americans. Violent American videos aside, Berchidda hosted Fresu's world-famous jazz festival, as we have learned, attracting American jazz musicians and fans for three decades. Chilivani had been named by the legendary Welsh train engineer Benjamin Piercy, who not only devised the first railway system through Sardinia—and parts of France, England, Wales, and India, which had beguiled Theroux in those countries—but made Sardinia his home for agricultural experiments for decades.

I picked up a new book published in those same years by British journalist Charles Richards, *The New Italians*, which reproached Italy for omitting Sardinia (and Sicily) from the country's map, as it took over the European Community presidency in 1990. Despite its good intentions, the book only mentioned Sardinia in a chapter about criminal gangs and kidnapping.

Funnily enough, the president and prime minister of Italy in that period was also a Sardinian, Francesco Cossiga—who attended Liceo Azuni in Sassari.

21 | *SA VITTA ET MORTE*

Non lis reparat sa tessida historia
De sos heroicos gestos, qui voltende
Anniquilat su nomen, e i sa gloria.

They are not protected by the weaved history,
of the heroic deeds that, changing,
annihilate his name and glory.

—Hieronimu Araolla, "A Vision," *Rimas diversas spirituals,* 1597

Our veranda overlooking the port in Alghero became our main living space. Alghero was an outdoor city, the temperature never veering too extreme, either hot or cold. Outside of July and August, when it reached into the 90s, the temperatures remained in the 60s and 70s most of the year, similar to the coastal areas of northern California. The morning coffee was peaceful, when the port was still quiet and the fisherfolk had not returned from their early roundup of the nets. A limpid air hung over the bay. The traffic along the boardwalk was minimal. Later in the day, we ate our meals outside, and continued to do so late into the fall. In the evenings, once the tourist activity along the beaches slowly faded away, the city fortress lit up like a movie set, the bending palm trees and bastion towers casting the shadows of Casa Blanca—or so it seemed. The lights from the port and bastion walls reflected onto the sea like little boats of fire.

For a landlubber like myself, the sea continued to beguile, the different ships forever changing; the light shifted throughout the day, as if Capo Caccia and the gulf coast floated in and out with the tide. There was a clarity along the coasts in Sardinia that I had never seen in any other country.

And then there were the winds—*il maestrale*, or *bentu maistru*, in particular. My youngest son had done some wind surfing, so he had the jargon down on the various winds—*mistral, sirocco, grecale, libeccio, ponente, levante*—but it didn't take long before it became the main topic of conversation. Will there be *il maestrale* tomorrow? This question was not silly chitchat. I understood why geologists referred to "wind landscapes," after we went through a particular rough mistral wind one morning. Within minutes, our plastic chairs launched across the veranda, and then off the balcony walls. Anything not tied down became a flying object: the books, the coffee cup, the hat—all took off in flight.

The brigades of kite-surfers in the bay, however, rode the white caps like carnival performers. Sardinia was a paradise for these wind surfers.

Arriving from the northwest, the mistral winds featured prominently in sailing chronicles for centuries. The positions of the winds framed the medieval compass for a reason. Numerous ships, from the Carthaginians and Romans to Muslim navigators and various Italian colonizers, were lost in storms. The great Arab chronicler and traveler Ibn Jubayr encountered a windstorm in 1185 off the western Sardinian coast that he noted as the most "perilous" in his life.

Nonetheless, the veranda remained my reading quarters for our sojourn. On more than one occasion, after a fall storm, a rainbow (or two) would arch across the bay like a natural arbor.

"I no longer recognize the sound of the wind," poet Lucia Pinna wrote in Nuoro. "If I want to find the path taken, I have to look for it in my verses."

Between the living and the dying—*sa vitta et morte*, in the poems of Antonio Cano in the 1400s, a clergyman from Sassari who wrote his pioneering works in the Sardinian language—so much of the treasury of Sardinian literature has remained in a locked chest for most of the world. Another Sassari priest, Hieronimu (Gerolamo) Araolla, added his own Sardinian poems a century later, religious verses for the most part, *sa vida, su martiriu e morte*: Life, martyrdom, and death. Over the next several centuries, untold reams of poems, novels, plays, songs, and histories had simply not been translated into Italian—or, if into Italian, they were not translated into English, French, Spanish, Arabic, Greek, Turkish, and all of the other languages in the Mediterranean, let alone Europe—and the world.

"To discover a prolific, but forgotten novelist is like stumbling upon a new species," social critic Todd Gitlin wrote in the *Chicago Tribune* in 1998. After his wife discovered a novel by Grazia Deledda on a lonely pile in the corner of a bookstore in New England, he searched for the rest of her works, only finding them in small and university presses. He declared it was long overdue for a "literary resurrection" of the once famous writer with the "emotional power" of her novels. In the end, he only found five of her thirty-three novels.

As I began to wade into the piles of books, which I had picked up like loaves of bread in my Alghero bookstores and in villages and museums along the way, I stumbled onto a haunting thread of death to the lives of so many Sardinian writers; an unreal number of Sardinians had been published posthumously, as if it was a requisite of the trade to leave a masterpiece in your drawer for another generation to discover. For me, it started with Deledda's last novel *Cosima*.

After her death in 1936, family members found that Deledda had literally left a carefully wrapped package in the drawer of her desk, the manuscript for *Cosima*, "written in ink on light-blue paper." *Cosima*, which was Deledda's middle name, recounts the life of a young woman's struggle to become a writer in Nuoro, amid the various characters of the village and countryside.

On that same road to Nuoro, wrote Salvatore Satta, "the spirit of the Sardinians lives." Indeed, the manuscript to Satta's masterpiece, *The Day of Judgment*, had also been found in a drawer after his death, buried among his papers and a diary, and published years later post-humously—initially, to little reception. The narrator of the novel even hints at its cryptic writing. "These pages that no one will read, because I hope to have enough clarity to destroy them before my death," the narrator says, adding, "this story that perhaps I should never have started . . . without measuring the risk to which I was exposing myself, to make myself eternal."

Though unimpressed with the translation from Italian to English, which he declared had failed to capture the "genius of Satta's prose, its marmoreal ferocity, the slow fire inside the stone," *The New Yorker* critic George Steiner wrote that the Nuorese author had left behind one of the literary masterpieces of the twentieth century. Literary and film historian Maria Bonaria Urban called it the "book of the dead." Susan Sontag, at Bruce Chatwin's insistence, eventually hailed Satta's work as "an improbable gift," and "a great European novel."

Well-known as a legal scholar and jurist, Satta lived most of his adult life on the Italian mainland, and was the author of several works on legal theory, including rewriting the country's bankruptcy laws. (He studied at Liceo Azuni in Sassari, too.) At the end of his career, he had spent years working on his novel, an ironic but unsparing family saga stitched into the turn of the century Nuoro and its cast of rather ignoble characters, all of whom share a similar destiny of oblivion, where even memory is a judgment. In many respects, the novel is the jurist's postmortem on Sardinia's twentieth century, from the perspective of his mountain town in the Barbagia, which Steiner compared to a prose version of Edgar Lee Masters' *A Spoon River Anthology*. "A stubborn documentary will," writer Giulio Angoni surmised, "aimed at reconstructing a world and a kind of life that has been broken and replaced."

It took a reissue of the novel by the larger Italian publishing house Adelphi for Satta's work to be widely read, compared to James Joyce's *The Dead*, and then hailed as an Italian masterpiece. The novel was eventually translated into nineteen languages.

Satta had actually written another novel as a young man, *La Veranda*, which had been chosen and then rejected for a literary prize in 1928. That manuscript, too, was found in Satta's personal papers (inside the folder of a lawsuit) and published after his death.

"And maybe while I think of their lives, because I am writing their lives," the narrator in *The Day of Judgment* concludes, "they think of me as some ridiculous god, who has summoned them together for the day of judgment, to free them forever from their memory."

That day of judgment came for so many other Sardinian writers.

Only a few years before Satta's novel was published, another Nuorese author, Romano Ruju, died at the age of thirty-eight, ending a flourishing career as a playwright, novelist, and journalist. He had written extensively about the infamous coal strike and massacre in Buggerru and the *Su Connottu* uprising in Nuoro in the nineteenth century, and he had written a novel, *Il salto nel fosso*, that won the Grazia Deledda Prize for Literature in 1968. But buried in a chest, fifty years after his death, his son found another manuscript, *La Legge*, The Law, which recounted the true story of a man from Orgosolo, a village in the Barbagia, who is falsely accused of a murder, sent to prison, escapes during the war, and then forgoes an opportunity to move to the United States in order to clear his name, only to languish years more in prison. It's an epic story, with death-defying moments.

Perhaps more than the novel itself, the publication of Ruju's posthumous work, which was based on his correspondence with the actual character, brought together the village of Orgosolo in 2021, in a shared act of contrition. "A meeting of the people, as it used to be many years ago," the mayor declared, "when Orgosolo was the crossroads of directors, photographers, intellectuals, actors, sociologists."

On the other side of the mountains, in the village of Bitti, the esteemed anthropologist and writer Michelangelo Pira also left his major works behind after a premature death, including his memoir and a novel, *Sos Sinnos* and *Isalle*. (We will discuss Pira later in the book.) In that same village, the great democratic statesmen Giorgio Asproni had grown up a century earlier, serving in the parliament in the latter part of the twentieth century after joining Garibaldi in his historic "Expedition of the Thousand" in Sicily in 1860 that galvanized the Italian Risorgimento. Asproni was one of only three people in Italy to have had a state funeral at the time of his death in 1876, when the government in Rome shut down to recognize his life. A century later, seven volumes of Asproni's *Diario Politico* (Political Diary), would be found in a chest in Rome and published as one of the fascinating eyewitness documents in chronicling the making of the new country—and the defense of his own Sardinia.

Such diaries were not unique for Sardinian writers. In 1947, a book drawn from Antonio Gramsci's *Letters from Prison* was published in Italian, along with excerpts from his *Prison Notebooks*, a decade after his death. Gramsci had been arrested in 1926, despite parliamentary immunity, when the "Exceptional Laws" passed by Mussolini's fascist government outlawed opposition parties. As a leading voice and publisher of the Communist left, Gramsci had openly denounced Mussolini on the floor of parliament; his fearlessness, as this short, hunchbacked truthteller from Sardinia, must have rankled the cowardness of the Black Shirts that marched on Rome in 1922. Once King Vittorio Emanuele III, the grandson of the last king of Sardinia, appointed Mussolini as prime minister, the fascist stranglehold over Italy would continue through the tragedy of World War II. Gramsci didn't survive that long. His already precarious health faltered quickly in the harsh conditions of the various prisons. He died at the age of forty-six in 1937.

Granted permission in 1929 to write in prison in Turi, near Bari, in southern Italy, after being sentenced to twenty years in prison, Gramsci methodically approached his views on philosophy, history, economics, and even Sardinia, in 2,848 closely worded pages in thirty-three notebooks. Even after he died, his work defied the prosecution's demand that the state "must prevent this brain from functioning for 20 years." Translated into English in 1971, Gramsci's ideas were introduced in countries around the world; his enduring belief in the "pessimism of the intellect, optimism of the will," transcended Communist Party dogma. (Interestingly, one of the main American translators of Gramsci's *Notebook*s was Joseph Buttigieg, the literary scholar, and father of American politician Pete Buttigieg.)

From poet Mario Pinna in Oschiri, to poet laureate Antioco "Montanaru" Casula in Desulo, the phenomenon of posthumous writing in Sardinia seemed to be found in every region. Pioneering linguist and writer Pietro Casu from Berchidda, a cleric who translated Dante's *Divine Comedy* into Sardinian, left behind a lifetime's work on his dictionary, *il Vocabolario Sardo-Logudorese-Italiano*, which would be published half a century after his death.

In 1995, novelist and essayist Sergio Atzeni died in a tragic accident at sea while swimming off the coast of San Pietro, an island off the main island in the southwestern corner of Sardinia. A week earlier he had written his editor that he had put the "final period" on the page and sent off the manuscript of his masterpiece, *Passavamo sulla terra leggeri*. The title had come from a line of Patrick Chamoiseau's novel *Texaco*: "The men treaded light on the earth." Atzeni had translated the incredibly original work by the author from Martinique, which was written in French and Creole, into Italian. Sardinia was a land of languages, "of shadow and light, and of diversity," Chamoiseau noted about his translator, who declared Atzeni understood his views on translations of oral tales that don't "fear the untranslatable."

If Steiner was in search of a "thousand years of solitude," a line shared by Nereide Rudas in her own essays in 1986 about Sardinian history, Atzeni's story should have been his choice, perhaps, rather than Satta's saturnine labyrinth of Nuoro. In the hands of oral storytellers, *Passavamo* traces Sardinia's history from its origins to 1409, when a disastrous defeat of Sardinian forces to the Aragonese led to the eventual end of the historic four judicadus that ruled independently over the island for centuries. Like Chamoiseau, Atzeni's novel is a tour de force of language, inventing terms, casting stories like spells that alter the way we see the world.

"You can add new explanations of the ancient facts narrated in the history entrusted to you and tell memorable events of the thirty years of your custody," the guardian of time tells the young narrator in *Passavamo*. "We guardians of time, from the day of the loss of freedom on our earth, have preferred to end history at this point."

Atzeni's tragic death was a bitter end. Published by Mondadori, one of the main publishing houses on the Italian mainland, a year after his passing, his novel marked the national recognition for the author that had eluded him most of his career. It also marked the growing role that Atzeni's original work would have on a new generation of writers of fiction, nonfiction, theatre, and film as a result of the "Sardinian Literary Spring" in the late 1980s and 1990s, a period of vibrant cultural activity that placed the island in the forefront of Italian literature.

Author of several works of fiction and nonfiction, including *Raccontar Fole*, an examination of the impact of foreign travel writers on shaping the historical views on Sardinia, Atzeni had worked intently as a writer, translator, and journalist to broaden the reach of Sardinian literature to readers outside the island. But he also called on his fellow islanders "to narrate about Sardinia in its entirety" beyond the folkloric stereotypes. For Atzeni, this meant more recognition of his own city of Cagliari and its voices, which he had captured in his novel, *Bellas Mariposas*, which was also published posthumously. A sardonic novel following the exploits of two preteen girls, Atzeni traverses a summer day in the working-class neighborhood of his capital city at the southern port to capture the conflicts of the times.

This search for descriptions of Cagliari, Atzeni had noted earlier, spurred him to describe the city from an internal point of view, setting each story in a different neighborhood. He was tired of "quoting authors who were not Sardinian." This discovery of his own city, Atzeni said, changed his life. It also changed Sardinian—and Italian—literature.

22 | *IN SOS LOGOS DE ANGIOY*

A ballad directed against the tyranny of the feudal barons (the worst features of feudal tenure were not abolished until 1835), contains stanzas which are magnificent even in translation.

—Charles Dickens, *Household Words*, 1856

The procession rode into the piazza with an air of triumph, the militia marching in front in ràgas, wearing their berritas, black jackets and vests, their flared white trousers under their black skirts, waving their hands to a ripple of red- and black-clad figures in the crowd, who cheered from the windows, balconies, and packed confines of the streets. The Sassarese revolutionary Gioacchino Mundula carried a flag alongside the armed peasants. Dressed in a white scarf, her traditional dress marking her village patterns, a young mother held her son and pointed at the figure on the white horse, a red cloak across his shoulders, as if he had triumphantly entered the city gates in victory. As clerics and nobles looked on warily from the sides, the marchers sang the words of a poem in the northern Sardinian language that had been circulating clandestinely all year: *Procurade 'e moderare, Barones, sa tirannìa.* Endeavor to moderate, oh barons, your tyranny.

"In Sassari," historian Francesco Sulis wrote in 1857, "the cry was that of 'down with the nobles, down with the priests, long live Angioy, long live the republic.' The representative of liberty and the Republic, Giommaria Angioy, sparkling the affection of the soul from his eyes, proceeded through the crowd at a slow pace and bareheaded, with a smile on his lip."

This was the image of the painting in the grand Sala Sciuti in the Palazzo della Provincia in Sassari, where council meetings were once held. Titled *L'ingresso di Giommaria Angioy a Sassari*, typically translated with a little more excitement as *Giovanni Maria Angioy's Triumphal Entry* into the northern city in 1796, the fresco returned to view in 2022 after a ten-year hiatus of restoration.

Somehow, symbolically, that delayed restoration captured a lot of Sardinian political history.

As I wandered the captivating streets of Sassari and its carnival of sights, I stumbled onto an itinerary of people and places in the history of the island. Walking in the towns of Sardinia was always a delight, and often an informative one. If you wanted to understand the layers of any city, one sought it at the source—its fountains, the piazzas, the streets, or the paths into the countryside, where decaying plaques or street names, even graffiti, gave a glimpse into a moment of history that mattered enough to mark its presence in our daily lives. Across a lovely white wall in Nuoro, for example, black spray paint zigzagged with a powerful message: *Sardigna Libera!* Free Sardinia!

Sardinia may boast more villages with murals than any place I have ever visited. A walk through towns like Oliena, Fonni, San Sperate, and Orgosolo, as we will see later, was like finding portals into another era, as street scenes and cubist visions played out on the walls. In fact, Bruce Chatwin's notable sentiment—"walking is a virtue, tourism is a deadly sin"—had an interesting twist on an island that had been a place of pilgrimage back to the Nuragic era. If anything, shepherds were pathbreakers by definition. One ambitious group, in more recent times, created the *Cammino 100 Torri*, an eight-hundred-mile trek that connected the paths from Byzantine to Spanish-era stone towers in the Middle Ages along the breathtaking coasts. The *Cammino Minerario di Santa Barbara*, in the southwest area, stretched for three hundred miles along mule trails and back roads through the historical mining towns of the region, in an extraordinary trek through nature and archaeological ruins in the Historical and Environmental Geomineral Park of Sardinia. Trekking in the Gennargentu mountain range, and throughout the island, as we will see a little later, made Sardinia a hiker's paradise, including the *Selvaggio Blu*, a twenty-five-mile trail of cliff-defying wilderness in the Supramonte range to the eastern coast of Baunei in the Ogliastra. In a line: Quite possibly the most breathtaking hike in Europe, and certainly a challenging one.

In sos logos de Angioy (In the places of Angioy), editors Antonello Nasone and Stefano Alberto Tedde actually presented an itinerary for a road trip through history, following the uprisings of the Sardinian Revolution in the 1790s in the affected towns and regions. Over the years, participants had gathered from Thiesi to Alghero to Sassari, and numerous villages and towns in between, to recount the uprisings and Angioy's role in theatrical, musical, and literary performances.

Here in Sassari, the piazzas spoke of patriots that carved their own trails.

In 1875, the provincial authorities of Sassari had selected Angioy's momentous entry as a key moment in Sardinia's history to adorn the walls of their great hall of councilors. Such a decision was not as simple or romantic as it might seem. In the mid-nineteenth century, Sardinian historians, under the sway of the Savoyards, had sought to "ennoble" the island's history while juggling its role within the greater Italian story. This led to a tendency to downplay Sardinia's feudal past under the Piedmontese—and its rebellions against the Savoyards. In his dictionary of "illustrious men of Sardinia," published in Turin in 1857, historian Pasquale Tola made a brief entry on Angioy, begging off that the rebel's intimate role in the "affairs of the nation" belonged to the historian "rather than the biographer."

As the painting in Sassari took form, the unification of Italy, too, was still in progress. The capture of Rome, as the final stage in the Risorgimento, had only happened in 1870 with the exodus of the French troops to the war in Prussia. When King Vittorio Emanuele II moved his residence to the Quirinale in Rome in 1871, his former Kingdom of Sardinia now renamed the Kingdom Italy, he preferred to communicate in French and the Piedmontese dialect, as much as Italian.

Tola himself walked a fine line; he didn't even include his brother Efisio Tola in his book of biographies. Efisio had been a Sardinian soldier and one of the first martyrs in the *Giovine Italia* (Young Italy), Giuseppe Mazzini's revolutionary secret society in the 1830s that called for a united, free, and democratic Italy. Discovered with "seditious books," the Lieutenant Tola was executed by a firing squad in 1833. He refused to disavow the cause or inform on his co-conspirators—or "shame his Sardinian name." The Piazza Tola, a fifteen-minute walk or so from the Provincial palace, was initially named after Pasquale in the 1870s, where he sat calmly as a statue in the middle of the square in a stone chair; his brother Efisio, with a plaque added on their family building in his honor, wouldn't be included as part of the piazza's name until years later.

In a national competition, the Sassarese selected the proposal of Sicilian artist Giuseppe Sciuti, whose Greek motif style of epic scenes in Greek and Roman history had already been exhibited in Rome, Naples, Milan, Catania, and the World Exhibition in Vienna in 1873. Sciuti took his assignment seriously; he met with villagers to study their traditional dress, he rounded up old weapons from the eighteenth century. He discussed the Sardinian revolutionary period from 1774 to 1796 with historians to capture the story of Angioy and the historic revolts of the times.

Like anything in Sardinia, those revolts were complicated.

But like so many pieces of Sardinian history, the creative works of artists and writers inspired those hinge moments on the island in ways that still played out in daily aspirations of Sardinian identity. As we will see, there has been a continuum of movements for independence and autonomy on the island over thousands of years that is rooted in the soil, as much as in the ports of the sea.

Born in the small town of Ozieri, which would become one of the literary capitals of the Sardinian language, Francesco Mannu composed his poem, *Su patriotu Sardu a sos feudatarios*, in the metrical pattern of the oral poetry traditions. Its forty-seven stanzas unfolded like a manifesto. Written in octaves, the poem was a searing address to the feudal lords and their Savoyard ruler, calling out the crushing taxation system and the plunder of the island with the meticulous attention of Mannu's role as a magistrate. Like Angioy, who he would join, Mannu came from the elite families. He had studied at the University of Sassari, and worked as a lawyer in Cagliari, eventually serving the military section of the parliament. His poem, which turned into a hymn, gave their bourgeois brethren a final chance to rein in the feudal system and the excesses of the Savoy administrators on the island. Invoking a local expression, it literally called for the lords to "get their feet back on the land." Yet, at the same time, Mannu embraced the rebellion of the bereaved vassals and peasants, burdened with unfair taxes and demands, trapped in poverty and famine, and addressed his poem to their fight. He raised their struggle to a unique Sardinian one, and a patriotic duty to unite as an island and overthrow a corrupt system.

By the time Angioy "triumphantly" entered Sassari in 1796, Sardinia had been in the throes of revolt for years. As author and antifascist leader Emilio Lussu wrote, while "it is generally ignored by Italians," the Sardinian uprising was the "first revolutionary movement to establish itself in Italy after the French revolution."

The French Revolution, funnily enough, was the first problem.

Only days after the New Year of 1793, the revolutionary French forces occupied the island of San Pietro, off the southwestern coast of Sardinia, and then commenced to bomb the city of Cagliari into submission from their ships. As the first military campaign of the new Republic, the French aimed to seize on the key location of the island in the Mediterranean, as a stepping stone onto the mainland of Italy. Wary of provoking the French and ensconced in his distant palace in Turin, the Savoyard ruler of Sardinia had failed to properly reinforce the island's military forces, making it a supposedly easy target.

The Sardinians, aware of their predicament, had already amassed an army of thousands of troops, including cavalry. While the island's *stamenti,* or parliament, had not officially met for years under the Savoyards, it still provided a structural form of administration under the viceroy. Established back in the fourteenth century by the Spanish—*stamenti* originated from the word *estamentos,* or estates— the stamenti had been divided between clergy, barons, and landlords, and officials from the royal cities. The vassals, beholden to the feudal lords, in an agro-pastoral economy, labored under a harsh system of servitude and taxation. They also dealt with the upheavals of plagues, climate disasters, periodical swarms of locusts, and the wars we already encountered.

"Positive cruelties no less than vexatious exactions, kept the vassal in a continual state of hatred of their lord, as well as fear of his agents; but their misery in many instances was only to be equalled by their degradation," wrote British traveler Tyndale in the 1840s. He interviewed peasants who witnessed acts under the feudal lords, which would only be abolished in 1836. Barons frequently called on their peasants to get on all fours, one recounted, where they were used as chairs outside the estates.

The French attack, however, did not galvanize a revolutionary spirit, but spurred the Sardinians to defend their lands from another invader. Despite their fleet of more than eighty ships, the French bombardment failed to dislodge the Sardinian spirit. Sending twelve hundred soldiers ashore outside of Cagliari, in the area of Quartu Sant'Elena, turned into a debacle. The prepared Sardinian forces hammered the invasion, drawing heavy casualties. Slammed as well by a storm from the sea, the beleaguered French finally retreated. They abandoned their southern campaign for another tactic in the north.

The young Napoleon Bonaparte, who hailed from the neighboring island of Corsica, saw his first serious military action as a commander, serving second-in-command under the nephew of Pasquale Paoli, the Corsican leader, who begrudgingly ruled under the French. The street of Via Pasquale Paoli ran down a hill toward the center of Sassari with a reminder of his neighborly role. Paoli, of course, would be no stranger to Americans either; in 1755, his island won its independence from France, as Paoli brought together the various factions, wrote the first constitution that rejected monarchy in Europe, and instituted a democratic parliament, with voting rights for all adult men. The American rebels closely studied his example of resistance. Benjamin Franklin wrote about his constitution. Thomas Paine dedicated a poem to the Corsican freedom fighters in his Philadelphia journal. One of the leaders of the Boston Sons of Liberty named his kid after Paoli. The Sardinians, however, might owe him even more.

The French and Corsican forces arrived at the end of February, 1793, in twenty-two ships, having sailed the Strait of Bonifacio, and immediately took over the smaller island of Santo Stefano. The

French assault on La Maddalena island, however, was rebuffed by the Sardinian forces, commanded by native La Maddalena officer Domenico Millelire. While Napoleon and Paoli's nephew clashed over strategy, the Sardinian forces utilized their cannons and the various advantages of the island to counterattack, eventually forcing the French and Corsicans to abandon the mission. Napoleon was humiliated. Whether or not Paoli betrayed the French forces, the future Emperor went down in defeat. Within a year, the British would align briefly with Paoli, who regained control of his island from the French.

When you depart from the ferry into La Maddalena port today, you soon step into the *Piazza 23 Febbraio 1793* for a reason.

The Sardinian victories galvanized the islanders. The Savoyard ruler, as King of Sardinia, was less impressed. He made a modest donation to the hospital in Cagliari, granted a handful of free places to the university, and basically rewarded the Piedmont barons and administrators on the island over the Sardinians who waged the counterattack. By the summer of 1793, the stamenti came together to issue its own "five questions," namely, to have their own representative in Turin, to run their own general courts to deal with the public good, to establish a council of state as opposed to a single secretary, and to gain the right of government jobs over the Piedmontese who had been sent to the island—and famously squandered or looted its coffers. In essence, the Sardinian nobles and emerging elite sought to shift the role of the ruling class, not necessarily break the feudal system. Despite receiving their questions in person, the King answered by suspending the stamenti, and rejecting the questions in the spring of 1794.

On April 28, 1794, the Savoyard viceroy sent his soldiers to arrest two Sardinian leaders in Cagliari, in anticipation of a rebellion, according to historians like Manno from Alghero. Whether or not that was true, the arrests triggered a rebellion in the process. By the night's end, armed citizens broke through the castle doors, seized the gates of the city, captured the viceroy (who had hidden in the archbishop's palace) and demanded the surrender of the Savoyard troops. Within a few days, the Sardinians rounded up the Savoyard officers, including the viceroy and hundreds of others from the Piedmont, loaded them on boats, and sent them back to the Italian mainland.

Here, Mannu's poem came into play, as he narrated the scene that the uprising faced prior to the arrests. Again, addressed to the absentee barons, as well as to the Sardinian elite and peasantry, he had called on the Savoyards and their feudal lords to "moderate" their tyranny, for if not, "war is even now declared, against oppressive power, and patience in the people, is beginning to give way."

Over 370 lines, Mannu provided one of the clearest breakdowns of the feudal system, unleashing a historical overview of the Savoyard's absentee rule and its devastating consequences on the island. In a classic Sardinian gesture of satire—forever with the sardonic smile—Mannu warned the noble readers to not mount their horses and run. The weak horses, so poorly treated by the Savoyards, would only throw them.

"Listen to my voice," he declared.

Su populu, the people, *finalmente dispertadu*, finally awakened, would now shake off the chains of feudalism.

Sos homines et feminas, Han bendidu cun sa cria. The men and women have been sold, even with their unborn babies.

Ten or twelve families have divided all Sardinia, he continued, by means unworthy.

Long before the feudal system, the villagers were the lords of the woods and cultivated lands. *Cuddu chi bos l'hat dada, Non bos la podiat dare.* Whoever gave it to you, had not the power to give it.

Sardinia to the Piedmont was a golden land, no different from what the Spanish found in the Indies.

Et a su sardu restada, Una fune a s'impiccare! To the Sardinian was left a rope to hang himself.

The island has been ruined by this race of bastards, he raged.

The Sardinian has expelled his injurious enemy. Though you still would be his friend, Mannu admonished his peers, oh, unworthy Sardinian barons.

Mannu then turned to the people of Sardinia.

> *Sardos mios, ischidade*
> *E sighide custa ghia.*
> *Custa, pobulos, est s'hora*
> *D'estirpare sos abusos!*
> *A terra sos malos usos,*
> *A terra su dispotismu;*
> *Gherra, gherra a s'egoismu,*
> *Et gherra a sos oppressores;*
> *Custos tirannos minores*
> *Est prezisu humiliare.*

> My Sardinians, rouse yourselves!
> And follow this your guide.
> This, oh people, is the hour
> To eradicate abuses;
> Down with all evil customs!
> Down with despotic power!
> War! War to selfishness!
> And war to the oppressor!
> It is time to humble now
> All these petty tyrants.

Whether it was published first in Corsica, where Mannu took refuge briefly, or clandestinely in Sassari, as historians now accept, the poem played an essential role in articulating and emboldening the rebellion across the island. In a nation of poets, a poem became their marching orders. Sung as much as it was recited, the poem evolved into a hymn of unity from village to village.

When the king sent a new viceroy to Cagliari to reclaim power, four Sardinians were appointed to prime positions in administering the island. A brief period of openness and discussions of reform ensued. The public took part in assemblies. City militias were strengthened. The king's appointments, however, managed to splinter the island into factions, including one side that essentially lobbied on behalf of the Sardinian landowners and lords, refusing to recognize the grievances of the peasantry.

By the summer of 1795, a second rebellion exploded when more royal appointments circumvented the Sardinian institutions, showing the king's disinterest in adhering to any reforms, and adding more support to the reactionary faction that had planned a repressive crackdown on the reformers. Two of the reactionary leaders were killed in a clash in Cagliari. More uprisings led Sassari to declare its secession from Cagliari, the final break between the two intense rivalries on the island, the *Capo di Sopra* from the *Capo di Sotto*. (The chief of above from the chief of below.) An armed militia of peasants from the northern ranks had assembled to take over Sassari, led by revolutionaries like Mundula.

Here, then, Angioy came onto the scene, appointed by the viceroy to restore order in early 1796. Raised as an orphan in the north of Sardinia in the village of Bono by his clergy uncles, Angioy had studied in Sassari, taught at the University of Cagliari, and climbed the ranks in the legal system to serve on the main court of the island.

Like many in Sardinia, he had closely followed the Corsican independence movement, the French Revolution and the growing embrace of Enlightenment beliefs across Europe. French revolutionary Jean-Paul Marat, who was assassinated at the beginning of the "Reign of Terror," actually had a Sardinian father. (So did President Juan Domingo Perón's family in Argentina. And so does Italian right-wing leader and prime minister Giorgia Meloni in our times.)

Historian Sabine Enders observed in Angioy's future works that he had also referenced *La Sardaigne Paranymphe de la Paix* (Sardinia paranymphe of peace), an unsigned mysterious text that appeared in 1714 as an overview of Sardinia's geography and history, written as a travelogue. In a clever twist, the book suggested the island deserved greater autonomy and a residing king, not an absent one. The writing was later traced to Vincenzo Bacallar y Sanna, a Sardinian patriot from Cagliari, who had fled to Spain. Sanna's plan was to coax a Bavarian prince to take power on the island; Angoiy had another vision.

Designated as the "alternos," with the power of a viceroy, he carried out the opposite of his orders. On his journey across the island, from Cagliari to Sassari by horse, Angioy saw firsthand the misery of the countryside, meeting with villagers, hearing the stories of the local representatives. By the time of his famed entry in Sassari, Angioy had amassed his own following, and called on the viceroy and king to end the feudal system. Villages along the *sos logos de Angioy* refused to pay taxes to the feudal lords, from Thiesi to Torralba to Ozieri, ransacking the storehouses in some cases. Within months, more than forty communities issued "instruments of union" that formally ended their recognition of feudal ways and demanded compensation in return.

By the spring of 1796, the French came back into the picture. With an armistice between the Savoy and French Republic, however, Angioy lost support from the French revolutionaries he had quietly been lobbying to intervene. The precarious alliance between the Sardinian nobles, newly empowered with a handful of promises from Savoy, and the larger peasantry seeking to end the feudal system, ultimately fell apart. Despite Angioy's attempts to institute reforms on taxation and land management, the reactionary forces gained the upper hand in the stamenti. In a desperate effort to force the question of feudal reform or abolition on the stamenti in Cagliari, Angioy marched the remains of his army south, meeting a growing opposition in the towns of Macomer, then Oristano, where news of the king's acceptance of the original "five questions" and an amnesty to those in the rebellion undercut Angioy's fraying movement. A bounty placed on Angioy's head forced him to escape and eventually take refuge in Paris.

The king's promises, of course, never came to fruition. By 1798, the French forces had pushed into the Piedmont, forcing the Savoyards to take refuge on the island. They even transported their Piedmontese bureaucracy with them. Within a few years, Vittorio Emanuele I became the King of Sardinia, ruling from Cagliari after his uncle had abdicated the throne and moved to Naples, plunging the island into a period of darkness, famine, and more revolts. By the time La Marmora wrote his first travel memoir in 1826, the population in Sardinia had actually decreased since 1796. "The main cause," noted *The Monthly Review* from London, in its review of his book, "is to be found in the oppression of the people by the privileged classes." The author, the reviewer added, found that "the nobility and ecclesiastics appear to be ignorant and numerous."

Similar to Thomas Paine's fate in the United States, a forgotten Angioy died in poverty in Paris in 1808. His ideas of a Sardinian era of enlightenment vanished in the shadows of the Savoyard upheavals in the early nineteenth century. It took 150 years before his dream of autonomy (or independence) for his island would take shape in a different form. On May 29, 1947, as the postwar Italian parliament debated the text for the new Constitution, granting the status of special autonomy to Sardinia, as well as Sicily, Friuli-Venezia Giulia, Val d'Aosta and Trentino, Emilio Lussu disparaged with his usual bitter wit on the limits of such autonomy within the context of the island's historical travails. "These autonomies of ours can fall within the great family of Federalism, just as the cat falls within the same family as the lion."

Sardinia, "even in a state of neglect," Angioy wrote in his memoirs in 1799, "would be one of the most prosperous states of Europe, and the ancients were not wrong to paint it as a country renowned for its size, for its population, and for the copiousness of its production."

In 2018, the Assembly of the Autonomous Region of Sardinia adopted Mannu's poem as the official anthem of the region. The decision was formally announced on April 28, *Sa die de sa Sardigna*, an official holiday set aside in 1993 as the "festival of the Sardinian people," recognizing the uprising in 1794. In selecting Mannu's hymn, the Assembly noted the enduring words: *Su mundu det reformare, Sas cosas ch'andana male.* The world must reform the things that go wrong.

23 | *SU PATRIOTU SARDU*

Pro difender sa patria italiana, distrutta s'est sa Sardigna intrea.
To defend the Italian homeland, all of Sardinia was destroyed.

—"Song of the muleskinners,' Camillo Bellieni, during World War I

To be a patriot in Sardinia was a complex reality. "I'm Sardinian," wrote author Sergio Atzeni, in an essay, "In what language should I tell my story?" He added, "I'm also Italian, and I'm also European." For the writer from Cagliari, the soul remained "rooted in the distant nation" wherever a Sardinian resided, in whatever language. Atzeni reminded his readers that the patriot Giovanni Maria Angioy wrote his memoir and history of Sardinia in French.

The reality of a Sardinian "nation," of course, dated back to medieval times with the original kingdoms and judicadus—even earlier. From the Latin nominative *natio*, the thread has always flowed between birth, birthright, a populace, and its homeland. Historian Attilio Mastino noted that Roman author Marcus Varro referred in 37 B.C. to earlier uprisings in the Sardinian nation by their dress: *Quaedam nationes harum (caprarum) pellibus sunt vestitae, ut in Gaetulia et in Sardinia.* (Some nations are clothed in the skins of these [goats], as in Gaetulia and Sardinia.) In 498 A.D., Pope

Symmachus listed his birth in the *natione Sardus*. In the 1390s, the
judges in Arborea contested their status with the Aragon officials as
representing the *nació sardesca* or Sardinian nation. In fact, Catalan
documents in 1355 had already called on the *sardica natio* to obey
the Crown's dominion over the island. Historian Carlo Livi considered this the first time for the recognition of the Sardinians as a
"nation" in historic times, and would be included in documents on
the enslavement of Sardinians rounded up from rebellions—or the
countryside—for labor on other Spanish-controlled islands or the
mainland into the 1400s.

One of the more fascinating paradoxes of Sardinia, especially in
the eyes of outside observers, has been its depiction as an isolated bastion on one hand, full of separatists and forever disconnected from the
mainland Italy, and then, on the other hand, an inspiring symbol of
national unity for Italy. Often the two conjoin.

Sometimes that could be for fun. When Italy won the European
soccer championship in London in 2021, for the first time in half
a century, Inter's midfield whizkid Nicolò Barella and Torino goalie
Salvatore Sirigu unfurled the Sardinian flag on the Wembley field in a
fit of pride in the Italian victory.

After leading the defeat of Napoleon at La Maddalena, Domenico
Millelire was awarded the first gold medal in military valor for what
would become the Italian navy, then serving the Kingdom of Sardinia
in Turin. He continued a long tradition of decorated soldiers from
the island that had served the Italian mainland that dated back to
851 A.D., when Pope Leo IV begged the ruling judges of Sardinia to
send armed soldiers to bolster Rome from attacks by the Aghlabids
and other Muslim forces. (The Pope also requested the treasured "sea
silk" that came from the rare byssus in the sea mollusks for his garments.) He granted the soldiers their own *vicus Sardorum* or Sardinian

community in Rome, hailing them the valiant youth from the island, and celebrated them as his personal guards. A thousand years or so later, the Sassari Brigade would enter the halls of military heroism for their service in World War I.

I had heard about the valor of the Sassari Brigade before I arrived in Sardinia. During one summer we spent in Gorizia, on the Slovene-Italian border, we had learned about their role on the brutal frontlines in the Karst region during World War I. A monument there had marked their sacrifice. Most historians noted 13,602 Sardinian casualties in the war, including 2,164 deaths, which averaged to 138.6 deaths out of every one thousand Sardinians called per year. The rate for the rest of Italy was 104 deaths out of every one thousand, by comparison. The Brigade's official motto—*Sa vida pro sa patria,* One's life for the homeland—was clearly written in blood.

A war bulletin in 1915 chronicled the bravery of the Brigade, which was the only battalion organized exclusively from one region—or one island in Sardinia's case: "The intrepid Sardinians of the Sassari Brigade resisted, however, firmly on the conquered positions and with admirable enthusiasm they conquered another important entrenchment nearby called the Rockets." In his *Storia della Sardegna*, Raimondo Carta Raspi wrote that the Brigade was "never spared, decimated and always reconstituted."

When Lussu's book, translated as *Sardinian Brigade*, appeared on the cover of *The New York Times Book Review* in 1939, the *Times* hailed it "an unforgettable" story of war, comparable to Ernest Hemingway's *A Farewell to Arms*. The review ended on an odd note: Even if the book had been imagined, the reviewer declared, it was pure "genius." Lussu wrote in the opening pages that his work was "not a novel, nor history." Writing about the battalion recruited from the island of Sardinia, "the most famous infantry brigade in the Italian army," Lussu declared the irony attributed to his writings was not his, "but Sardinian." Such irony and satire were at the crux of Sardinian literature—and they always had been. And for good reasons.

As an officer from the village of Armungia, Lussu's heroic actions became legend. "Anyone who saw him in the penultimate battle of the Piave recounts his deeds as those of a hero from a myth," wrote Camillo Bellieni. "On his feet, after seven nights of vigil, he cried out for the final counterattack. He proceeded among the bursts of the opposing machine guns, beating a high club to the ground, the shoulder strap loaded with bombs, intoning a song in our way. The whole enthusiastic brigade followed him, the gunners, taking up their pieces, shouted: 'Long live Sardinia!'"

In the early spring of 2022, a new monument to the Sassari Brigade was inaugurated in the Piazza Castello in Sassari. Shaped as a candlestick, another symbol for Sassari, the monument replaced an earlier one that had largely been ignored for years on the outskirts of the city. With the informative museum for the Brigade around the corner, this new monument brought the historical memory of their service back to center stage in Sardinia. That memory constantly needed refreshing. A plaque in the courtyard of the city hall in Cagliari, designed by the celebrated Sardinian sculptor Ciusa in 1919, and dedicated to the "heroism of the Sardinian people," was demolished during the bombardments by the American forces during World War II.

The Sassari Brigade, for the first time since Angioy's forces, brought Sardinian youth together in a Sardinian formation, as Lussu wrote in his memoirs of the war. The soldiers had been enrolled "en masse on the island, from which only the blind escaped, the whole of Sardinia passed there, no village excluded." Lussu estimated that 95 percent were peasants or shepherds or workers from the mines. Not all the officers were Sardinians, but everyone "sardized themselves," Lussu added. "And they too danced the Sardinian national dance and also sang the duru-duru."

From the first deployments on the northeastern front of the war along the Isonzo River in 1915, through the grueling battles in the Vicentine Alps on the Austria border in 1916, and numerous victories in the mountain range, the Brigade distinguished themselves in frontline battles until the war's end in 1918. As the most decorated Italian battalion, and the only one to be awarded four gold medals to the two regiments, Raspi noted, the Sardinians "gave the greatest contribution of heroism to the glory of the army and cause of the homeland, wherever there were sacrifices to be made and blood to be shed."

In his prize-winning novel, *Po cantu Biddanoa*, published in 1984 in his Sardinian language variant from the village of Villanova Tulo, author Benvenuto Lobina depicted the trenches as a meeting point for the rural Sardinians—and a rare moment to learn about the rest of the island. "From the stories of his companions from Campidano he had known the Campidano, land of cereals, village by village, from the Sulcisans the Sulcis with the mines, the Gallura with the cork, Trexenta, Parteolla, Ogliastra, Baronia, which must have been an unfortunate place," Lobina wrote.

For his main character Luisicu, Sardinia lived in its villages—and the battle to survive in that world continued to burn after the war. The soldiers in the Sassari Brigade went back to their villages and towns, the agricultural fields and pastures gutted in their absence, as the southwestern mines still churned out lead, zinc, silver, coal, and iron, as new Sardinians.

In the scenes of Lussu's novelistic memoir, the Sardinian soldiers returned with more than the wounds from a global conflict that pitted the poor against each other, and where sadistic commanding officers showed a disdain for the lives of those on the frontlines. As a counter narrative to the mythology around the Great War, Lussu's work aimed to dispel the heroism of war with the reality of chaos and atrocities. "It had already become unbearable for us," he wrote. "Every patch of land reminded us of a battle or the grave of a fallen comrade."

Perhaps Gramsci best captured this clash between being national Italian heroes and Sardinian patriots in an article in 1919 for the *Avanti* newspaper in Turin, which would be censured and only discovered decades later. As the Sassari Brigade marched through Turin in a parade, cheered by the Turinese elite and military authorities, and sent to clamp down on expected demonstrations by workers, Gramsci narrated his version of the scene: "Turinese gentlemen, the bourgeoisie of Turin, who have always considered Sardinia a colony of exploitation," he began, "together with the descendants of those Piedmontese barons against whose vexations and ferocity the revolutionary songs of Giomaria Angioy are still sung today by shepherds and peasants—all of this riff-raff, elegant and well fed, now celebrate the peasants, the shepherds and the artisans of the Sassari Brigade.

"We believe, however," Gramsci admonished, "that the bourgeois and the aristocrats are greatly mistaken about the feelings of the Sardinian peasants and shepherds."

Within two years, the veterans of the Sassari Brigade, led by Lussu, would launch their Sardinian Action Party. Instead of the traditional flag of Sardinia—the flag of the four Moors, which dated back to rather unsure origins in the Middle Ages—some members had suggested a new flag based on a wood carving by Sardinian artist Mario Delitala, who would become one of the island's celebrated painters at the Venice Biennale. Using the same four quadrants with the St. Charles Cross, the four Moors were replaced with a shepherd, a farmer, a fisherman, and a miner, as symbols of an equitable economy on the island.

The flag wasn't adopted. The Sassari Brigade, one of four brigades not disbanded after World War I, carries on as a mechanized infantry brigade in the Italian army. In 2019, Christian Solinas, as the leader of the Sardinian Action Party, in a center-right political alliance, became president of the Autonomous Region of Sardinia.

"Sardinia will rise again, and we Sardinians will be the architects of our future," Lussu wrote in a searing essay titled "The Future of Sardinia," in 1951. "But without the solidarity of the nation state, it is fantasy to dream of rapid rebirths. And such solidarity is in vain to beg for it. Nor can it be spontaneous. It can only be a conquest of the political struggle, inseparable from that of the rest of Italy. And, like any conquest, it will require long and hard sacrifices."

PART FOUR

MONTES INSANI
THE INSANE MOUNTAINS

Buscos chi mai b'haiat intradu
rajos de sole, miseras sacchettas
hant bestid'e su log'hant ispozzadu.
Arvures chi pariant pinnettas,
pro ingrassare su continentale,
affrontadu hant undas e marettas.
Inue tott'es passada s'istrale pro seculos e seculos,
de zertu si det bider funestu su signale.
Vile su chi sas giannas hat apertu
a s'istranzu pro benner cun sa serra
a fagher de custu log'unu desertu.

In woods where never had entered
rays of the sun, miserable uniforms
were proffered, and the land stripped.
Trees that looked like pine groves,

fatten the continent,
faced the waves and swells.
Wherever the hatchet passed
for centuries and centuries, of course,
the trace will be fatal.
Vile is he who has opened the doors
to the stranger to come with the saw
to make this land a desert.

—Peppino Mereu, "A Nanni Sulis II"

24 | SAVING THE COASTS

Many days have passed and still that beauty continues to burn.
It is extraordinary. I would never have had Sardinia in my life,
if it hadn't been for your insistence, and it is strange how now a
reflection, a glimmer remains—more like an event, a war, than
a journey.

—Elio Vittorini, *Sardegna come un'infanzia*, 1932

From the spur of Punta Artòra, overlooking the easternmost point of
the island like a balcony, the sea expanded into the horizon with the
gentle fade of blues. Little dots of sailboats were in the far distance
of the deep; the shallow turquoise and light blue waters off the sand
dunes of Capo Comino to the north shimmered like crystals. The
stacks of rocks nearby, on the other hand, poked through the green
shades of the Mediterranean brush. Boulders cascaded down the hills
amid the leaps of mastic, myrtle, juniper, and even cork trees, until
they reached the jagged edge of the coastline like a thin white line of
a border between the mountain and the sea. The beauty of the open
sea left us in awe every time, as if it were our first time to see the mag-
nificence of the foundations of the water, but this time was even more
spectacular from the lookout in the hills in the Baronia region.

Our Nurnet app, of course, prompted a look under our feet, the Nuraghe Artòra long since surrendered to the concrete floors of a World War II platform. Other nuraghes or sacred wells or tombs dotted the landscape in every direction; the valley along Monte Albo toward the interior looked like a Nuragic highway on the app. The nearby Bronze Age temple at Janna 'e Pruna stacked its square basalt blocks into a sacred place.

The essence was the same: the Punta post of observation, today, in the war of the mid-twentieth century, or three thousand years ago, a Nuragic sentinel watching the same currents, the same colors, the same horizon, with the same mix of wonder and trepidation. The sea, of course, might have deigned a sense of isolation, on first glance, but history was a reminder of its easy connection to the rest of the world.

That view across the sea also provided historic breakthroughs in telecommunication. Farther up the coast, outside the port of Olbia, Guglielmo Marconi and his team installed a transmitter with a short-wave radio on the promontory of Capo Figari in 1932. Marconi had been awarded the Nobel Prize in 1909, for his pioneering work on transmitting radio waves across long distances. Fashioning a thirty-foot directional beam radio system at an old lighthouse, and with equipment on a yacht positioned in the Gulf of Aranci, Marconi successfully received and sent microwave transmissions to another installation on the Rocca di Papa, off the coast of Lazio, 167 miles away, advancing the research in wireless communication.

Every trip to the eastern port of Olbia, one of the growing cities and busy airport terminals of Sardinia, always had an air of innovation about it. Perhaps it was tradition. In 2006, a two thousand-year-old gearwheel was found in the historic center, attesting to some sort of connection to the Archimedes Planetarium. Overlooking the bay, the Rio Mulinu Nuraghe and its fortress walls dated back to the thirteenth century B.C. The Museum of Archaeology itself, wonderfully located on the Peddone Island near the port, felt like a vessel through time, from the pre-Nuragic to Phoenician and Greek, which gave the city its name—Olbia translating into "happy"—to the medieval age.

We were the last ones on the beach by the time we walked down from the Punta. We followed a trail along the coast, seeing bunches of rock roses and *elicriso*, an explosive plant that bloomed into a tiny yellow flower, the leaves and petals used for herb teas with healing and anti-inflammatory properties. Many travelers had picked elicriso, the everlasting flower, as a symbol of Sardinia. Its perfume in the spring filled the air with a curry smell. The Sardinians used it in more than teas, adding it to fava beans and rice, seasoning chicken with its flavor, or even grinding it into a pesto for pasta.

We were not far from the Capo Comino lighthouse, winding between the thick Mediterranean brush and an occasional juniper or maritime pine that leaned back with its branches as if protecting itself from the gregale or *bentu de soli* winds on the east coast. The outer lights of a restaurant illuminated like its own version of a lighthouse for those emerging from the rolling sands or the solitary road that snaked through the countryside to the coast. We looked forward to plates of local oysters seasoned with *pompìa*, the wild citrus found only in this region, and dill. To find a restaurant on these outer banks was more uncommon than one would imagine.

That might have been the most exceptional realization of this stunning view from the Punta—there was so little ugly development along the coast. From the overlook, we could count the beaches that revealed their beauty in total freedom and nature—S'Aliterru, Cala Mialli, Su Tamariche, Cala S'Archimissa, and on and on until you could see nothing but the sheen of blue and green. It was the same feeling that overcame you with a breathtaking sense of serenity at

Porto Ferro, north of Alghero, where the rugged cliffs were broken into wedges of beaches and the forests ringed the area like a green fortress. It was the same astonishment that met you in Piscinas, where some of the highest sand dunes in Europe climbed to nearly two hundred feet and stretched for miles along the rugged *Costa Verde*, or Green Coast, in the southwest section of the island. Pick your "pearl" of a beach in Sardinia—there were hundreds of them, literally. (The shallow waters along the coast on the island of Asinara on the northwest corner, as a nationally protected zone, might be the most divine.) If Sardinia was the Caribbean pearl of the Mediterranean, every region had its own pearl and trademark favorite; the list of most beautiful beaches in Sardinia was as long and debatable as lists for favorite wines in Italy.

Some of the most striking beaches didn't even appear on the map. And some of the most incredible secrets of the coast, like the exquisite Grotta del Fico, which provided the last shelter for Mediterranean Monk Seals in the 1970s, were hidden from sight and required a boat.

The entire island of Sardinia deserved to be recognized as a World Heritage Site, if only to acknowledge the unique preservation of its great natural resources—its nature, its coasts, its mountains. This didn't happen by accident, of course. It also didn't happen without paying a huge price for the slowness and complexity of sustainable development and village revitalization instead of rapacious tourist developments and speculation.

And this might be one of the great stories we never expected in Sardinia. In the fall of 2006, newspapers around the world ran similar headlines: "Sardinia's coastline protected from developers."

Not all of Sardinia had gone unscathed, however. Not all of the island was impenetrable to the pirates of grotesque tourism or immured from the sprawl of high-rise concrete that lined so much of the rivieras on the rest of the Mediterranean—or California, for that matter. The whims of speculation and uncontrolled development led to boneheaded monstrosities of concrete from the Italian heydays of the 1970s to the 1990s, an occasional tourist village of summer homes or camping facilities, and, of course, the thirty-odd-mile clip of Monti di Mola (Montes de Mola) on the northeastern coast that cashed in its chips in 1961 to become the Costa Smeralda strip of resorts.

In his novel, *L'amore del figlio meraviglioso*, Sardinian author Baschisio Bandinu wrote about the implications of the name change on the region itself: "Costa Smeralda is the name of water and comes from the sea, it says of a color and a landing. Monti di Mola is a voice that resonates in the orality of time, bounces off the crest of the rocks, sinks into the abyss of the valley, is buried in the roots of the olive tree. It is the name of the earth, born from the quality of the stone with which the grinding wheels were made to grind the grain and to sharpen the blades of the knives."

Funnily enough, malaria played a major role in the development of tourism in Sardinia, especially the Costa Smeralda. Researchers traced malaria back to the invasions of the Carthaginians and their infected workers, sometime in the fifth century B.C. One scientist even suggested that the nuraghes might have been built as defensive forts against infected invaders. Not a single traveler or writer in Sardinia failed to mention the "insalubrity" of the island over the next two thousand years. *Malaria—mal aria*. Bad air. The "very breathing of the air by a foreigner at night," a fellow traveler warned writer Thomas Forester in 1858, was considered "certain death." *Harper's Monthly* reported that one out of eight residents on the island had reported a case in 1917, though most survived; still, an estimated 3,800 Sardinians died from malaria between the two world wars.

However, an important little detail should be noted: thanks to land reclamation, drainage, and the greater accessibility to quinine, mortality rates declined from an average of two thousand from 1890–1900 to 138 in 1939 and 88 in 1940, according to one study.

In the aftermath of the war, working with the United Nations Relief and Rehabilitation Administration, the Rockefeller Foundation shifted their malaria eradication programs to Sardinia. They had noted success with using DDT to fight mosquitos in Brazil and the South Pacific. But their work didn't happen without controversy. Scientists noted the still uncertain toxic repercussions. In the clash of postwar politics, the Communist Party accused the Americans of setting up their own fascist operations in every village. Assembling a wartime-like operation, more than thirty thousand people mounted donkeys, trucks, jeeps, helicopters, and airplanes to spray every inch of the island with DDT.

Writing in *Fortune* magazine in 1953, Sardinian artist Costantino Nivola, who was living in New York City, praised the campaign for finally conquering the scourge of the island. "No building," he declared, was left unsprayed. Workers actually stamped DDT on the buildings when finished, including the nuraghes. "If Lawrence were alive to write a sequel," Nivola added, the British writer would record that "U.S. money and leadership" had subdued the Sardinian mosquito. By 1950, Sardinia marked the first time in its history without a case of malaria. The long-term health impact of the toxic DDT on livestock, crops, and the Sardinians themselves, however, remained unclear, even decades later. In 2009, a report noted that "no studies of the environmental effects have been conducted."

Following up funding support from the World Bank for the campaign, English banker John Duncan Miller visited Sardinia in 1958. The beauty of the island's coasts overwhelmed him. Now freed from the malaria fear that had once made travel guides like Baedekers warn travelers to avoid the island from July to October, Miller put together an investment group to purchase areas of the coast for development. The Mediterranean riviera, of course, was burgeoning. As one of the potential investors, a young student who had just graduated from Harvard University joined Miller for a ferry trip to the island. At first, the twentysomething Aga Khan (Prince Shah Karim Al Hussaini, Aga Khan IV) didn't appear as impressed as his British counterpart. But on a subsequent journey on his yacht along the northeastern coast, the Aga Khan became enraptured by the island's charm. By 1962, he would break ground on his plans to turn the wilderness and pastoral areas of the coast into his vision of the "Emerald" coast. "There are scores of fine, sandy beaches with not so much as a cat on them," he recounted in 1964. "Rugged green and gray mountains drop abruptly toward the water. A carpet of purple and yellow, and red and blue flowers perfumes the air. The climate is semitropical, much warmer than in the overcrowded resorts of southern France."

The Costa Smeralda was not the only exclusive tourist venture, of course, to seize on the stunning beauty of the coasts. But not all enjoyed the same success. One of the most exquisite beaches in Sardinia, the red rock cove at Su Sirboni in Gairo along the Ogliastra coast, was a marvel of both nature and human folly. On our way to a lovely cove, we walked passed a tourist complex that been built in the 1970s and then abandoned and reclaimed by slopes of juniper, pine, mastic, and macchia, peering behind the gated walls at the beachcombers today with the longings of tourist industry dreams.

An estimated half of the coastline of Sardinia had been earmarked for development, until a coalition of academics, organizations, and political parties in 2002 came to the realization, in the words of Renato Soru, "that in a short time, everything would be lost, and we would become an island of regret, of remorse."

As the billionaire founder of an internet and communications company, Soru led *Il Progetto Sardegna* (The Sardinia Project), a movement to transcend old concepts of extraction or development of natural resources and upload "innovation with the preservation of the environment and identity." In effect, a cultural revival was also brewing to increase bilingual education programs and Sardinian cultural initiatives. In 2004, the Progetto Sardegna and its coalition of center-left political parties won the regional elections, putting Soru into office as the president of Sardinia's autonomous region. The Progetto's agenda emphasized the saving of the coasts and protecting the environment by launching economic initiatives to increase communication with the world, increase sustainable tourism, and reorganize regional government bureaucracy.

By 2006, Soru and his coalition passed a law to make the Sardinian language, *sa limba sarda*, the official language. Within four years, everyone on the island had access to high-speed internet; a significant shift of public spending went to the health-care system and education; and employment levels rose. The discount airlines began to ramp up flights to the island for tourism.

The big leap came with the writing and passing of the first Regional Landscape Plan in Italy in 2006, which developed a ring of protection of the coasts, as well as new rules for locally administered plans. "Now Sardinia is safe," Soru declared. "There is a strip of coastline covering on average three kilometres from the sea where it is not possible to build anything. The Sardinian territory will no longer be consumed."

Two years earlier, Soru and his administration had put all development on hold, and then brought in a committee of experts, including archaeologists, naturalists, sociologists, and art historians, to reconsider the concept of landscape. This had gained as many enemies as advocates, including former prime minister and media tycoon Silvio

Berlusconi, who had built a "James Bond villain-style underwater entrance" and classified the construction as a "state secret" at his massive villa playground on the Costa Smeralda.

"The new law brings an end to a period of anarchy on the island," *The Independent* in London reported. It gave the last word to Soru: "All that has been saved from assault during the previous decades will remain intact. The beauty of nature is a patrimony that can be exploited only if it is not violated. We were given the task of turning the page, and we have done so. The island's Wild West period is over."

The question would be for how long. In 2009, Soru lost in his campaign for reelection.

25 | POMPÌA

Sardinia has hot springs that bring healing to the sick and
blindness to thieves if they touch their eyes with this water after
an oath has been given.

—*Etymologies of Isidore of Seville*, 626 A.D.

We had stayed up until 2 a.m. with our hosts, Pina and Franco, who
had left behind the town of Siniscola for a small permaculture farm at
the foot of Monte Arbu (Albo). The plates of food, served on cork platters, never ended; the rows of local sheep and goat cheeses, roast pork
and lamb, figs, veggies from the garden. The stacks of *carasau* flatbread
were devoured. The Cannonau wine flowed. An offer was floated for a
local dish, *Sa Suppa Siniscolesa*, the lush bread pudding with *sa lorica*
bread, made from durum wheat semolina, soaked in a broth of veal
or pork or mutton, and mixed into a sauce of tomatoes, an assortment
of cheeses like pecorino, Fiore Sardo, and Dolce del Montalbo, and
regional herbs like chives, thyme, garlic, and parsley, and cooked over
a low fire for hours. Perhaps for another time.

In the 1620s, a French writer questioned why historians had disparaged islands like Sardinia with a sweeping claim of cruelty and dis-
trust. "They live in great friendship and harmony among themselves,"

he wrote, "and are extremely civil to strangers." In the 828 A.D., the sailors with Bonifacio II from Tuscany—the namesake of the Strait of Bonifacio—referred to Sardinia as the *insula amicorum*, or friendly island. On an island where the lore of banditry filled a lot of chronicles in the twentieth century, the culture of hospitality in Sardinia remained legendary; in 1916, the *National Geographic* magazine mocked the bandit obsession of the newspapers, declaring Sardinia was safer than the rest of Italy. For the past three centuries, Perdasdefogu, a village in the Ogliastra, had even celebrated an annual day, *Sa Strangìa*, to welcome foreigners, including the Piedmontese, to their village.

Not all travelers were happy, of course. In Siniscola, dear D. H. Lawrence found a "narrow, crude, stony place, hot in the sun, cold in the shade," where a "barbaric" woman served him at a restaurant, holding her own and "ready to hit first."

Our s'arrogliu of stories seemed typical for our journeys around the island. The Sardinians we encountered seemed anxious to provide a more complex picture of their village or region than the mere postcards of sun, sand, and wine. They pulled out books and introduced their favorite writers, poets, and singers. They promoted the traditional festivals. They told us the archaeological sites to visit—and knew them well.

The insightful Sardinian writer Dessì once warned against the commodification of folklore. "Writers are slaves of folklore and they themselves then create this folkloric-journalistic tradition that slowly becomes a miserable thing," he declared, pointing his finger at the emphasis on the costumes, dances, and music that tended to sweep the island's crises under the rug of tourism.

But I found that today's writers, artists, and artisans used the traditional arts as a departure for their own contemporary expressions and the crises of their own times. Whether it was artwork that protested the NATO military operations on the island, or the basket makers in Castelsardo working to preserve the waterways and native

reeds, dwarf palms, sea grass, and myrtle from environmental pollu-
tion, or the workshops of weavers in Armungia, where the Casa Lussu
believed that "innovation lies within tradition," we saw how the arts
played a strong role in not only shaping a Sardinian identity, but also
in providing a narrative of viability in the villages and small towns in
an age of globalization.

As an island of 1.6 million inhabitants, with one of the lowest
density populations in Italy, more than half of Sardinia lived in areas
defined as rural. The old ways of *città chiusa e campagna aperta*, closed
city and open countryside, where the urban areas depended on and
dominated the rural areas of farmers and shepherds, no longer defined
the island today. And yet, the viability of rural life, for those who had
left the cities or for a small but growing movement of young people
staking out a new economy of regenerative agriculture, tourism, or
telecommuting, there remained a question for an island where unem-
ployment rates still ranked among the highest and migration abroad
continued as the default option.

We also felt this in Alghero. Many of our friends, or the parents
of our children's friends, straddled a precarious line of seasonal tourist work and the off-season hustle to find some sort of employment to
remain in town through the winter.

Pina and Franco's home was framed with cubist artwork by one
of their sons, an artist now living in Alghero, who drew on Sardinian
designs, ancient masks, and contemporary scenes. Ceramic plates and
homemade baskets contained piles of drying herbs, like lavender, that
reflected their engagement in the Slow Food Movement and the restoration of the land from prior abuse. Fruits trees surrounded their lovely
home, including the pompia, wonderfully named the *citrus monstruosa*
in the science books, which looked and tasted like a cross between a
wrinkled lemon and a grapefruit.

Pina, as a child of immigration, recounted the family departure

to Belgium, her father working in the mines and factories with other
Sardinian immigrants; and then, the reintroduction to her own region of Baronia, as tourism brought urban European fashion to the
beaches and villages in the 1960s in an exchange with Sardinian traditional ways.

The nearby town of Orosei, one of our favorite places on the eastern coast, had enticed us to this region on several earlier trips. Artists
abounded with their displays in the historic center. The medieval
streets came alive in the evenings. Farther up the road, the gorgeously
restored cobblestoned warrens through the village of Galtelli wound
with its *parco letterario* dedicated to Nobel Laureate Deledda, who had
based her novel *Canne al vento* there.

There was a thread through so many Sardinian family experiences.
The experience of migration on one end balanced the influx of global
tourists on the other. In the process, this had evolved into a sort of third
culture on the island. To be sure, there was always a strong emphasis
on Sardinian traditions needing to be preserved; and, Sardinia, itself,
needing to protect its autonomy at all costs. An element of separatism
still thrived on the island—*Sardigna Libera*. But the majority of people I met and interviewed had a fairly common sense approach to the
island's autonomy and basic rights of sovereignty. "We are Sardinian,
we are Italian, and we are European," Pina told me, echoing what I had
heard all over the island, "but the bottom line is that we should have
control over our natural resources and lands."

We enjoyed a similar evening farther down the Ogliastra coast,
on the opposite side of the Gennargentu mountain range. The thick
tangle of the trees and bush gave off its own fragrance—*murta, ogiastu,
theria*—like bookmarks, as a half moon showered the boulders on the
coast with grey light. We were so close to the sea, a few miles south
of the town of Tortolì in the Ogliastra, that I could hear the waves

crashing on the rocks like neighbors. *"De s'Ozastra, sa perla 'e diamante, sa natura sa sorte l'avvalorat,"* as an old poem declared: "The region's precious nature is our fate."

Our host, Gianni, a burly man with a big smile, a cigarette in one hand and a glass of Cannonau wine in the other, had opened one of the first hotels in Tortolì in the late 1950s with his siblings, and watched the evolution of the modern tourist industry. He didn't want to talk about the famed Costa Smeralda. He had better stories—about his father in the heroic Sassari Brigade during World War I, about the role of fishermen from Ponza, about the real bandits in the region. Like a great storyteller, he commanded our attention, as his wife and cousin and others looked on, ready to take their turns.

Gianni flicked his cigarette, reached down, and placed a thick book on to the table. *Tortolì, Celu Inferru,* by Paolo Pastonesi, a history of the area. I turned to the first page: "The lack of awareness of the past is an affliction if a people don't defend and validate their patrimony."

"The central Italian administration has always sent its worse functionaries, as some sort of punitive measure, to Sardinia," Gianni said, taking up the same question of autonomy. "And this has resulted in negative consequences for us Sardinians."

As we drove into the Supramonte mountain range, I thought about our hosts, and the inexorable debates over the control of the land and the island's resources. It wasn't until 2008, under Soru's administration, that the American military bases, including the stationing of nuclear submarines on the island of La Maddalena, were closed down. "The real issue for us is, after 30 years, we still have an American base here in our archipelago. Is that necessary?" Soru had asked in 2005. "We love American tourists," he added. "We are good friends with the U.S. But would you want a nuclear submarine next to your house?"

Still today, more than 60 percent of the Italian military operations took place on the island; large areas were restricted for military use, including the war game operations of NATO countries. One of the most popular beaches in the glistening blue coves of Teulada, in the southwest Sulcis area, was called the *spiaggia degli Americani*, because it fell within the military zone.

In 1952, only a few years after the end of World War II, the *New York Times* ran a startling headline: "Fleet of 4 Powers to 'Bomb' Sardinia." The largest single naval task force unleashed "intensive bombardment" on the Sardinian shores, led by eight cruisers and ten destroyers. Over the next seven decades, opposition and protest movements had marched, fishing boats had waded into military zones off the coast, and citizens' groups had taken military officers to court over the severe health and environmental damages from the bombing ranges. In 2018, an investigative film documentary, *Balentes*, by Sardinian-Australian director Lisa Camillo, examined the consequences of the fallout on families and communities. In the fall of 2022, according to *L'Unione Sarda* newspaper, NATO forces from five nations launched the "Open Sea" exercises "at sea, under the surface, in the air and on land," with "approximately 4,000 military personnel and more than 45 ships and submarines." They were met in protest by A Foras, an alliance of groups, calling for "a Mediterranean of peace and for popular sovereignty in our islands."

Those annual war games and bombardments continue today.

26 | TISCALI

We are attached, like oysters to the rock for millennia,
and the rock is something of ourselves; if it weren't there,
we would never be there.

—Giovanni Lilliu, at Su Nuraxi Nuraghe in Barumini

We were en route to Tiscali, a Nuragic site that stood inside the crown
of a limestone ridge in the rugged Supramonte mountains.

We had known about Tiscali, or at least the name, for years.
And this was thanks to Renato Soru and his telecommunications
company. He grew up in the town of Sanluri, the site of a historic
battle in 1409 between the Aragon forces and the Sardinian judicadu
of Arborea, which effectively led to the beginning of the end of the
last rulers of the traditional judges. Soru did not come from nobles,
but a mother who ran grocery stores and a father who was a school
administrator. After studying at the prestigious Bocconi business
school in Milan, he expanded his mother's supermarkets in Sardinia,
worked in banking, and then stumbled into the world of telecommunications in Prague.

He returned to Sardinia in 1997 to launch his own telephone and
internet company in Cagliari, which he named Tiscali. The name
fascinated Soru after he had heard about the Nuragic settlement

hidden inside the limestone cliffs, as envisioned in the novel by Atzeni, *Passavamo sulla terra leggeri.* "An ancient hero named Mir hid there," Soru recalled in an interview, escaping from invaders "in a place where the Sardinian people had hidden in silence. We used it in reverse. We didn't want to hide, but we wanted to talk, and talk to the world."

By 1999, taking advantage of deregulation in Europe, Soru had already leaped ahead of the competition by offering cash phone cards in Italy, a country where credit cards were still difficult to obtain. Then, he became the first free internet provider on the continent; but his service was limited to Italy. Taking the company public in order to expand across Europe, Soru became a billionaire as one of the pioneers in internet service. The prime minister at the time, Giuliano Amato, called him the "Bill Gates of Italy." The news media hailed the *miracolo dei nuraghi.*

Keep in mind that Marconi, back in 1932, had already used Sardinia as a launching pad for wireless microwave experiments. Antonio Ticca, a graduate student at the Center for Advanced Studies, Research and Development in Sardinia, actually created the first website in Italy in 1993. A year later, the *L'Unione Sarda* newspaper in Cagliari became the first online newspaper in Italy—and one of the first in Europe.

"What could be a better name for the company that was supposed to be a miracle and a mythical warrior against the giants of the sector?" one Italian newspaper asked.

For the first time in Sardinia, I felt the magnitude of the island's mountains, as we drove toward the foot of Tiscali. Monte Uddè appeared on the horizon like a fortress of limestone. While nearly 80 percent of Sardinia would fall under the category of hills or mountains, the chains across the Supramonte and Gennargentu reached nearly five thousand feet. They reminded me of the smaller ridges of the Rocky

Mountains in the western United States. From Dorgali in the east to Oliena and Orgosolo in the west, and Urzulei and Villagrande in the south, the Supramonte range rolled along in a series of peaks and boulder cliffs, divided by thick valleys of forest, gorges, and canyons. While marketed as the "Grand Canyon of Europe," the deep gorge of Gorropu curved through the high cliffs more like a Sardinian version of Utah's Zion and Canyonland parks.

In the late 1990s, a movement led by national environmental groups to create the National Park of Gennargentu was met with widespread protests by hunters, shepherds, wood cutters, and tourist operators, who all objected to restrictions on an area that had been considered a public commons. While the park was officially established in 1998 as the *Parco Nazionale del Golfo di Orosei e del Gennargentu*, stretching along the coast from Dorgali to Baunei, and across the Supramonte and Gennargentu ranges in the eastern mountains, various legal challenges kept it from being instituted. But that certainly didn't stop locals, the region's forestry service, and organizations in Oliena, Orgosolo, and across the island from continuing conservation efforts, as well as eco-tourism endeavors to appreciate and protect the land.

We met Mariangela, our trekking guide, at the Su Gologone pools, at the foot of Monte Uddè, where an intense blue spring of water surged out of the karst rocks. An estimated five hundred liters of water flowed per second, funneling into the largest underground waterway on the island. Hopping out of her jeep, a day pack on her shoulders, laced up in boots and shorts, the twentysomething Mariangela rounded up the trekkers with the hustle of a shepherd.

Originally from the nearby town of Orgosolo, Mariangela had studied and graduated in languages and communication at the University of Cagliari, traveled the world, and then decided to return to the region to pursue her dream job as a trekking guide. As part of a new generation involved in the growing ecotourism industry, Mariangela moved easily between the languages of Italians and foreign tourists as she led kayak, caving, and hiking tours across the island, as well as Corsica and Sicily.

Climbing into Mariangela's jeep, we scaled the narrow dirt road, which had been used for decades, if not centuries, by the wagons and trucks carrying loads of wood for the charcoal industry. She handled the curves without looking. Her arm pointed out the window at too many landmarks to remember; she recounted stories of the recovery of the Griffon vulture, which had nearly gone extinct after World War II from the setting of poisoned traps. "See the *leccio* tree," she called to the back. The holm oak, which appeared to be vibrant all over the island. That tree withstood the wood cutters, she remarked, because it was valuable to the shepherds for the acorns.

The deforestation of Sardinia, dating back to the Romans, was no secret on the island. In medieval times, forest communities were required to provide thousands of carts of wood every year to the coastal towns and feudal lords. In modern times, the Savoyards in Turin began selling off rights to the forests in the early 1700s. In his novel *The Forests of Norbio*, based in his southwest area near Villacidro, author Dessì chronicled a land grant to a Swedish noble to take coal and wood for the foundries, "thus destroying the forest heritage of the region." Within a century, virtually every travel writer remarked on the fury of logging across the island. The prelude to deforestation, as anthropologist Fiorenzo Caterini wrote in his book, *Colpi di scure e sensi di colpa: Storia del disboscamento della Sardegna dalle origini a oggi*, was the infamous Edict of the Closures of 1820, which allowed for the division of the lands into private plots, literally through the construction of stone fences—many taken from disassembled nuraghes—and the privatization of lands that had been held communally.

The blind poet Melchiorre Murenu from Macomer, hailed as the "Homer of Sardinia" for his wandering stories and narrative poems, bitterly mused in the mid-1800s: "If sky had been on earth, they would have closed it, too."

A traveler "cannot but be filled with grief at the sight of such great destruction of trees, of forests, of woods," Pietro Ballero wrote in 1805, after a journey from the Nurra region in the northwest through the Barbagia in the central mountains. In the mid-1800s, La Marmora spoke against deforestation of certain species of trees, noting the loss of deciduous oaks. British writer Tennant called for the "arrest" of cutting down the forests, agreeing that "large areas have been completely denuded," leading to more flooding and the creation of new swamps infested with malaria.

By 1868, forest cover in Sardinia had been reduced to only 12 percent across the entire island. According to most estimates, the island had lost four-fifths of its forests in the nineteenth century. At the turn of that century, the poet Peppino Mereu, a former Carabineri officer from the Barbagia village of Tonara, excoriated the "vandals" from afar that had plundered the forests and left this "painful state of affairs." Mereu himself finished destitute, a socialist critic of the corruption and destruction of his region, who died at the age of twenty-nine from illness. His epic poem, "A Nanni Sulis," among many others, continued to be performed by tenore groups and contemporary bands.

"The destruction of the woods was in fact entirely in function of the needs and interests of Northern Italy, which needed coal for industries and sleepers for railways," historian Casula noted. "With the unification of Italy, the game ends with a monstrous acceleration of the pace of destruction."

What wasn't felled for industrial interests was loaded into trains for charcoal, according to one writer in the early 1900s. He counted eighteen tons of charcoal being loaded in a single day at one train depot—the same depot where Lawrence had passed on his journey.

In 1919, Gramsci took up the deforestation crisis in his *Avanti* newspaper. "The island of Sardinia was literally razed as if by a barbarian invasion," he wrote. Like Tennant a half century before him, among other observers, Gramsci also pointed out the aftermath of the destruction on the island's climate: "We inherited today's Sardinia alternating long dry seasons and flooding showers." This included malaria, as Tennant and many others noted.

Strangely enough, the Roman writers dating back to Titus Livius did not only fear the malarial swamps in the lowlands of Sardinia, but also the tempestuous winds of the *montes insani* or *insani montes*—the insane mountains. Writing in the first century A.D. about an earlier expedition in 200 B.C., Livius narrated the disaster of a fleet coming from Corsica, which encountered a storm along the eastern cliffs and mountains and shattered into pieces. Ptolemy continued that narrative, though he shifted the montes insani to the north, following a chain into the central highlands. When the poet Claudian recounted the Gildonic revolt in North Africa four centuries later, he also set a storm that rolled over the eastern mountains in Sardinia to scatter a Roman fleet, as if the winds among the mountains were propelled by some supernatural entity: *insanos infamat navita montes*. Scholars largely agree now that his reference was to the larger chain of mountains in the Supramonte and Gennargentu.

And then there was the mountain of Tiscali.

Once we arrived at the base of the Lanaittu Valley, we began our ascent of the mountain, straddling the border of the Supramonte in the Dorgali and Oliena districts. Mariangela, as our trekking guide, led us along narrow trails that had been broken by either mules or sheep. The forest was not lush, but thick; we now recognized the family trees of the island, the mastic, the oaks, the juniper, some pines. Mariangela pointed out the plants that could heal or harm; the milk from one plant was used by fishermen to stun the fish. At the first summit on the trail, we looked back into the expansive valley enclosed on either side by the limestone peaks. The deep forests filled in the valley like a bivouac of evergreen. There was no human habitation in sight. Yet, we knew that was a delusional thought on this island.

The Corbeddu Cave sat just over the ridge, where the middle finger of a Paleolithic man had been found—waiting on humanity to catch up for the past twenty thousand years. The phalanx bone had not been lonely. The cave became the infamous hideout of one of the legendary bandits in the region, Giovanni Corbeddu Salis, the king of the Mediterranean macchia. Gunned down by the Carabinieri police in 1898, Corbeddu Salis had spent nearly two decades roaming these ridges, negotiating disputes and earning a reputation as a sort of Robin Hood.

Among the nearly fifty nuraghes and scores of Nuragic settlements in the Supramonte mountain range, the Sa Sedda 'e sos Carros Nuragic village interested me the most. As a metallurgical center with a Bronze Age foundry, it featured the remains of a round building fashioned with stone blocks; the side walls were lined with a stone bench. A fountain flowed into the round house through the carved mouth of a ram or mouflon-shaped protome and into a central basin. Along with iron slags, stores of bronze objects had been found for smelting. In effect, this was a mining and metallurgy village, churning out bronze and iron products more than three thousand years ago. The woods in that period were indispensable, of course, in order to fire up the furnaces to smelt the ore.

After two hours of walking, our trail suddenly turned into the cliffs. A little wood sign pointed into the rock face of a mountain. Mariangela hopped across the rocks, leading us through a steep narrow passage in the cliff, where we squeezed through the side of the mountain. We gripped a rope ladder and pulled ourselves atop the stones. Looking down, we could now see into the cauldron of a karst sinkhole, which dropped dramatically below us. Following a mule trail along the ridge, we slowly descended into the side of the cliffs and sinkhole, where the Tiscali dwelling suddenly came into view like a secret world opening into a natural fortress. It was strangely calming, and otherworldly. Walking into the open-air cavern, it reminded me of the prehistoric cliff dwellings in the American West; though, the dwellings here were stone houses along the cliffs, not attached to them, and a central area spread out in the middle of the arena like a mound settlement that was now forested. They were also three thousand years old.

While shepherds—and bandits, of course—had known about the Nuragic site for centuries, archaeologist Ettore Pais first examined it in 1910. Born in Turin, Pais had actually grown up in Sardinia. He famously sat on Giuseppe Garibaldi's lap as a child. As a young man, after the university, he became the director of the museum in Sassari in the 1880s, and then moved on to Palermo and Rome, where he emerged as the dean of Roman history in his era. Pais's views on Sardinia had evolved over the years, especially during his tenure in Rome. In his earlier writing in 1880, "Sardinia before the Roman period," he noted the Roman devastation of the island; by 1923, in his book, *Storia della Sardegna e della Corsica durante il dominio romano* (The History of Sardinia and Corsica during the Roman Dominion), he depicted the Roman occupation as bringing civilization and order to the island.

"To understand the importance of Tiscali," Pais wrote, "you have to take the classics in hand." By that, of course, Pais relied on the Greeks and Romans, not the Sardinian stories. In fact, Pais wrote that the island "possesses very little authentic history," though the archaeological material was "abundant." The celebrated archaeologist surmised the site was one of refuge, fleeing the Carthaginians or the Romans, who hunted down the Sardinians in their campaigns in the second and first centuries B.C. Eventual research, however, also pinpointed an earlier founding of the site, dating back to the fourteenth to tenth centuries B.C. in the Nuragic civilization.

The mountain was called *t'Is kal'i*, Atzeni wrote in his novel. "The mountain, and in the forest, is the only possibility of salvation," for his Nuragic characters, who gathered for the dances at the sounds of drums.

There was certainly an air of serenity in the confines now. I could imagine rituals. I could see the dances. I could hear the launeddas. The drums would have echoed off the cliff walls. (Such an image, and the sound of ancient instruments, would come alive in the town of Pula, outside of Cagliari. The Muspos museum of popular Sardinian instruments had created a multimedia experience to see and hear the ancient reed, string, and drum instruments from around the island.) A large opening in one of the walls provided an incredible view into the valley, like a natural outpost for the Tiscali sentinels. Little black marks along the cliffs noted fires. The stone huts themselves spread out in disarray, after centuries of abandonment and honeycomb digging by visitors. The site itself now only had a single attendant, who collected a ticket and watched as we followed Mariangela along a narrow trail.

While other archaeologists visited the site in the 1920s, the first extensive excavation took place in 1999, and an analysis of the materials and artifacts was finally carried out in 2005. Among the forty or so remaining huts, archaeologists assumed the karst dwelling held a population of 200–250 inhabitants at any given time.

We quietly descended another trail, following Mariangela. I thought about Soru naming his internet company after a Bronze Age site, and it somehow made me smile. In the end, he had taken Pais's patrician advance—to take the classics in hand. In this case, of course, he took a Sardinian classic, not one from the islands of Greece or the corridors of Rome.

The Sardinian gift of weaving their ancient histories—and mythologies—into contemporary stories removed the veil, so to speak, of the stultifying orthodoxy of some archaeological theories. Tiscali was truly an "otherworldly" place, its dramatic setting defying any tidy explanation for its existence. And yet, it seemed perfectly in place in Sardinia's landscape.

This also made me consider the long-standing controversy in the world of Sardinian archaeology over the storytelling narrative by journalist Sergio Frau, who had staked out a claim to the Atlantis allegory recounted by Plato over two thousand years ago. Frau, as one of the founders of *La Repubblica* newspaper in Rome, did not only take a classic in hand; he put a map on it and pinned it to Sardinia. With his storytelling prowess and media contacts, Frau had managed to create his own museum in Sorgono, churned out a couple of bestselling books, and attracted global attention for his belief that the "Pillars of Hercules" did not indicate the Strait of Gibraltar but the Strait of Sicily, leading to Sardinia as the famed island of Atlas that had been struck by a tsunami. The remains of the nuraghes, and all those still buried, were part of this story.

Frau's popular work, including an exhibition at the UNESCO headquarters in Paris, struck a hornet's nest in academia; in 2005, a group of Sardinian archaeologists published a rejoinder, placing his work into the field of "fantasy" archaeology. The indefatigable Frau continued with another book, *Omphalos*, that placed Sardinia and its story as the center of the world.

"Prehistory is always one step away," Dessì had written. "Solitude and sociability correspond to millennia of European history, but perhaps even only to a night's sleep."

27 | BITTI

At this point in our history, continuing to leave this literature out
of the mainstream school and new mass communication channels
would quickly lead to a mutilation of our cultural identity.

—Michelangelo Pira and Manlio Brigaglia, *Il meglio della grande
poesia in lingua sarda*, 1975

I seemed to be doing everything in contrary fashion in the hill town of
Bitti, halfway between Siniscola, Tiscali, and the main town of Nuoro
in the Barbagia. I took a back road, which included the usual thousand
curves through the Sardinian countryside, bordered by a savannah of
oak, cork, mastic, and the occasional vineyard or farm. When I finally
arrived at the town, which perched up on the side of a hill, I parked
at the bottom, not far from some mounds of sand. The town was still
recovering from an apocalyptic storm, which had bounded over the
crest of the hills and poured through the streets of Bitti with torrents
of mud, taking three lives in the process. The tragedy had been com-
pounded by the collapse of roads, and the inundation of homes on the
lower part of the town.

Unfortunately, this had not been the first disaster in recent memory. In 2013, a similar flood swept through Bitti and other villages in

the region. In an act of "sarditudine," a group of writers came together to publish a book as a fundraiser—*Sei per la Sardegna*. It included works from Sardinian writers such as Francesco Abate, Alessandro De Roma, Marcello Fois, Salvatore Mannuzzu, Michela Murgia, and Paola Soriga, who wrote a short story about a young woman who is given a book, "a classic of world literature," though her family views it as a waste of time, an act that would leave "crickets in her head."

In fact, I had come to Bitti for numerous reasons. (The fascinating multimedia museum of the famous Tenores di Bitti, for starters.) But, as a writer, I had also come to walk the Caminera Literaria of Michelangelo Pira, one of my favorite Sardinian authors. The problem was: I had arrived at lunchtime, and not a soul was on the street, and the illusive Caminera map, after the flood, had left me disoriented on where to turn.

I opted for lunch. I found a rustic restaurant in the lower town, where workers from the cleanup were taking their rest. While I was far from the sea, I still ordered the *spaghetti alla bottarga*, the specialty of ground mullet eggs that turned the pasta into a bowl of treasure, and enlivened it with a smooth but intensely rich flavor of Sardinia's golden caviar. But this was a dish for the coast, the waitress reminded me. *Butàriga*, in Sardinian, was best in Cabras and Oristano, she kept pushing. "*Pecora in cappotto*," she countered. That was "sheep in a coat," which was a traditional stew of the shepherds. I nodded. I understood that we were in the uplands of the island. But no place in Sardinia was far from the sea. I went with the *butàriga*—and it was tasty.

In the eternal question of the agnostics—Who would you like to invite to lunch?—I would include two writers from Bitti: Pira, and the rebel politico of the Risorgimento, Giorgio Asproni. As for the other spots, the list would be long, but Maria Carta, Maria Lai, Antonio Gramsci, Paolo Fresu, Pinuccio Sciola, Paskedda Zau (who led an uprising in nearby

Nuoro), and Emilio and Joyce Lussu, among many others, were certainly contenders. I'd probably change my mind and add more in the next village. Perhaps I needed a lunch in every village—in nearby Orani, I'd love to time travel and sit across a table from poet and independence activist Marianna Bussalai, novelist Salvatore Niffoi and the celebrated sculptor Costantino Nivola. (Nivola's grandson, by the way, is the American actor, Alessandro Nivola.) We would have room for a chair for sculptor Albino Manca, from the Ogliastra village of Tertenia, whose massive "Diving Eagle" sculpture became central to the East Coast Memorial in Battery Park in New York City during an inauguration with President John F. Kennedy, and whose designs adorned parks in Rome, Brooklyn, and Queens, including the "Gates of Life" at the zoo. Such a lunch in Sardinia would be more like a banquet—the *convivio*, as Dante liked to say.

After lunch, I asked around for help on finding the Caminera for Pira, but no one seemed to know where to begin, or they pointed me in opposite directions. As I wandered up a backstreet, slowly climbing the steps of the town, I nearly bumped into a woman who was chasing a little kid down an alley. He appeared to have escaped his post-lunch nap. So, I asked her. She stopped, clamping her grip on the kid's arm, and nodded for me to follow her. Walking down an alley, no one in sight, she turned left then right, and then left again. She looked up at the wall, to see if I had noticed anything. Suddenly, little plaques appeared on the fraying plaster and old bricks, with quotations from Pira's books, as if the neighborhood had unfolded into pages of stories, wall by wall, building by building, until I arrived at his small childhood home.

I thanked the woman as she dragged away the kid. He shot one last look at me, either out of envy or pity. I went back and looked at the first plaque: *Il mondo intero e' quel che mi pareva fosse il villaggio quando ero bambino.—M. Pira, Il Villaggio Elettronico.* The world is what I thought the village was when I was a child.

Pira wrote a fifty-odd page novella called *The Electronic Village* in 1970. It deals with a world connected by computers. Whether it was coincidental or prophetic, Pira's story captured the need to communicate through whatever channel our minds can create. When Renato Soru launched his Tiscali company nearly three decades later, he declared: "Michelangelo Pira's dream of the electronic village finally comes true."

"The last thoughts of Martino, ninety years old, founding father of a new company that connected computers in a planetary network," Pira wrote. "My candle is at the end. You are here to see how one of the founding fathers of the community dies. When you can no longer communicate, it is easy to die." Pira's visionary story continued:

"Consciously or unconsciously, everyone tried to communicate to as many of his fellow beings as possible, his thoughts and experiences of his travels, but the spoken word was not enough, cinema was not enough, radio was not enough, phones were not enough, schools were not enough. Everyone considered themselves a terminal, but there was no central nervous system . . . because each extension had its own brain in contrast to those of the others. Thus, electronics and communication and science began to meet and seek common ground of application and implosion and to form new sciences.

"We were a definitive answer to the human fear of happiness . . . not a day went by that new computers were not built and that new terminals were not connected to them and that computers did not connect to each other. The system managed to slow down this process by spreading 'the fear of the computer'; that is, trying to transfer its fears to the citizens who were to benefit from it. It became defined as excessive, the wisdom of computers and the dangers for privacy. But (referring to computers and the network) man's wickedness, not his goodness, must have been afraid of it. Where information is collected there is power, and the concentration of information is dangerous. The computer made the information available to everyone. This was revolutionary."

Born in Bitti in 1928, Pira moved to Oschiri as a child to join his father, a shepherd. His mother had died, leaving Pira with no other family. He ended up at the famed Azuni high school in Sassari, and then the University of Cagliari. As a journalist, cultural anthropologist, novelist, and playwright for radio and theatre, Pira taught at the university and also became one of the most prolific and active writers in Sardinia in the 1960s until his sudden death in 1980. His 1968 book on language and bilingualism, *Sardegna tra due lingue*, addressed the impact of a society losing its native language. In a groundbreaking analysis of the shift from the agro-pastoral society to the demands of industrialization, his book, *La rivolta dell'oggetto*, became a classic.

Pira wrote in Italian, and in his native Bitterese language.

B'at cosas chi pro las cumprèndere bi cheret tempus e isperièntzia; e cosas chi cand'unu at isperièntzia no las cumprendet prus. Cosas chi pro furtuna s'irmentican e cosas chi pro furtuna s'ammentan; e cosas chi si creden irmenticadas e chi imbetzes una die a s'improvisu torran a conca.

There are things you need time and experience to understand, and things that when one has gained experience, one no longer understands. Things that fortunately are forgotten and things that fortunately are remembered; and things that are thought to be forgotten and that instead one day suddenly come back to mind.

Among his many stories, radio plays, and essays, Pira wanted to recover his family's history, as well as his own. In his novel, *Sos Sinnos*, which was published posthumously, he wrote in the Bittese variant of the Sardinian language, in a phonetic style of his own making. The story began with his actual name—not Michelangelo Pira, but Milianu. His father, Bachis, having decided to name his son after the Mexican revolutionary Emiliano Zapata, ended up arguing with a municipal employee who informed him that his son must be registered with an Italian name. The employee treated Bachis as if he was ignorant of the rules. The story unfolded:

> "Milianu, I put him."
> "Milianu? E-mi-lia-no."
> "You write in the register what you like. I continue to call him
> Milianu, Milianu Pinna."
> "Pinna is fine, but Milianu is not. And I bet you don't even know
> what this name means. It means born in Emilia, and instead your
> son was born here, in Sardinia."
> "The municipal employee made the process difficult and polite.
> Remunnu, who had given nicknames to the whole country, had put
> him 'Ispantamiseros,' which could not be more just than that. But
> Ispantamiseros was a miserable man, too, and frightened himself."
> "Bachis Pinna knew the reason for the name he wanted to give
> to his son, the seventh. From the vet, once, in the fold, he had
> heard the story of Milianu Sapata, who as a shepherd, or a peasant,
> had become a general making war on the rich, who, in the end,
> treasonously, as they know how to do, had killed him like a wild
> boar, but before dying he had given them a lot of trouble and wars.
> And Bachis Pinna, who felt what had remained in his ears, liked
> the story. And now he wanted to give his son the name of Sapata,
> but in secret, that the rich did not notice, because otherwise the
> son would have got him killed immediately."

As I walked around the back alleys of Pira's home neighborhood, only an occasional cat out during the afternoon siesta, I read the little plaques of excerpts from his stories on the walls. A mural of a boy reaching for a bird looked back from the opposite side of his home, a little one-room abode. A couple of shepherds peered at the boy, telling him stories.

"Emiliano, continue," the teacher tells him in his novel *Isalle*, published after his death. "But careful with literature. You can learn as much from the farmers as the books."

28 | THE BARBAGIA

I see you descending the Gennargentu,
with one horse in front, and the other after,
and bold, with your brass pipe.

—Sebastiano Satta, "A Vindice mio figlio," *Canti Barbaricini*, 1910

Back in Alghero, I occasionally dropped by a cultural center in the old town, ResPublica. Based in the former barracks of the Carabinieri, off the Piazza Pino Piras, the center functioned as a free-wheeling arts hub, with concerts, literary readings, and art shows. There was a very casual walk-in feel to the center, unabashedly political and radical, where a collective of numerous arts, environmental, and social groups also sponsored political events. On the first time I visited, I saw a poster of Nelson Mandela next to a few paintings of abstract Sardinian land-scapes and a display for "poetry found." Bookcases lined one side of the walls with an open library.

During one art show, I took a seat next to an older man and then struck up a conversation about the paintings. He was one of the artists. He came from a village near Nuoro, in the central Barbagia mountain region. As we drank our wine, he looked around in a curious manner, and then turned back to me, as if divulging a secret to a foreigner.

"You know, we are different from these people," he said. "In the Barbagia, I want to say."

I nodded. The "we" referred to the *barbaricini*, not me, of course. He winked. We raised our glasses and drank.

We had made a few trips into the Barbagia. As a writer who had chronicled the travails and largely overlooked contributions of mountain cultures in Appalachia, the Sierra Madre of Mexico, and the Western Ghats of India, I felt more at home in the Barbagia, as much as anywhere in Sardinia. The rural communities resonated with the history in my own forests in southern Illinois, where my family had resided for two centuries. Saddled with the stereotypes of being violent, indolent, somehow deficient (as "hillbillies" in modern depictions), our "backwoods" region had also gone through a similar period of "local color" writers in the nineteenth century, alternating between portraits of quaint folklore and unhinged feuds and banditry, and the bloody mess of the coal mines. I grew up in a family that both denied and embraced the stereotypes. It wasn't until I spent a summer working on a West Virginia farm and folk school in 1983, listening to stories and interviewing coal miners, that I saw how the recovery of "hidden histories" in the mountain regions could reshape a historical record that had allowed the exploitation of the land to go hand in hand with the marginalization of its people. Far from being in the "backwoods," Appalachia had played a leading role in the American Revolution, the anti-slavery movements, the labor and civil rights movements, and it churned out an extraordinary range of writers, musicians, and artists that had defined the American experience. Appalachian poet Don West once warned me about romanticizing mountain cultures, which he considered another curse. Contrary to the tropes of isolation and insularity—or some sort of "other" reality—West saw Appalachia's conflictual history as quintessential, not exceptional, and connected to mountain cultures around the world.

The *Civitates Barbariae*—this was how the Romans referred to the interior mountainous area of Sardinia. In the western areas of Sardinia, archaeologists found a stone inscription with the *Civitates Barbariae* moniker from the time of Emperor Tiberius in 19 A.D. near the Roman thermal baths in Fordongianus. The pools and vaulted ceilings of those baths, and their porticos, remain a great attraction today. The hot springs still flow at contemporary spas in town, as well. The Romans had left a lot of thermal baths around the island. They also left—or imposed—their language of Latin. Sigismondo Arquer, the hapless first Sardinian historian who ended up on the Inquisition rack in the mid-1500s, pointed out that Sardinians spoke "a large number of words that are not found in any language," though he added their language "retains many words of the Latin dialect, especially on the Barbagia mountains, where the commanders of the Romans had military garrisons."

There are numerous references in ancient times to "barbarians" in Germany and all over Europe, of course. The actual term derived from "babblers" in ancient Greek, a term borrowed by the Romans as an indication of the uncivilized.

The *Barbagia* name in Sardinia remained fairly unique in modern Europe, codified and embraced by the region, and celebrated as a heroic part of their heritage of resistance. To be sure, inhabitants in the Barbagia were not called "barbarians" but the *barbaricini*. (Some Sardinian linguists and advocates also posited another view that the word "barbaricini" might even have pre-Roman origins, signifying people of the mountains.) The geographer Ptolemy, among others, actually gave names to the mountain populations as the Ilienses, Balari, and Corsi. Diodorus and Strabo, writing around the turn of the first century A.D., chronicled the stories of Nuragic populations that "fled for safety to the mountains," where they raised herds with

"food in abundance." Strabo also identified four "nations" of mountaineers, who took the "customs of barbarians" and plundered the
lowland areas.

Historically, the Barbagia had been divided into at least six can-
tons, so to speak—from Mandrolisai to Nuoro to Ollolai and Belvì,
and from Seùlo to the Barbàgia Trigònia in Ogliastra. Several of the
larger towns included Nuoro, Orgosolo, Orani, Gavoi, Mamoiada,
Fonni, and Tonara. If you looked at a map of Sardinia, all of these
townships ringed the central-eastern mountain areas like beads
on a necklace, each with their own identity and legacy: Gavoi and
its Fiore Sardo cheese and literary festival, *L'isola delle Storie*, to
Mamoiada and its masks and rituals, to Fonni and its murals and
pastoral culture as the town at the highest elevation on the island,
and Seulo, with its array of waterfalls and caves, and the Ecomuseum
of Altoflumendosa.

Over a century before Cicero's tongue lashing of the Sardinians
as barbarians, Roman poet Naevius inscribed the word "sardare" in
the third century B.C., as formed from *sardo* or *sardus,* meaning "intelligent" and denoting an ability to "speak clearly." And Marcus Varro,
in the time of Cicero, lamented that the Romans were too lazy and
busy with theatre and circus to farm, so "we hire a man to bring us
from Africa and Sardinia the grain," he lamented, "with which to fill
our stomachs."

Nonetheless, Cicero taunted the Sardinians in one famous trial
as "brigands dressed in sheepskins," as if the mountaineers were
wildly savage. The *Sardi pelliti.* This description appears in numerous
chronicles, especially referring to the *mastruca* dress in the mountains.
One ancient Greek writer, Ninfodoro from Syracuse, actually complimented the Sardinian dress from sheep or goat skins as uniquely
suitable for the climate.

Even as Cicero turned the *mastruca* into a belittling part of the Roman vernacular, the Romans feared the Sardinians' resilience. Two thousand years later, it still endured.

In Ottana, a small mountain village in the Barbagia, we heard them first, the large collection of bronze cowbells on their backs and around their chests, clanking step by step. *Sos Merdules and sos Boes*, the shepherds and the oxen, dressed in their respective costumes of white sheepskins, wearing hand-carved masks from pearwood with the grotesque faces of some underworld vision.

In the village of Mamoiada, *sos Mamuthones* lined up in two rows of six, their dark presence in the January night casting an air of intrigue and tension. The large crowd stepped back, careful not to be swept up into the action. The Mamuthones masks were black as night, with wild expressions of contorted lips and high cheekbones and protruding noses. Their sheep garments were dark as well, and once assembled in a formal gathering, they began a dance back and forth. All of them wore the headscarves of women as a symbolic touch. They danced back and forth until they clanked *sa harriage*—these sixty-pound chains of bronze cowbells—cueing *sos Issohadores*, dressed in red jackets with a leather bandoleer, and white pants, their faces covered in a carved white mask, who responded in their role of the ritual with ropes.

Throughout Sardinia today, these ancient masks and their rituals, dating back to the Nuragic period or most certainly pagan times, often drew the largest crowds during the Carnival period. They had long been culled into Christianity, though the pagan symbolism still rang out on those harsh cowbells. Whether the masks veiled the truth, as the expression went in Italian, or reflected a larger truth about winter rites into spring, the distorted smiles on the masks celebrated a ritual of death and rebirth.

Cicero, like most Roman observers, took his invective one step further with another charge; he also referred to the Sardinians as "Punics, mixed with African blood." They were somehow indigenous and African transplants at the same time, both equally abhorrent to the Roman.

To make things more complicated, Procopius of Caesarea wrote in the sixth century A.D. that *Maroúsioi* (Moors from North Africa) had been sent to Sardinia by the Vandals, and remained in the mountains—and were called barbaricini, too. There were also the *Barbari* or Berbers of North Africa, known in modern times as the Barbary Coast.

All of these depictions—let's call them calumnies of barbarism—were not merely filed away in the ancient chronicles like epithets. The image of the ill-clad plundering highlander remained a vibrant proto-type for the next two thousand years. The historical sources of conflict in the region were rarely discussed. This included, for starters, the oc-cupation and colonization of the land by outside invaders and feudal lords, privatization and enclosure of land in the 1820s, the disruption of ancient pastoral rights, the devastating consequences of deforesta-tion, the displacement of poor shepherds in the burgeoning cheese mar-kets, and the lack of investment in cottage industries in modern times.

Arriving in Sardinia in the late 1890s, on the heels of a brutal government campaign to crack down on banditry, a twenty-one-year-old Alfredo Niceforo, as a Sicilian student of the racial criminology theories of the era, roamed the villages and mountains in the Barbagia with a measuring tape in hand. He pinned down the villagers, calcu-lating the size of their skulls; he tabulated the color of their skin and the thickness of their hair. He filled his notebooks with observations to determine whether the Barbagians were "born" criminals.

"We have discovered the imprint of atavistic stigmata to a surprising degree," he declared. The key word—*atavistic*, as some sort of ances-tral trait—would become nearly inseparable with the Barbagia. (Even

Emilio Lusso, writing about the failures of the island into the 1950s, declared Sardinians suffered from "complexes" that were "largely ata-vistic.") Publishing his results in 1897, *La Delinquenza in Sardegna,* which needs no translation, Niceforo provided a pseudo-scientific ex-planation for the high rates of livestock rustling, land conflicts, and violence. Even the children were "morally inferior," Niceforo wrote. "Some form of organization in their nervous system pushes them to fatally draw blood."

For the next several decades, Niceforo's unabashedly racist work, among others, would provide the sociological foundations for reams of government reports—and also poems, songs, stories, novels, and films—on banditry, feuds, and crime in the mountains. As a young writer, Deledda even dedicated one of her first books in 1896, *La Via del Male,* to Niceforo, "who lovingly visited Sardinia." Within a decade, however, the famed novelist would remove such a dedication.

The clash between the state authorities and criminal bands, includ-ing periodical dragnets and shoot-outs by the police and Carabinieri, would fill the headlines until the 1990s. The lore of lawlessness, similar to my own southern Illinois and Appalachia, churned out more than enough books to fill a library. In 1954, Franco Cagnetta's controversial work, *Inchiesta su Orgosolo* (Inquest on Orgosolo), which was a village in the mountains infamous for its violence, presented a wild, alien, and mysterious world where "three thousand years" of "permanent mili-tary and police siege" had battled an "incredible primitiveness" inside a "frightful Eden." Sardinian historian Maria Bonaria Urban called Cagnetta's dispatches one of the twentieth century's most influential works on Sardinia. (She also reminded us that the first Sardinia-set film was about bandits in 1905, *I briganti in Sardegna.*)

Gramsci, as would be expected, had already analyzed the por-trayal of his islanders' depictions as criminals as bereft of any deeper historical context. Writing in his newspaper in 1920, he excoriated the "cruel dictatorship" of the Italian state for "crucifying, quartering, shooting, and burying alive the poor peasants that mercenary writers tried to shame by branding them 'bandits.'"

One of my favorite bandit movies, though, Vittorio De Séta's *Bandits of Orgosolo*, about the ill-fated descent of a desperate shepherd into rustling, had some beautiful scenes in the Supramonte range. Using shepherds as actors, De Seta's black-and-white film won acclaim at the Venice Film Festival in 1961; Martin Scorsese called the Sicilian filmmaker, "an anthropologist who spoke with the voice of a poet." The impact of the film was tangible. The Italian journalist Roberto Saviano wrote that De Seta told him in an interview that the famed historian Indro Montanelli "wrote that the criminals on the Supramonte of Sardinia should be firebombed."

On that note, let us return to the ancient stories.

The origins of the Sardinians, especially in the Barbagia, always confounded the classical historians and their readers in modern times. The Greeks assumed the island had been settled by the Libyans, the sons of Hercules; the Romans assumed it had been settled by the Greeks; that Ioalus and his flock planted the fruit trees and built the stone towers and temples, and Aristaeus introduced agriculture, cheese-making and beekeeping—Sardinia's famous bitter honey.

The classical writers simply refused to acknowledge any indigenous culture that merited note. We can "pass over" the native tribes, the Latin writer Solinius wrote in the third century A.D., and for the most part writers did so for the next fifteen centuries, largely repeating the classical stories as fact, almost to absurdity. Sardinian historian Giovanni Fara noted in his "first book of the Sardois" in

1580 that the crab-legged Phorcys, the primordial sea god of the Greeks, served as the first King of Sardinia. Even into the twentieth century, the farcicalities of classical tales mixed into modern history. "The large proportion of persons of very low stature," British historian Edmund Spenser Bouchier added in his history of Sardinia in 1917, "leads some anthropologists to assume an early incursion of African pigmies, who by mingling with the other inhabitants have lost their most marked characteristics."

The recent studies of DNA told another story on the island, including an analysis by the University of Chicago in 2020. As part of the Neolithic migration period around 7000 B.C., settlers hopscotched their way across the lower seas and islands off Tuscany, then Corsica, arriving in Sardinia. While other waves of migrations continued across Italy and Europe, the Sardinians maintained a unique ancestry over the next several thousands of years. This DNA story, therefore, informed a key point in the island's progression of development. The pre-Nuragic and Nuragic periods, according to the study, were "not marked by shifts in ancestry, arguing against hypotheses that the design of the Nuragic stone towers was brought with an influx of people from eastern sources such as Mycenaeans."

In effect, the results suggested that Sardinia's sophisticated Bronze Age ways, such as the stone towers, water temples, and Nuragic cultures, emerged on their own. They certainly rose within the context of exchange with other civilizations, but without any other waves of migration and occupation until the arrival of the Phoenicians around the tenth and ninth centuries B.C.

Therefore, it was important to return to the Nuragic monuments to help untangle the ancient histories and myths that still defined much of the narrative in the Barbagia and all of Sardinia.

One of the most captivating Nuragic sites, in fact, was near Bitti, and strangely named after the Romans—the sanctuary village of Su Romanzesu. Winding along the hills, following through a magnificent forest of cork trees, whose denuded bottom red trunks stood under the canopy of branches and foliage and thick bark on the upper part of the trunk with the look of some sheared beast of the woods, we seemed to be heading into an unknown hinterlands. But this road, or the contours of the natural geography, had been followed for millennia as a route of pilgrimage.

As usual, it baffled me that only a handful of us toured the site. These extraordinary places, dating back thousands of years, would have been key destinations in other parts of Europe. A single site dating back to this period in the United States would have been a national park. Here in Sardinia, with its abundance of Neolithic and Bronze Age remains, it was almost too easy to bypass a gem of ancient art or architecture that had watched from the roadside for untold generations of travelers.

Our guide, Francesco, had left behind an office career to pursue his passion. As we began to make our way through the forested community that dated back to the eleventh to the ninth centuries B.C., he reminded us to not look at the ruins with "modern eyes." Spread out over eighteen acres, tucked under the canopy of cork and oak trees, laced with ferns, the compound of temples had an almost mystical feel of a ceremonial center. The ruins seemed laid out with an intentional design; a large step-stoned amphitheater, the sacred well, the walls of a round house with a labyrinth, a *megaron* temple and a temple to heroes, clearly showcased a park of ritual. Other temples and over one hundred round houses abounded. You had the sense that the sanctuary was not simply a community, but a sacred place of destination.

I had been curious to visit Romanzesu—my first Nuragic "sanctuary" and sacred well—for a long time. In a critical period of shift on the island, as the Bronze Age worlds in the rest of the Mediterranean and Near East were collapsing into chaos in the twelfth century B.C., ornate water temples and *pozzi sacri* (sacred wells) began to appear across Sardinia.

By far, the most spectacular example of the sacred well was Santa Cristina, in the village of Paulilatino on the upper plateau between Oristano and Fordongianus—about fifty miles southwest of Romanzesu. We had visited that sacred well once, after a trip to Oristano. Dating back to the eleventh century B.C., this Nuragic site sat inside an elliptical enclosure that would appear like a keyhole from an aerial shot, and then descended twenty-four steps down a triangular staircase, into an underground chamber that looked back up through the beehive tholos of a nuraghe tower design. A pool of water, once surging from the spring or well, perfectly framed the bottom of the chamber; there was a bench or landing for someone to stand or carry out a ritual.

The Santa Cristina sacred well, three thousand years later, remained in a stunningly refined condition, its chiseled ashlar stones from basalt creating a staircase and side walls in an isodomic technique that appeared almost too perfect. "One might indeed be overwhelmed by the impression that this building is not Sardinian—or that it is too Sardinian," Maud Webster observed in an archaeological study of water temples. While similar stone techniques created the marvels of the Parthenon in Greece and untold numbers of Roman buildings centuries later, the antiquity of Santa Cristina—and its utter faultlessness—was nothing less than astonishing in Sardinia. It was truly a masterpiece of architectural genius.

It had not always been so evident. While travelers like La Marmora had noted the well and staircase by the mid-1800s—Spano, the pioneering archaeologist, thought it reminded him of a Roman prison—the first photographs by a Dominican priest in 1898 showed the staircase to be almost completely covered in rocks and rubble. The first excavations didn't happen until the 1950s.

As part of a larger tourist complex, the site was now a major destination on the Nuragic circuit. Our guide even had a tattoo of the well on her arm.

The sacred well back at Romanzesu stood out as a larger sanctuary compound, which had been established on the plateau as a pilgrimage destination in a period of clear upheaval and transition. The sanctuary was quite near the source of the Tirso river—the most important river on the island.

Writing in the fourth century B.C., Greek historian Herodotus pinpointed an enduring drought as the cause of famine, displacement, conflict, and even the collapse of societies in the Bronze Age. Recent studies in the Mediterranean, including the island of Cyprus, confirmed a three-hundred-year period of megadrought, though scholars still remain in disagreement over the drought's primary role in the Bronze Age upheaval.

In Sardinia, many archaeologists pointed to a similar drought on the island. Some, like the Websters and Maria Fadda, suggested the sacred wells emerged along the "ancient roads of transhumance," where "ritual practice fused with economic interests" took place at the sanctuary villages, characterized by a "need to resolve the grave problem of the scarcity of water which could compromise local economies."

At the beginning of the Iron Age, "the picture changes radically," according to most archaeologists. The sanctuaries became hubs of wealth, including the concentration of the bronzetti. Some assume an elite emerged, though their reign appeared to be short-lived; within two centuries, as coastal trade within the Mediterranean and connections with other cultures trickled throughout the island, Sardinia began to see the integration between the traditional Nuragic economy and outside markets. By the time the Phoenicians docked into the ports with their wares and ideas in the tenth to ninth centuries, the Nuragic civilization had transformed significantly from the Bronze Age and entered the early Iron Age with rapidly changing territorial and cultural ways.

Fast forward five hundred years: With the arrival of the Carthaginian and Roman fleets and their soldiers from 500 to 237 B.C., the Nuragic civilization faced the most important threat to its actual survival. This brings us back to the Barbagia.

"Since our island of Sardinia occupies a central position with respect to other lands," wrote Giovanni Arca Sardo (Ioannis Arca Sardo) in 1598, in *De Barbaricinorum fortitudine,* "constituting—so to speak—the key and bulwark of the kingdoms of Europe, it was conquered and destroyed by almost all peoples and nations; nevertheless, the Barbaricini never lost their ancient freedom."

The Barbagia didn't just have its own history; it had its own historian in the late sixteenth century. From the same village of Bitti, where four hundred "fires" (or households) were noted during his childhood in the 1560s, Giovanni Arca had gone on to study as a Jesuit in Cagliari, and then served as a teacher in Sassari. He didn't get along well with the Spanish-controlled clergy. By the 1590s, he submitted his resignation and asked for a horse to return home to the Barbagia. Having read a copy of Fara's and Arquer's pioneering histories, Arca decided to write his own from the view of the Barbagia. He ended up writing several books. In fact, he became the first published writer outside of the coastal cities in Sardinia. He added "Sardo" to the end of his name, as if to differentiate himself from the other writers, especially those from Spain, who ruled over the island.

Whether you would call it fiction or nonfiction, Arca was

fabulously resourceful. He took ancient Roman poems and histories and altered them into first person narratives, adding some dramatic details. He lifted entire sections from Fara. In recounting battles between the Romans and the Sardinians, including the mountain populations, Arca sought to show how the Barbagia retained its cultural and social integrity in the face of the onslaught of the Roman campaigns, until the region's final conversion to Christianity in the sixth century A.D.

"This clearly demonstrates with what courage and valor the Iliensi defended themselves," Arca narrated, after one battle, identifying one of the Barbagian populations. "Despite having lost so many men in these battles, nevertheless they took away the lives of as many Romans." The "fear of the heroism of the Barbaricini," Arca declared, made the Roman prefer to leave them "free rather than fight them with so much damage."

The rise of the defiant Barbagia, in contrast to the conquered coastal areas, became a defining narrative for the region.

Arca drew from classical Greek and Latin sources, including Pausanias, the Greek geographer from the second century B.C. Going back before the Romans, he claimed the Carthaginians conquered all of Sardinia, with the exception of the "Ilians and Corsicans, who were kept from slavery by the strength of the mountains."

In the face of his "enthusiastic mythicization of the Barbaricini," historian Maria Teresa Laneri observed, it was hard to say whether Arca appreciated more the Barbagia's eventual conversion to Christianity with "the consequent pacification" or rather he "regretted their indomitable pagan pride and belligerence."

The writer from Bitti, having broken from the Spanish domination in Sassari, clearly wanted to send a message from the past to the present (and future): If the other Sardinians had risen to the occasion with the "warlike virtue of the Barbaricini," they could "always remain free and masters of all their wealth."

Despite their unique role, Arca's Barbaricini still followed the thread of classical literature. The Bitti writer made it clear, Laneri added; his Barbaricini didn't descend from the "rough and barbarous people who contaminated the northern part of our island," but by the "very ancient and noble Trojans." Led by Iolaus, the grandson of Hercules, Arca concluded, "the beginning of those people we know today as Barbaricini" came to Sardinia.

Regardless of their entwined ancestral mythologies, what mattered most to Arca was *De Barbaricinorum fortitudine*—the fortitude of the Barbaricini.

29 | ASPRONI, GARIBALDI, AND THE PRINCE OF SATIRE

Sardinia wrote in 1792 and 1793 one of the most glorious pages of our history . . . They should tell their fellow citizens not to look at the Piedmont, but at the Italy that is becoming, and which, just done, will keep Sardinia as one of the most splendid gems of its diadem.

—Giuseppe Mazzini, *L'Unita' Italiana*, 1861

The village of Bitti tagged along with me on numerous trips, even outside the Barbagia. That included the island home of Giuseppe Garibaldi, who had worked closely with a revolutionary figure from Bitti in the Risorgimento.

Standing on the fortress walls of the Garibaldi museum in Caprera, I could see the outline of Corsica toward the northwest, hopscotching across La Maddalena archipelago and its varying shades of sea-blue that scurried between the rocky islands. On the opposite end, the undulating hills on the mainland came into view, as if the "hero of two worlds" had managed to keep Sardinia at a distance, and also within reach of his command.

The far northern island of Caprera, as the place of refuge for Italy's national hero, was a serene windswept nature reserve floating in the Mediterranean. Boulders stacked like monuments along the stretches of pine and oak forests. Crystal-blue coves ringed the island with an incredible sense of calm. And yet, on this northern outpost of solitude in Sardinia, the commander of the insurgent forces mapped out his plans to invade Sicily with an army of a thousand volunteers, and liberate the rest of Italy for its unification in 1860–61.

The English writer Jessie White Mario, a pioneering journalist, wrote about her monthlong hunting trip with Garibaldi in Sardinia, where the banished followers of Mazzini, and former soldiers under Garibaldi's earlier defense of Rome, had "thronged around him," anxious to take action.

It was hard to imagine that there on Caprera, tending to his farm after recognizing Vittorio Emanuele II as King of Italy, Garibaldi had turned down an offer from the Union forces in the American government in 1861, during a pivotal moment of the Civil War, to become a general of one of their units. Garibaldi, who called for the abolition of slavery as a condition for his military role, would later write President Abraham Lincoln an open letter in the *New York Times* from his island in 1863, commending him for following John Brown's aspirations, signing the Emancipation Proclamation, and reminding him of the "robbery of Mexico." Over the years, his island would entertain revolutionaries from around the world, including Russian Mikhail Bakunin.

The treasury of literature on Garibaldi, including his own memoirs, is vast. Longtime Italian observer and British author Tim Parks recently followed the path of the insurgent's flight from Rome and across the Apennines in 1849, in his book, *The Hero's Way*. English historian A. J. P. Taylor referred to Garibaldi as "the only wholly admirable figure in modern history."

Operated with the help of volunteers, the museum in the old Savoyard fort on Caprera, along with Garibaldi's home by the sea, did an excellent job in walking visitors through the legacy of this towering figure of the nineteenth century. It also reminded me of his connection to Sardinia—and the role of Sardinians themselves in the Risorgimento. In one of the displays, I noted the name of one of the revolutionaries, Giorgio Asproni, who had secretly worked with Garibaldi to raise the arms for the famed "Expedition of the Thousand" in Sicily. Another Sardinian from Cagliari, the famous tenor "Mario" (Giovanni Matteo de Candia), whose leading role in the world of opera was immortalized in James Joyce's *Ulysses*, also provided funds and support for Garibaldi.

In the late spring of 1876, an ailing Garibaldi had disregarded the instructions of his doctor and hurriedly returned to Rome to bid his farewell to Asproni, one of his legendary red shirts and now a parliamentarian. Garibaldi didn't arrive in time; Asproni's funeral at the Campo Verano shut down Rome for days. One of the main oppositional figures on the left in the parliament, Asproni had been a powerful voice of reason over three key decades in Italy's transition in the mid-to-late nineteenth century.

Born in Bitti, and representing the Barbagia region in parliament, Asproni had juggled a tenuous relationship with the island and its mainland through the Kingdom of Sardina and its evolution into the Kingdom of Italy. (Another one of my favorite maps was from 1860: *Il Regno di Sardegna*, which showed the entire country of present-day Italy, with the exception of Veneto, Tirolo and the *Stato Pontificio* of the Vatican, as the Kingdom of Sardinia.) In Turin, Asproni once told the English journalist White that he had found "neither soul nor sentiment" in that northern city, and that he would have preferred "a thousand times" to go to Sardinia.

Over 350 years after Arca's tributes to the Barbaricini, whose

writing would largely be forgotten, *La Nuova Sardegna* newspaper ran
a commemorative headline about this other writer from the same village: "Giorgio Asproni 80 years after his death," with a fiery summary
of the article at top: "The combative Bittese canon from the ranks
of the Thousand to the first Italian Parliament—Friend of Mazzini
and Garibaldi—Sardinian deputy on the attack—He clearly saw the
need for an autonomous administration of Sardinia, but no one today
remembers him."

Like Arca, Asproni had also opted for the route of the Jesuits, after
the death of his parents in Bitti had left him in the hands of his uncle,
Melchiorre Dore. A clergyman and respected poet, Dore's poem *Sa
Ierusalem vittoriosa* was considered a classic of regional literature.

Bitti, for a small village, certainly had its share of writers—and
satirical ones, even today. In 2004, Albino Pau's novella *Sas gamas
de Istellai* recounted a village's struggle with modernity when cows
start producing chocolate milk. Over the past four decades, Bitti
author Bachisio Bandinu had written numerous novels and books,
including *Lettera a un giovane sardo sempre connesso* (Letters to a
Young Sardinian Always Online), seeking to illuminate stories in *sas
intragnas* or the penumbra of the Sardinian experience. Born to a
poor family of peasants in 1797 in Bitti, Diego Mele had managed to
study as he worked, eventually entering the priesthood. Befriending
Spano, the pioneering archaeologist and linguist, Mele's true love
was poetry, both oral and written works in the Logudorese variant of Sardinia; biting satire was his talent, especially aimed at the
Savoyard policies and barons that left his Barbagia region impoverished. German traveler Von Maltzan hailed Mele as the "prince
of Sardinian satire," during his trip through the island in the mid-
nineteenth century. Accused of "inciting the people to support the
wandering cattle, and to spread territorial communism," in protest

of the closure laws that broke up the ancient commons, Mele was banished by the archbishop to remote villages in the Barbagia, with a particular association in Olzai, where he wrote his poetic defense of the shepherds, "In Olzai non campat pius mazzone." His work continued to spread, and was eventually published in numerous collections and translated in German, French, and Italy.

Asproni was no less prolific as an author. In 1849, he defended himself in a pamphlet after La Marmora accused him of being a "champion of communism," according to *La Nuova Sardegna*, "because he had defended those Nuorese who had opposed with riots the payment of taxes," and that "he understood well, however, that the small property, protected by taxes and helped by appropriate measures, would be the fundamental formula of the Sardinian economic awakening." Trained by the clergy, Asproni had also studied law. While serving as a canon in the Nuoro area, he was first elected to parliament in 1848, but forced to decline due to the rules of his religious order. Once the Mazzini uprisings occurred, Asproni could wait no longer; he renounced his canonry, and then ran again for office in 1849, representing the Barbagia in the parliament. Taking part in the parliamentary discussions as a noted orator, Asproni became one of the leading voices against the Savoyard stranglehold on the island.

He compared the "wicked domination" of the Piedmontese to the Turks' aggression in Greece, denouncing "the ruthless government" that had "inflicted, are inflicting and will inflict upon Sardinia." The former clergyman, who would also step off in an armed duel in Napoli, didn't mince his words. He charged that the Savoyards sought to keep Sardinia "permanently depopulated, barbarian and a slave."

As one of the first advocates for autonomy, not independence, Asproni wrote that he believed the islands of Sardinia and Sicily "should have their own government with their own and independent administration." Sardinia, in his mind, could "always subject to the bond with mother Italy, which will be represented by a government and a national parliament in Rome." His bill for the "Improvement of the Island of Sardinia" of 1850 failed, however, to shift any change. After joining Garibaldi's force in Sicily, Asproni directed Mazzini's political newspaper *Il Popolo d'Italia* in Naples, and then eventually took his seat again in the new parliament, where he became deeply involved in worker societies and unions across Italy.

His advocacy on behalf of Sardinia resulted in investments for the railroads, among other improvements, but a commission set up in 1868 to study the needs of the island turned into a colossal disappointment. Asproni wrote to his constituents in a letter:

> Why don't we leave to Sicily and Sardinia the faculty to
> satisfy their own supreme needs? As long as they are governed
> and administered by the proconsuls, by telegraph, as long as
> they use the buttons of fire, the states of siege, the formless
> shootings, the judgments on the drum, they will be unhappy
> and will be a disturbance, a gangrene for the State. By eternal
> and immutable law the islands are and will be what nature
> made them, that is, sui generis.
>
> We Sardinians proclaimed our Italianness in the innocent
> demonstrations of 1847–48; Sicily in the barricades of the
> heroic Palermo. But this happy union cannot be consolidated or
> cemented by violence or by Leonine societies; but with justice,
> with equal rights and with freedom.

"The fundamental themes of his political action concerned problems, most of which are not yet resolved today," *La Nuova Sardegna* opined in 1956. It concluded: "The issues concerning communications with the Continent, public security especially in Nuoro, the agrarian question and the ademprivili, the administrative decentralization within the region, almost all await a solution that Asproni pointed out with the help of a deep knowledge of the historical, economic, and social causes."

30 | *L'ATENE BARBARICINA*

It is a period when the Belle Epoque does not spare even this little, neglected, out-of-the-way capital of the Barbagia district, where the people of Nuoro are busy creating their own vision of themselves. Reckless and unshakeable, not conformist but worldly. No pure metals but alloys, stronger or weaker according to the composition of the mixtures from which they have been made. A touch artistic and a touch stingy, inclined to fuss over details while remaining completely ignorant of the wider picture. But this is not the story we have to tell.

—Marcello Fois, *Stirpe* (*Bloodlines*), 2009

We walked up and down the old town shopping district of *il Corso Garibaldi* like characters in *The Day of Judgment,* Salvatore Satta's spirited send-up of his native town of Nuoro. The Caffé Tettamanzi buzzed with patrons, both inside and at the tables on the street, just as it had in his time. The décor had not changed much in a hundred years. Books hung from the ceiling like lanterns. We took our coffee and brioche, and watched the waves of strollers. There was something gritty and unadorned about Nuoro that was appealing. "Don Ricciotti spent his life at the Caffé Tettamanzi, the very place where his father had gambled away his whole fortune," I read in Satta's novel. He never ate or drank. "But his suffering was of the kind that required witnesses, and above all people whom he could involve in the hatred bottled up in his heart for so many years."

"There is nothing to see in Nuoro," Lawrence wrote. "Which, to tell the truth, is always a relief."

A hundred years later, we argued over our itineraries for the day—I had lined up a dozen more nuraghes. Fed up with prehistory, the family had ranked their preferences for seeking out food or visiting the Art Museum, the MAN Museum of Art, the National Costume Museum, the National Archaeological Museum, and Grazia Deledda's Museum (which also featured a room for poet Sebastiano Satta, I was reminded). I had put the Spazio Ilisso on my list—a combination of a publishing house, art gallery, and event space. Publishing houses abounded on the island. There were almost too many to note, but I appreciated the fine work of Ilisso, Carlo Delfino, Il Maestrale, Condaghes, Edizioni della Torre, Arkadia, Centro di Studi Filologici Sardi, Domus de Janas, CUEC, Alfa Editore, and Sellerio (in Sicily), among many others that specialized in Sardinian writers and themes.

Not far from Spazio Ilisso, and across the street from the Museum of Sardinian Ceramics, remained a burning ground for modern Sardinian history—the Piazza Su Connottu, where Paskedda Zau, a sixty-year-old peasant and widow, led an uprising against the auctioning of common lands in 1868. "You cannot understand the riots that broke out in Nuoro with the cry of Paskedda Zau, 'Torrausu a su connottu,'" noted Gianluca Medas, author of a biography on Zau and an actor and director from Cagliari, "if you do not summarize the history of the Savoy monarchy, who invented private property where it did not exist." Outraged that state authorities planned to auction lands that had always been used as a public commons for shepherds and farmers,

Zau led the attack on the town hall, burning the list of lands up for sale. Her demands to return to *su connottu* or "the known" became a motto for ancestral rights and traditions.

As we entered the Piazza Sebastiano Satta, however, a haphazard square that was neither square nor rectangular or triangular, these massive stones like menhirs stole our attention. Designed by the acclaimed artist Costantino Nivola in the late 1960s, the square fanned out in large blocks that looked like tiles. On carved-out shelves on the granite stones sat little bronze statues of Satta, among others, like contemporary bronzetti.

Born in 1867 in Nuoro—his mother came from the village of Mamoiada—Satta had been one of the most compelling poets on the island around the turn of the century. He, too, studied at the Azuni high school in Sassari, and then in Bologna, only to return to Sardinia to study law. Poetry was his passion; he published his first collection, *Nella terra dei nuraghes*, in 1893. As a lawyer, journalist, poet, and radical socialist, Satta played a role in the lively period when Nuoro, full of artists and writers, was considered the Athens of Sardinia.

I had first read Satta's masterful work on the coal mining strike in the town of Buggerru on the southwestern coast. Today, Buggerru was a gorgeous little hub, with nearby beaches. In 1904, known as "Little Paris" for the comforts that greeted its mine owners and upper class, Buggerru sat at the bottom of a breathtaking cliff in a winding hill town of miner shacks. Women and children worked alongside men for twelve hours a day; accidents were frequent. When the miners went out on strike in 1904, the mine owners called in the soldiers. A clash broke out. The guards gunned down four miners, injuring a dozen others. When news of the massacre was finally reported, syndicalists in Sicily and other parts of Sardinia went on strike, but the protest didn't end on the islands. The cause of the Sardinians sparked the first ever general strike in Italy, signaling a dramatic shift in the labor movement across the country. Satta's *"I morti di Buggerru"* poem drew national attention to the tragedy:

> *Sardegna! dolce madre taciturna,*
> *Non mai sangue più puro*
> *E innocente di questo*
> *ti bruciò il cor.*

> Sardinia! sweet taciturn mother,
> Never has blood more pure
> And innocent than this
> Burned your heart.

After suffering a stroke in 1908, at the age of forty-one, the poet was forced to dictate his verses to his wife and assistant. His greatest work, *Canti Barbaricini*, appeared in 1910 as a tribute to his mountain region. Satta died in 1914.

Nivola's unusual piazza inspired us to pursue a different journey than we had planned. We mapped out a few days of art in the area, from the Francesco Ciusa museum in Nuoro, to the murals in Orgosolo, to Nivola's own museum of sculpture in his village of Orani.

Critics tended to say that modern sculpture in Sardinia began with Ciusa's haunting piece in plaster, *La madre dell'ucciso* (The Mother of the Murdered), which won acclaim at the Venice Biennale in 1907. But as Emilio Lussu once pointed out, one of the most poignant bronzetti in the Nuragic age had also been known by the same title, with a mother holding the body of her slain child. Ciusa had never known of such a bronzetti prior to his exhibition. Against the wishes of his dear friends Sebastiano Satta and Deledda, who preferred his striking nudes, Ciusa had entered his Barbagia-based artwork in the prestigious competition. According to one reviewer, *La madre dell'ucciso* was "one of the strongest works of sculpture of our times." Ciusa's success propelled him to a national and international status as an artist.

La madre captured the anguish of a thin, aged, and hooded mother in *sa ria*, the wake, sitting down, her arms crouched around her knees, her lips tightened into silence. Ciusa said the image of the mother had come from a real story he had witnessed as a teen, the grief of a mother over the loss of her murdered son, which had profoundly affected his work as an artist. The original now appeared in the Galleria d'Arte Contemporanea in Cagliari, while a bronze copy was placed in the permanent collections at the Galleria d'Arte Moderna in Rome.

Born in 1883 in Nuoro, Ciusa had studied in Florence, but decided to return to L'Atene Barbaricina, where he joined Satta and other writers, artists, and activists on the island at the turn of the century. While famous for his sculptures, Ciusa also did illustrations of Deledda's novels and magazine covers, as well as paintings. And while he continued to exhibit his work in Sardinia and Italy, including other Biennale shows in Venice, the fame of *La madre* continued to overshadow his other pieces of work. Satta had encouraged Ciusa to move to the United States, to seek out more success, but he remained in Sardinia.

Half a century later, Nivola, on the other hand, had fled to France and then the United States in 1938, when the grip of fascism had clamped down in Italy.

It wasn't hard to find Nivola's museum, which perched on the opposite side of the valley of his nearby hill town of Orani like a white monastery. Born in 1911 to a poor family, Nivola had trained as a stonecutter, eventually finding work in Sassari. Falling under the guidance of painter Mario Delitala, also from Orani, who had designed that unique flag from a wood print for the independence party and won considerable attention for his paintings and frescoes, Nivola eventually entered art school in Monza, near Milan. After marrying his wife, Ruth, a fellow art student from Germany who had been affected by the Racial Laws for being Jewish, Nivola left the country for Paris, where they met with anti-fascists. Concerned with being arrested, the couple flew to New York City, where they became part of the leading circles of artists. Nivola's first art show took place in Greenwich Village in 1944.

Outside the Nivola museum in Orani stood his most famous pieces—the great mothers. "For some time, in my sculpture emerges a simple, essential force," he explained. "Here spirit and senses collaborate in giving shape and meaning to matter. There is a female form as a result, but not necessarily as a starting point. The potbellied wall of a rustic house, in my magical childhood, always hid a treasure: the flat and thin bread that swells with the oven heat, the promise of satisfying an everlasting hunger." Echoing *la dea madre* patterns from the Neolithic sculptures at Monte d'Accoddi, and other sites, Nivola's oversized figures, *Dialogue* and *Widow*, were minimalist forms of women in marble and bronze.

Working first with the Italian Olivetti company in New York City, Nivola had actually shaped a unique career collaborating closely with architects on large-scale graphic design installations, including the Olivetti showroom, as well as the façades for various buildings. In the 1950s and '60s, Nivola created sculptures and installations for Yale University and McCormick Place in Chicago, among other buildings around the country. In 1972, he became the first foreign-born artist to be admitted into the American Academy of Arts and Letters.

The connection to Sardinia never wavered, though. He returned in the 1950s for a visit; in 1958, he created a fascinating graffiti design on the façade of the Church of Sa Itria in Orani, which still remains today. Along with the piazza sculptures for Satta in Nuoro, Nivola had also designed a special monument for Gramsci, whom he considered a personal hero, as well as the Sassari Brigade, though neither project came to fruition. One of his last works took place in Cagliari, as part of a special sculpture event in 1987. He died a year later.

In a poem in his memoir about Orani, Nivola had written: *Anch'io come te non ero nato / per vedere il mare . . . Sono tornato a Orani / annunziate dalle tue comari / "ricco e potente e'" hanno detto / "meschino" hai risposto / "costretto a vivere in terre straniere."* I, too, was not born like you / to see the sea . . . I returned to Orani / announced by your merry wives / "rich and powerful is he," they said / "pitiful" you replied / "forced to live in a foreign land."

Crossing over the hills on the opposite side of Nuoro, we set aside any stories of bandits to arrive in Orgosolo. Instead, we read from Maria Giacobbe's memoir, *Diario di una maestrina* (Diary of a Young Teacher). "And now it has been three years that I teach in Orgosolo," she began, writing in 1957. "Three years in which a lot of clichés I had when I arrived have disappeared, and new sentiments have replaced them." Orgosolo, she declared, "is no longer the 'university of crime.'"

The town perched on the side of a hill, as if to hide its secrets. A fabulous boulder met you at the last bend into the town, where a painted figure stared at your ascent. The anonymous postwar effect of the housing blocks could have been anywhere in Italy, as if masking the Sardinian ways of the Barbagia. But once we parked our car on a side street and started walking through the old town, we felt like we were entering another dimension of one of Nivola's or Ciusa's art shows. This time, however, the art was on the facades and walls and back alleys of the buildings, effortlessly left behind like stories or postcards from those behind the closed doors and windows.

The murals of Orgosolo deserved their own books and films—and I imagined there were plenty of documentaries. Far from any neat and tidy framing of the murals, the streets of Orgosolo sprawled intentionally out of the box of any control, scenes reaching over windows and doorways, climbing up walls and to the side of windows; oversized faces and images splattered across entire side streets. And like graffiti poetry, the shaking hand of a writer's words danced across the sides of the murals, as if inured to any concept of staying within the lines.

The anarchy, of course, was intended. The first mural, according to an older woman we met on the street, had been done by a collective called Dionisio, but the real work and the bulk of the more than 150 murals had been painted "by the teacher." That teacher was now famous in Sardinia—Francesco del Casino, who had won a *concorso* in 1964 for a teaching position, and agreed to move to Orgosolo from his native Tuscany after seeing the film, *Banditi a Orgosolo*. More importantly, del Casino had trained as an artist, and fallen in love with cubist works. In the early 1970s, in preparation for the anniversary of the liberation of Italy, he rounded up his students and began to paint scenes on the walls of his adopted town to "break the wall that divides school from society."

His paintings took on an unmistakable style. His choices of topics were defiantly political—and radical. Imagine a mixed Sardinian version of the *Guernica* by Picasso, imprints by Banksy and graffiti done by students and local artists, with tributes to Sardinian, Italian, and world events. The scenes ranged from Angioy's rebellion, to Garibaldi and Gramsci, to protests against weapons testing in Sardinia and a satire on Niceforo's racist studies. The broken plaster and uneven layers of bricks played into the art. The writing couldn't be contained by a single wall, often trickling over to the next buildings. The murals celebrated shepherds, families, traditional artisans and musicians and poets, food and wine, women's rights, and even a playbill for the *Banditi* film. It covered international episodes, such as the overthrow of the Allende government in Chile or even the 9/11 attacks in New

York. Walls dealt with immigration and migration, displacement and poverty. We stared at untold street scenes of various locals in Orgosolo, as if eavesdropping on their conversations.

One of the most compelling murals for me placed the revolt of Pratobello on the stage of a building. In 1969, after government officials told shepherds to move their flocks from the Pratobello area near Orgosolo, because it had been slated to become a shooting range for NATO and the Italian army, thousands of people from the area came out in protest. After several days of occupation, the army threw up its hands and canceled the shooting plans. The victory for Orgosolo, and shepherds, became a powerful story in the narrative of resistance in the Barbagia.

The murals depicted an older man blocking the vehicles of the soldiers. A second mural showed a procession of marchers in red, behind a banner of *rinascita* or "rebirth," with scenes on the side of shepherds being arrested by the soldiers, as sheep flocked in the fields. The image of a man on the balcony depicted him dropping posters. To the right, an oversized image of Emilio Lussu peered on intensely, with the Sardinian patriot's famous words of support to the protestors:

> *Quanto avviene a Pratobello contro pastorizia e agricoltura è provocazione colonialista, perciò mi sento solidale con pastori e contadini. Rimborso danni e premio in denaro è un offensivo palliativo che non annulla, ma aggrava l'ingiustizia. Se fossi in condizioni di salute differenti sarei con loro.*

> What happens in Pratobello against pastoralism and agriculture is a colonial provocation, so I feel solidarity with shepherds and farmers. Reimbursement of damages and cash prizes is an offensive palliative that does not cancel it, but actually aggravates the injustice. If I were in different health conditions, I would be with them.

We dined in Orgosolo that night on *porceddu*, the roasted suckling piglet specialty, for the meat eaters, and *culurgiones*, the ravioli-like pasta stuffed with potatoes, pecorino cheese, mint, basil, and garlic. The mountain cuisine was divine; the wine was Cannonau from Oliena.

We did, of course, eventually visit Deledda's museum and home back in Nuoro. Hailed in the American newspapers in 1902 as the "George Sand of Sardinia"—though, George Sand never won the Nobel—Deledda's role in Sardinian literature occupied its own realm. "Why should anyone feel doubtful about the future of fiction," the American reviewer noted, "when young authors are rising every day, to show us the world as it appears."

The world appeared very differently to the young woman writer in Sardinia. After elementary school, with the assistance of a tutor, she had published stories as teen, much to the chagrin of her family, who saw such work as a scandalous activity for a young woman. Deledda never looked back. Her first novel, *Fiori di Sardegna* (Flowers of Sardinia), appeared in 1892, at the age of twenty one. She went on to write more than sixty works of fiction, nonfiction, and poetry. In 1926, as the first woman and second Italian, she received the Nobel Prize for her "idealistically inspired writings which with plastic clarity picture the life on her native island and with depth and sympathy deal with human problems in general."

The main newspaper on her island, *L'Unione Sarda*, ran a few lines on the prize at the bottom right corner of the front page. It seemed as hesitant as her parents over Deledda's success. Mussolini's attempts to engage the author resulted in little attention; she simply asked him to release a friend of hers from Nuoro from prison. After moving to Rome in 1900, the author's relationship with her home remained as tenuous as ever. In her novel *Cenere* (Ashes), she wrote:

'Aren't you ever going to return to Sardinia,' he asked Maria Obinu one evening. 'Me?' she answered, a bit gloomily. 'Never again.'

PART FIVE

SEDD'E SU DIAULU
THE DEVIL'S SADDLE

Hanno già tutto cantato, scudi scintillanti, spade feroci,
pallidi amori, passioni e sangue, ricchezza, fame, lonza di
maiale,
tegole che cadono in testa all'erede sfortunato, caviale,
bluegrass, bestemmie e l'imperizia a vivere del poeta.
Che mi resta? Un tamburello, una vita.

They have already sung everything, shining shields,
ferocious swords,
pale loves, passions and blood, wealth, hunger, pork loin,
tiles falling on the head of the unfortunate heir, caviar,
bluegrass, blasphemies and the poet's inexperience to live.
What do I have left? One tambourine, one life.

—Sergio Atzeni, "Due colori esistono al mondo:
Il verde è il secondo," 1997

Our village never had the Sardinian charm of troubled events and wild ravines, and instead of a book by Grazia Deledda it looked more like something out of a western film after the bad guys passed by, only that none of our men went on horseback, or had a gun in his belt.

—Milena Agus, *Un tempo gentile*, 2020

The promontory at the base of the Devil's Saddle captured the grandeur of the gulf into Cagliari. The view from our window at the apartment in the Castello quarter, though, reminded us of the sweep and many layers of stories in this invigorating capital city, including the *Bellas mariposas* of author Sergio Atzeni. In that novella, his two young female characters that set off on a journey to make sense of their unforgiving, beguiling, and complicated backstreets. Written in the dialect of the Cagliari neighborhood, often in a stream of consciousness, the young Caterina finds solace on the beach and in the sea:

> *quando nuoto dimentico casa quartiere futuro mio babbo*
> *il mondo*
> *e mi dimentico*
> *dovevo nascere pesce*

> when I swim I forget home neighborhood future my dad
> the world
> and I forget myself
> I should have been born a fish

The city and its sea—it pulled like a tide for everyone. Cagliari was a working port, and it felt like it. In his award-winning novel, *Sardinia Blues*, Flavio Soriga's young and disaffected characters also attempted to make sense of their island in a postmodern world. He wrote:

> *Sono riuscito a tornare che e' ancora buio ma non durera' molto, tra poche ore arrivera' il sole e le famigliole si sveglieranno, si prepareranno al mare, povere vita ordinate senza sorprese e sballi e rimorchi e notti in bianco, scendo i gradini verso la spiaggia e mi spoglio ed entro in acqua, non lo faccio mai, nuotare la notte, non d'estate, a maggio si, mi piace moltissimo, si nuota come in un sogno*

> I managed to come back when it's still dark but it won't last long, in a few hours the sun will come and the little families will wake up, get ready for the sea, poor tidy lives without surprises and highs and trailers and sleepless nights, going down the steps towards the beach and I undress and enter the water, I never do it, swim at night, not in summer, in May yes, I love it, you swim like in a dream

Writers and historians had been trying to make sense of Cagliari and its origins since the Phoenicians pulled their ships into the gulf in the eighth and seventh centuries B.C. In the summer of 2022, archaeologists, including the venerable Giovanni Ugas, uncovered the foundations of a nuraghe wall on Monte Urpinu in the city that dated back to the fourteenth century b.c. Ugas referred to it as the possible "missing link" in the pre-Nuragic timeline that attested to the "central role of Cagliari in the Sardinian panorama of ancient history." That link remained underground for now. Such a massive excavation in the city still required several doors to open.

"How many Ulysses disguised as Norax, Daedalus, Hercules, Iolaus, with myths and knowledge, coming from west," archaeologist Maria Antonietta Mongiu had asked years earlier, "lapped Sardinia because its inhabitants and resources were known? The Gulf of Cagliari has always been a welcoming gateway. That it has become irrelevant in its sea because it is denied a place where it can cross the shadow line of identity simplifications to recognize itself as a synthesis of Mediterranean epics?"

Never one to wait for permission, in 1934 French playwright Antonin Artaud opened his classic essay, "The Theatre and the Plague," with a story in Cagliari, about the "astonishing fact" of the premonition of a plague in the dream of the Viceroy in Sardinia in 1720. The dream spurred him to block the entry of foreign ships arriving into the Cagliari ports. The dream, Artaud wrote, effectively saved the island from the scourge that would ravage Marseilles and much of Europe that year—except, the story never happened. It was simply Artaud's imaginary plague story, most likely based on an incident on the coast of Tuscany.

Such health quarantines did happen, though. Quinto Tiberio Angelerio, the Protomedicus of Alghero, published a book in Cagliari in 1588 on how to handle the plague, based on his successful practices in Alghero. (It was published in Latin, with an addendum in Catalan, and then republished in Spain in Castilian.)

Five hundred years later, in the late morning of July 2, 2020, having departed the day before from Eagle, Colorado, a private jet landed at the Elmas airport in Cagliari, on the southern tip of Sardinia. The view of the Gulf of Angels on its descent would have been splendid from the aircraft's window, the mythological clash between good and evil unfolding onto the limestone promontory of the Devil's Saddle. In the ancient story, the celestial army had cast Lucifer from the beloved island of angels. Within hours, having been denied entry due to COVID-19 restrictions, the five American travelers (and some British cohorts) were forced to reboard the plane and depart for England.

Displaced travel plans in the time of a plague are an old and generous story in Italy, and particularly on Sardinia.

Americans have always had a tenuous relationship with Cagliari and Sardinia. In 1767, John Dickinson wrote "Letters from a Farmer in Pennsylvania," holding up Sardinia's revolt from unfair taxation by the Carthaginians (in today's Tunisia) in 400 B.C. or so, as an example of undue repression. In 1798, a self-proclaimed noble from Cagliari, Francois de Navoni, began a series of letters to President John Adams, offering his services as the trading agent for the new United States of America. Salt was high on his list. Navoni kept up a prolific pen for years.

In 1804, Navoni complimented President Thomas Jefferson and the Secretary of State James Madison for having paid off the ransom of a young Sardinian woman kidnapped by Tunisian pirates—except, the American government had never agreed to such a pricey gesture. Navoni was referring to a massive attack on the smaller island of San Pietro, where hundreds of Sardinians had been carted away. "The Sardinian people will always esteem the U.S. for such a great and beneficial gesture," Navoni declared.

In truth, a rogue American officer and consul in Tunisia, William Eaton, outraged by the piracy of the Bey in Tunisia and the extortion that served as American policy for safe passage in the Mediterranean, saved young Anna Porcile's life from slavery by promising to pay her huge ransom. After the young Sardinian was released, Eaton failed to provide the cash, claiming the American government would eventually abide by the agreement. The Bey demanded Eaton's dismissal as the consul. Within a year, though, Eaton returned, serving as the commander of a platoon of mercenaries and U.S. Marines, and defied the Bey's authority in the region in the final chapter of the first "Barbary War." Marching his forces across the desert in Libya, Eaton became a hero in the famed Battle of Derna. The Marines' anthem, which triumphantly sings to the "shores of Tripoli," originated from this strange little piece of history connected to Sardinia.

Navoni's pen pal relationship with the American presidents aside, the Americans insisted on their own representatives in Sardinia. Navoni claimed the commander of the U.S. Navy in the Mediterranean had appointed him as the consul agent, however, when the king of Sardinia came aboard the ship in Cagliari in 1802. Within two years, Madison appointed his own consul, but he never showed up. Relentless as ever, according to documents, Navoni ended up serving as an agent, official or otherwise, until his death in 1825. It wouldn't be until 1839 that Anthony Thorel arrived as the first American consul in Cagliari, but his tenure was brief as well.

Perhaps one of the most chilling incidents between the American officials and Sardinia took place in 1931. Michele Schirru, a naturalized American citizen who grew up in Pozzomaggiore, near Alghero, was arrested for attempting to assassinate dictator Benito Mussolini that year. The anarchist had apparently divulged his plans in advance at a hotel in Rome; he had also been betrayed by loyal fascists back at his home in New York, when they learned of his sudden trip back to Italy. "American Is Shot For Plot On Il Duce," ran the *New York Times* headline. The "doomed man" showed little emotion, the reporter observed. He left behind a two-year-old daughter.

The American Schirru understood his legacy on the island: "I certainly inherited impulses and ideas," he wrote in a letter to his

Sardinian family. "It must be certain that perhaps in the past centuries, perhaps in the times of Spanish domination, some of our ancestors, rebellious to the tyranny of his time, will have retreated to the mountains and forests, and with other generous fighters for the freedom of Sardinia."

The American embassy, "acting on instructions from Washington," did not attend the trial. Schirru was executed by a firing squad—without a single word of protest by the United States.

E tue, zente, patria, isolana,
Senza istruzione e senz'iscola,
No istes prus che ainu de mola
Chi rezzit colpos canto nde li dana
Ma legge sa cummedia mundana
Tu'e sa tua discendente prola;
Legge, ca cun su tempus, incontrare
Podes sa vera via 'e camminare.

And you, folks, island and fatherland
Without education and without schools,
You are no more than a beast of burden
that takes all the blows it is given.
Read the worldly comedy,
You and your offspring;
Read, because with time
You may find the true road to walk.

—Salvatore Poddighe, "Sa Cummedia Mundana," 1924

At a bakery in the lively Stampace District, I found *sa panada* for the
first time. Shaped like a breadbasket, the pie made from *pasta violada*

was typically packed with eel or lamb and herbs. I managed to find one with artichokes and potatoes, mixed with parsley, dried tomatoes, and peppers. The nearby town of Assemini was considered the panada capital—though it appeared to be common in other areas, including Alghero. It reminded me of chicken potpies, though the tradition in Sardinia dated back to the pre-Roman days. The panadas in Cagliari were ornate, appearing in the display case with their cooked "lids" like little ceramic pots.

At first, Cagliari seemed like a panada, a mix of so many architectural styles, sloping up the hills in stages of history. But the panada was too tidy for this port city. The streets possessed the allure of the morning after, as if the city lived at night. The port churned at all times. Cagliari thrived on the sea, and therefore it presented itself like the delicious *Burrida a sa Casteddaia*, this smorgasbord of fish—such as the bottom-feeding catfish or type of sharkfish—stewed in a sauce of vinegar, extra virgin olive oil, walnuts, garlic, parsley, and its own livers.

The walking story of Cagliari began underground, in the crypts of churches in the Stampace District of the city, including the chamber where Saint Efisio had been held before his martyrdom as a Christian in 303 A.D. Every May 1, thousands of people converged on the streets from around the island on horses, oxen, chariots, and foot, representing nearly one hundred communities in their traditional dress in one of the most spectacular events in Sardinia. Spread out over several days, the extraordinary march acknowledged Efisio's ceremonial role in 1656, when Sardinians appealed to their saint to intervene against the ravages of a plague. Over three hundred and fifty years later, the colorful procession, with its musicians and rituals, continued to unfold as one of the longest promenades in traditional costumes in Europe.

The time-bend walk went even deeper in the Marina District, under the Gothic church of the fourteenth-century Catalans, Sant'Eulalia, where a staircase took walkers down to the paved road in the fourth century A.D. in Roman times. The name of the city may have changed with languages, but a continuum of its role as a key port over thousands of years remained vibrant. The vault below was not a tunnel but a massive chamber. Along with the colonnade that once protected the chariots and wagons that moved between the markets and workshops of the Roman city of "Karales," you descended further back into time, where the sacred temples and areas of the Punics in the city of "Krly" or "Karaly" had been traced to the fourth to third centuries B.C.

But there was another underground in Cagliari, like all of Sardinia, that fascinated me—the political and literary underground. I found it on Via Raimondo Carta Raspi in the Sant'Elia area. In 1923, Raspi had quietly founded a publishing house, Il Nuraghe, to promote Sardinian literature. As fascist laws clamped down on Sardinian languages, Raspi published *Sardegna terra di poesia: Antologia poetica dialettale sarda*, among other poetry, fiction, and historical works in Sardinian over the next decades.

Other writers and publishers were not so fortunate. Salvatore Poddighe, a self-taught miner who lived and worked in Iglesias, in the southwest mining district, had joined fellow poets in the taverns and piazzas for the oral poetry contests. By 1917, he was performing parts of his *Su Mundana Cummedia*, a satire on the *Divine Comedy* that blasted the treatment of workers and the complicity of the clergy. In 1924, as priests colluded with the growing fascist movement to shut down oral poetry contests that attacked the church, Poddighe published thirty-five hundred copies of his poem, with nearly two thousand verses. In some of the first lines, the poet declared:

> *Sa Divina Cummedia leggimos;*
> *E noi Sardos proite non faghimos*

Un'attera Cummedia mundana?
Pro dare lughe a sa zente isolana

We've all read the Divina Commedia;
Now, why wouldn't we, Sardinians, make
Another comedy, a worldly one,
To bring the light to us, island dwellers?

In 1935, Cagliari authorities banned the poem, proclaiming that "it incites class hatred and the contempt of religion and its ministers." All copies of Poddighe's works were rounded up. The desperate poet, unable to shake the depression from the crackdown, took his life in 1938.

Not far away was Via Raffa Garzia, named for the radical young writer, journalist, and Liceo Dettori high school teacher of Antonio Gramsci in 1910–11, who would help to shape one of the most important political thinkers of the century. As an editor at the *L'Unione Sarda*, Garzia made it possible for Gramsci to publish his first story as a high school student—*A proposito d'una rivoluzione* (Talking about a revolution)—a short spoof on election turmoil near Gramsci's hometown of Ghilarza. Garzia went on to teach linguistics at the University of Cagliari and published an important anthology of poetry, *Mutettus cagliaritani*. He remained an important influence on Gramsci.

Via Emilio Lussu celebrated the Sardinian patriot, though his home in Cagliari had been the site of an attack in 1926. Warned that a fascist mob was marching on his home, chanting "Death to Lussu," the member of parliament from Sardinia made the decision to hunker down alone. He sent away his friends, fearing for their safety. Lussu had spoken out against the kidnapping of journalist and fellow parliamentarian Giacomo Matteotti, who was killed by a fascist gang in

1924. With Mussolini consolidating his power over the next two years, Lussu had faced further threats. He had already been knocked unconscious in an earlier attack.

In the fall of 1926, after a failed assassination attempt on Mussolini in Bologna, columns of Blackshirts raged through the streets of Cagliari. Refusing to flee, the former military officer from World War I made preparations for defense. "The idea of flight has never appealed to me," Lussu wrote in his memoirs. "The unexpected always contains an element of success, whether on the stage or in real life." He set aside a sporting rifle, two revolvers from the army, and a supply of ammunition. When the mob descended on his house, attacking from three areas, Lussu wrote in his memoirs about his "quandary." Racing from one side of the house to the other, he noted, "I confess that, in the course of my life, I have found myself in pleasanter circumstances." When one Blackshirt broke through the window, Lussu fired and immediately killed the man. The mob fled instantly. Within minutes the police arrived, arrested Lussu, and took him to the prison in Cagliari, where he was eventually acquitted in his first trial, and then charged again and convicted. Sent off to prison on the island of Lipari, Lussu made a dramatic escape in 1929, and joined the resistance.

In an earlier trip, we had visited Lussu's family home in the mountain town of Armungia, about an hour's drive away. Lussu's grandson Tomasso and his wife, Barbara, had launched Casa Lussu, a dynamic center for weaving and the arts. Having left behind a career in Rome, Tomasso moved with a sense of mission to protect Sardinia's cultural heritage in an innovative way; Casa Lussu participated with organizations and movements across the island. We spent an evening at the Lussu home, where Lussu's son Giovanni recalled his parent's role in the resistance. Emilio Lussu had once offered to lead a raid on Gramsci's prison, Giovanni had been told.

Emilio had met Joyce, a writer and translator from central Italy, during the war in Switzerland, where he was recovering from an illness. She took a leading role in the resistance, as well. "The love for a Sardinian brought me to Sardinia," she had written in her book, *L'olivastro e l'innesto*, "and this love was also the acquisition of a world, with its history and its present, its ancestral crystals and its future buds. I grafted onto Sardinia, and we have grown together ever since."

Far from the remote village of Emilio's times, the beautiful streets of Armungia now shimmered with their cobblestoned renovations and the tidy back alleys of ancient stone houses. The unexpected mountain ranges of the Gerrei region jutted off in every direction like a trekking crossroads. An unusually well-maintained nuraghe sat at the top of the village, as if part of the civic center. In fact, the Casa Lussu ran its looms and workshops at a center adjacent to the fifteenth century B.C. tower. As a connection to that ancient past, the multimedia museum dedicated to Joyce and Emilio Lussu might have been one of the most informative on twentieth-century politics on the island. Armungia, indeed, perched in the mountains, had the feeling of a modern sanctuary town awaiting pilgrims.

But one of the murals in the village, done by the Orgosolo artist del Casino, captured a scene I had never crossed before in Sardinia: the cubist vision of Gramsci sat on one side, villagers and workers reading the newspaper in the middle, while Lussu perched on the opposite side. Two of the main pillars of Sardinian resistance had finally come together—back in Sardinia, back in their mountains, back on their frontlines of history.

33 | OF STELES AND ISLANDERS

From the neo-Hittite citadels, to the eastern vertex of the "triangle" between Cyprus, Cilicia, the Near East, bristling with a people of statues that lined the city streets frequented by Phoenicians, Aramei, Eubei, Cypriots, the inspiration of the monumental statuary must have come to the Sardinians, translated into the agalmata of Mont'e Prama (Cabras-OR), which dominated the road that bordered to the east by the heroon of Sardinian heroes, represented by warriors, archers and boxers of calcarenite.

—Raimondo Zucca,
Storiografia del problema della 'scrittura nuragica,' 2012

At the top of Cagliari, like the capstone of the lively city, the National Archaeological Museum held some great treasures in this renovated citadel. Taking visitors from the Neolithic to the medieval periods, the museum moved from floor to floor with the thread of the thousands of years of continual residence on the island. To the contrary of Atzeni's endearing novel, the Sardinians did not "tread lightly" on this earth; they had left behind an array of fabulous monuments and memories of their times. The idea of the "empty stage" of Sardinia, suggested by the Greeks and Romans and modern-day writers, became laughable. The landmarks of several dynamic civilizations, forever changing, mounted with so many phases and shifts in cultures that it would take several museums to adequately display the complexities of the island's habitation.

In effect, all of Sardinia, with its wealth of archaeological remains, was truly the "open museum" we had been urged to see for ourselves.

Wonderful museums like this one in Cagliari, of course, were reminders to take these little nuggets of artifacts and go back out into the remote countryside—or nearby urban underworld, in the case of Cagliari—and visit their stomping grounds of origin.

Like an immortal page out of history, the Nora stele in its corner case was one of the treasures of the national museum—and all of Italy and Europe. As a writer, I found this stone slab to be riveting; I tried to imagine the hand on the chisel, choosing her words that would be hammered into eternity. It wasn't simply the oldest Phoenician text in western Europe; the inscription on the stone, in all of its controversial interpretations, recognized "in print" the existence of a Sardinian people on this island over three thousand years ago.

The concept of steles—as inscribed slabs of stone or wood or whatever material—predated the worldly Phoenician scribes, of course. As the Neolithic displays indicated in the museum, a visitor only needed to travel to the menhir stones of Pranu Muttedu in Gona in the Ogliastra or the extraordinary array of similar menhirs at Biru 'e Concas in Sorgono, which left behind Neolithic roadmaps of steles from five thousand years ago. We found such sites to be sacred places in Sardinia, almost as if the ancients had decidedly chosen the remote lookouts of hills and ridges and plateaus as suitable stages to capture the grandeur of their rituals. Across the island, travelers could also see the domus de janas, such as the Su Crucifissu Mannu in Porto Torres, which showcased stunning inscriptions and symbols of narrative from the fourth millennium B.C.

The exhibit of the "giants" of Mont'e Prama, the towering statues that once lined the necropolis and ancient streets of an essential
Nuragic focal point, had journeyed from the town of Cabras on the
western coast region near Oristano. While a new museum in Cabras
was in the making, the site awaited the national and international
recognition that it deserved for its contributions to humanity. That
story had already been written in stone; now, all of the site, including
what remained to be discovered underground, just needed to be uncovered, excavated, and revealed to the public for the final chapters.

Earlier models for Cabras, perhaps, could be found at the excavated nuraghe sites like Barumini or Genna Maria or Arrubiu,
which accompanied their spectacular towers and Nuragic villages
with updated multimedia museums. The Losa Nuraghe, not far from
Oristano, was one of my favorite places, a sprawling basalt stone
library from the fifteenth and fourteenth centuries B.C. that sat on
the Abbasanta plateau in the shape of a massive triangular ship. Atop
its hill in the southern Marmilla area, Genna Maria provided a connecting view from Cagliari to the Gulf of Oristano, as if keeping
three thousand five hundred years of history within its reach. As
a UNESCO World Heritage site, Barumini and the Casa Zapata
Museum remained one of the star attractions on the Nuragic circuit,
excavated by the pioneering archaeologist Lilliu in his own backyard.
Beyond its sixty-foot tower, dating back to the fifteenth century B.C.,
Barumini's expansive village with paved streets included one of the
oldest sewer systems in Europe—centuries before the Romans.

Far from a fleeting moment in history, or a stack of stones, the
open museum of Sardinia recounted a story of foundations; a story of
birth and rebirth, of endurance and resilience and re-use, and a story of
rituals and cultural ways that had made the island the staging ground
of civilizations that not only shaped its own peoples, but the rest of
the Mediterranean.

34 | ON THE RIM OF THE WORLD

Mi trovo di stessa nascita; e l'isolano antico.
I am of the same birth; and the ancient islander.

—Salvatore Quasimodo, *Sardegna*, 1934

One of the most thrilling drives in Sardinia was along the Costa Verde on the southwestern coast, which hugged the route along the cliffs and then maneuvered through the forested hills to reach the ancient mining sites and villages. We found the return trip north to be more delightful. You were able to lean against the white line and walls carved into the side of the hills, instead of the white-knuckled edge of the narrow outer lane heading south, which curved a thousand times on the edge of oblivion below.

At times, you did feel like you were driving on the rim of the world.

Each mining site with its history beckoned a visit. But winding down the narrow road to the harbor off the coast near Nebida truly unveiled one of the most dazzling views on the island. The *Concali su Terràinu* in the cove of Masua—also known as *Pan di Zucchero* (Sugarloaf)—was a limestone rock island that hovered in the sea like a glistening monument. It was probably one of the most photographed sites in Sardinia.

While mining, as we have learned, dated back to the Nuragic, Phoenician, and Roman days, the construction of the Porto Flavia in the cove in the 1920s appeared like something out of a fantasy movie. The first documented foundry in the area actually dated back to 1614. For the next three hundred years, the ore from the mines in the area was transported by mule and men and loaded by hand onto the ships. The precariousness of the winds and storms took a costly toll; the lead, as well as zinc and other materials, was heavy. It often took weeks to load a ship, many of which either sank or failed to depart in a timely way.

When a Belgian company bought the rights to the mine, it brought on an Italian engineer who designed a plan to sink two long tunnel shafts, which ran nearly two thousand feet. Linked by an electric train, the shafts fed a reservoir, which was then connected to a conveyor belt that loaded the ore directly onto the ships in the harbor. The door of the loading terminal at Porto Flavia was truly awesome. Carved into the cliffs, it resembled a mini version of a door into the Erebor stronghold of the dwarf kingdom in *The Lord of the Rings*. Or so it seemed. The engineer had named it after his daughter, Flavia.

Those ships loaded with ore headed to Carloforte, on the southwestern island of San Pietro, where it was easier to harbor. The history of that island and its inhabitants was almost as unusual as the Porto Flavia.

At the basin of a range of hills, the port of Carloforte greeted us from a distance, as we arrived on the ferry from Portoscuso. We left our car at the port parking lot, and then followed the *caruggi*, or narrow alleyways, until we reached our place to stay on our first visit. As a tourist hub, the port was packed, especially along the boardwalk *corso* and in the main streets into the Piazza Repubblica. We passed a monument to King Carlo Emanuele III, which made sense for the first time in Sardinia.

Meeting with Antonio, a jovial retired ship commander in Carloforte, I learned why the port felt so vibrant. Antonio arrived with an album of photos and a stack of books. He had written his own books, including a chronicle of a passage through the Suez Canal. In 1736, he recounted that Ligurian families (from the Genova area), who had been living in the coastal Tunisian town of Tabarka for the past two centuries as coral fisherfolk, had petitioned King Carlo (Charles) for the right to settle on the island of San Pietro. With the island un-occupied, permission was granted, and in 1738, the first Tabarchino families arrived. Within the year, 126 families with 466 people began to build the new town on the banks of sand. While coral fishing con-tinued, the real wealth of the island came with the eventual devel-opment of the port to serve the ships from the nearby mining areas, where the steep cliffs and dangerous coves kept any long-term ports from being stationed.

There was an infectious enchantment about Carloforte and its eighteenth-century architecture; it was a charming town, full of restaurants and shops and side streets. That cheerful air continued along the roads that traversed the island and its quiet beaches. Two natural columns jutted out from sea on the southwest side, immor-talized as stone sea monsters in some legends to protect the island. Perhaps one of the most poignant views on San Pietro—even in all of Sardinia—came at the end of the road on the far western side of the island. The lighthouse of Capo Sandalo, the westernmost point of Italy, hunkered down on the windswept cliffs, as another rim of the world. The understory of the Mediterranean macchia, along with patches of myrtle and the strawberry trees, held tight nearby, edged by an occasional prickly pear.

In the late 1860s, the nautical handbooks alerted mariners that the signal from the lighthouse was visible from twenty-eight miles away.

That made me wonder about the view from the islander's mind; what incursion or invader, or trader or friend with new goods and stories, was about to arrive from the sea?

As I ate my *curzetti* with tuna, the medallion-shaped pasta that had Ligurian roots, I heard the Tabarchino language swirl around me from the locals. The Ligurian variant had remained strong over nearly five hundred years after being transplanted in Tunisia and now Sardinia.

While four nuraghes, at least, appeared on our Nurnet maps, the island of San Pietro, adjacent to Sant'Antioco and its archer, had also been occupied by the Phoenicians, who had named it after the Accipiter sparrowhawk. The Phoenician experience in Sardinia—from Sant'Antioco to the city of Nora, the spectacular port of Tharros on the western coast, all the way to Alghero at Sant'Imbenia—deserved its own book, of course. Several great volumes existed. The same case could be made for the Roman experience in Sardinia, and that of the Spanish and Catalans.

But one place brought all of these clashing civilizations together in a poignant and very powerful way. Having passed Carbonia and Iglesias, we returned north toward Fluminimaggiore and the Costa Verde, heading across the rolling valleys in the Iglesiente mountains, with *Monte Conca s'Omu* in the background. It felt like we were back in the Supramonte, albeit a smaller area.

For centuries, the search for a temple dedicated to Sardus Pater, the mythological figure of the Sardinian father, had transfixed the island. The venerable archaeologist Raimondo Zucca called it "the most exciting question of ancient topography in Sardinia." An image to Sardus Pater had been forged onto Roman coins in 37 B.C. In the sixteenth century, the clergyman and historian Fara had conducted a search around Oristano. Four hundred years later, Lilliu, among other archaeologists, still did excavations in the western coastal areas, chasing the Sardus trail. Pausanias, the Greek writer in the second century B.C., had noted the appearance of a statue of Sardus Pater at the Delphi in Greece; the statue had been sent "by the Barbarians who are in the West and live in Sardinia." Writers in the Greek and Roman chronicles recounted the journey of Sardus, the son of Hercules, who had arrived from Libya to occupy the island.

Our pioneering travel writer La Marmora, back in 1838, had stumbled on to a site in a dark green forest, but he was unable to move any rubble to closely inspect the ruins of what appeared to be Roman columns at Antas. To be sure, ruins from a Nuragic village from the ninth century B.C. were on the edge of the area. Scientists would later confirm that silver, traced in the lead isotopes, from sinkholes in the nearby Antas valley had been found in hoards in the Levant as early as the ninth century B.C.

In the 1960s, however, archaeologists uncovered inscriptions at the same site where La Marmora had first visited. The discovery revealed a Roman temple from the first century A.D. that was dedicated to the deity Sardus Pater. Another inscription, dated to the second century, commemorated the second restoration of the temple to Sardus under Emperor Caracalla. However, the original temple had been built by the Punics in the third century B.C., in honor of Sid Babai, a deity many scholars associated with an attempt to overlap Nuragic, Phoenician, and Punic religious rites. The temple was abandoned after the Roman period, as Christianity spread across the island. Pope Callixtus had actually worked in the nearby mines in Sardinia, as part of his earlier persecution.

At the crossroads of mythologies in Sardinia, the Temple of Antas now stood in this forested valley like an arena of serenity—and wonder. It felt protected, not hidden, by the mountains. I noticed quite a few tourists lingering around the columns, almost all in silence. Whether Sardus Pater had indeed been the father of Sardinia, the gods of the Nuragic, Phoenician, Carthaginian, and Roman worshippers had certainly found a magnificent place to call home.

 EPILOGUE

THE DESIRE TO RETURN

For when we ourselves do not change at all in our thoughts, or when we have not noticed our thoughts changing, then time does not seem to us to have passed—just like it does not for those whom the stories tell slept among the heroes in Sardinia, when they wake.

—Aristotle, *Physics*, fourth century B.C.

I found Sardonicus in his orchard. At the foot of a mountain, south of Alghero, on his family's ancestral lands, he had been tending to his agro-forestry project for years. There were numerous agro-forestry and regenerative agriculture projects on the island—a true movement—including the work of Tenute il Maggese in the Ogliastra, where young farmers planted ancient grains, legumes and saffron, along with fruit trees, to restore a family farm. A local organic food movement flourished in Sardinia, as well. The open food markets, like those we found in Alghero, overflowed with regional farmers and vendors. No matter what kind of adventure one had in Sardinia, the traveler ate well and heartily.

Sardonicus had been at work on a new essay based on his experience, "Small Practice Suggestions for a Sustainable Green Revolution." The outdoor work kept him fit, and with a perpetual grin above his white beard. Trees from Afghanistan and Japan mixed with the native ones like myrtle, olive, and strawberry; fruit weighed down the branches of numerous trees. He held a basket of pears and figs. He motioned toward a table and chairs under a carob tree. We watched the chickens that had escaped their pens; the donkey brayed in turn, the cicadas raised their volume. A slice of the sea appeared in the valley, from a wedge into the cliffs that continued along the horizon. The beach nearby was his playground.

In his home, a former barn, books lined the shelves for weeks of reading, alongside art he had collected from around the world. A long table served the assembly line of his homemade pasta regimen. Piles of baskets made from palms stacked in all corners. A fire burned in the corner, as if it had never stopped.

It was never easy, and never so fun, to report on our journeys to Sardonicus. He frequently held court for lunch with his cadre of elders. An old school friend quietly helped on the farm, muscles rippling from his arms like hoop rings on a barrel, as if he were a young man, not a retiree. The others appreciated the homemade pasta, the plates of fish and meat, garden veggies and greens, the abundant fruit and wine. The conversations blended one into the other. Forever the jester, Sardonicus always had more questions than answers.

"There was this women's collective of weavers in Muravera," I once began, or the story about the shepherds on motorcycles whose flock blocked our country road. "Yeah, yeah, we know that one," someone would say. "We finally visited the castle in Burgos," I would go on, where Adelasia died in 1259, having juggled the judicadu of her times—like Eleonora, Elena, Benedetta, the noble Sardinian women who took their turns as judges. "Yeah, yeah, she had more husbands than Liz Taylor," someone offered.

Sometimes I would read aloud from a book to gauge the response: "The history of the *giudicati* in Sardinia is a history of internecine wars and fratricide," according to historian Gian Giacomo Ortu. "From the late twelfth century on, there was not a single *giudice* who did not concoct a plan to rule the island under one scepter."

That generated a new discussion on contemporary politics.

Our journeys, like our exchange of stories, never really ended. The trips became more beguiling; the discoveries were more complex. In the sixteenth century, the Spanish referred to the Sardinians as *pocos, locos y mal unidos*—few, crazy, and disunited. Spanish writer, Tirso de Molina, responded with a fanciful Baroque play in the 1600s about an arcadian world in Sardinia. "I do not know why the ancients discredited the fame of Sardinia," he wrote, "because I affirm to you, with truth, that in abundance, benevolent climate, goodness of air, fertility of fruits and water health, it can compete with the most intoned provinces of Europe."

It was certainly easier to write natural history, Dessì once fumed in the late 1960s, than talk about the history of the judges in Sardinia. Therefore, when he thought of humans, "I see them as ants and bees; I see them as a species that remains unchanged over the millennia."

On the way home from Sardonicus, I often stopped at the Nuraghe Palmavera on the outskirts of town, where the tower dated back to the fifteenth century B.C. Reflecting on how "myth and its story have always been an inseparable complement to history," Nurnet cofounder and vice president Giorgio Valdès once cited Louis Godart, the Belgian-Italian archaeologist. "The old legends have their roots in history and it is certain that at the basis of any myth narrated by the Ancients there is a historical truth that modern criticism must try to find and explain."

The second phase of Palmavera, after the collapse of the Bronze Age, fascinated me. Around the ninth century B.C., the Nuragic inhabitants added a "meeting hut." Lined with stone seats, like some ancient roundtable of the knights or kiva of elders, or perhaps a Nuragic version of s'arrogliu storytelling, the meeting huts reminded me that civilizations rose and fell and transformed through a collective exchange of stories. A model of a nuraghe sat on an altar in the middle of the hut as a living memory of their past, and its presence in their lives in that moment.

Memory is neither a perception nor a conception, Aristotle taught his students, but a state of affection. He singled out the stories of "incubation" among the "heroes" of Sardinia as an example, where the islanders carried out rituals at the tombs of their ancient ones to conjure some sort of understanding or healing; to halt time, for a moment, to commune with their ancestors, their land and nature, and their place in this world.

Perhaps the most poignant story of such a modern-day ritual for me, though far from any "sleeping" at the tombs of our "heroes," was in the village of Desulo. Cascading down the deep Barbagian forests like a quilt, the mountain village emerged from the road on the western range of the Gennargentu. The exquisite traditional dress of the villagers held almost a hallowed spot among folklorists; it drew observers from around the world, including the Disney film crew in the 1950s. Along with a walk in the woods, we had ventured to Desulo to learn about *Montanaru*, the "mountaineer," the poet laureate of Sardinia in the twentieth century, Antioco Casula.

Like many places in Sardinia, we stumbled onto the right people as our Virgil—in this case, Alberto, the grandson of the famous poet, who left behind a plate of pasta on his lunch table and agreed to take us to the poet's home for a visit. Near the top of the village, we entered the home as if we were visiting an old friend. At least, that was how Alberto made us feel. The front walls immediately greeted us in poetry:

> *Desulo*
> *Fiera e ruzza, in mesu a sos castanzos,*
> *Seculares, ses posta o bidda mia;*
> *Attaccada a sos usos de una la,*
> *Genereosa, ospitale a sos instranzos.*

Proud and rough among the chestnut trees
secular, you are placed, oh my village;
holding the uses of the past,
generous, hospitable to foreigners.

The home felt as if Montanaru had left earlier that morning—not in the late 1950s. Born in 1878, Montanaru had studied in Cagliari, served in the Abyssinian war, and then worked as a Carabiniere in various towns. He quietly began to send off his poems, which were published in his native language. Wanting to have more time to concentrate on his writing, he returned to the mountain village, where he worked as an elementary school teacher and postal worker. His poetry, though, had already attracted the attention of fellow writers like Sebastiano Satta and Deledda. In 1922, the year after Lawrence visited Sardinia, Montanaru published *Cantigos d'Ennargentu* (Songs of Gennargentu), which would become one of his most famous volumes. The celebrated artist Filippo Figari praised the collection for the "fraternal, almost humble voices, with the language of women and ancient fathers, the poet speaks to the heart and intellect of all Sardinians."

As we moved through the rooms of paintings, bookshelves, and display cases of costumes and artifacts, we learned about the life of the poet, including the role of his grandmother, Michela, who had been an influential oral poet, like so many unnamed women. In one room, pages of a manuscript hung from the ceiling like spoken words waiting to be performed.

In Montanaru's office, though, I felt like I had walked into a giant's tomb. The musty smell of the room of books befitted an ancient archive. Stacks of books and papers still weighed down his desk. A personal letter from Pasolini overlooked his chair. A copy of *Sos cantos de sa solitudine* (The Songs of Solitude) sat on the edge of the desk, as if inviting a reader.

Having resisted fascism's edict to stop writing in his native Sardinian language, Casula had defiantly declared: "The Sardinian language has the strength, the ductility and the brilliance of metal and therefore leaps alive like a fresh spring from the heart of the people to sing the pains and joys, the strength and hope."

His works, of course, outlived fascism's stranglehold. He participated in the independence party movement, his poetry dealing with the struggles of the times. Montanaru beseeched Sardinians to keep their rich cultures vibrant: *Una die che perla ses cumparta, subra sos mares ricca d'onzi incantu.*

His grandson Alberto, like other grandkids, had carried on the poet's legacy. A longtime guide into the mountains, where Montanaru had found his inspiration, Alberto collected flowers and herbs and made organic drinks and elixirs; his Arbisos company, named after the Desulo word for "ideas," had even made an elixir in the name of the poet, Montanaru, to keep alive the traditions of the Gennargentu.

Returning back to Alghero for the sunset stroll along the bastion, I would often end up on that flat perch on the tower walls, overlooking the port. The sleeping giant of Capo Caccia rested in the background with its silhouette.

It was hard to imagine living without this city of Alghero, without this island of stories, poems, and songs. Without the sea and mountains. Without the nuraghes. Without the *mirto*, that delicious nightcap of the evening, and the friendships of s'arrogliu.

Sitting back and watching the boats in the gulf—sometimes with a book, sometimes not—I would think about the other parts of the island I needed to discover. The desire to return. Just like the kid in the black-and-white photo from the 1890s, wondering what travel story awaited with the tide, or the next page.

ACKNOWLEDGMENTS

You take delight not in a city's seven or seventy wonders, but in the answer it gives to a question of yours.

—Italo Calvino, *Invisible Cities*

The writing of this book, over several years, has been a wonderful journey, albeit a hard one with some health issues, and I deeply appreciate all of the kind souls in Alghero and across Sardinia that have helped me along the way, as well as the support from our dear friends and family in Bologna, Falconara and Consuma.

For translation help in Sardu, Algerese/Alguerès, Italiano, Français, thank you so much, Sara Chessa, Angela Mameli, Valerio Mameli, Christopher Rundle, Glen Alessi, Guy Lydster, Licia Catapano, Sara Porqueddu, Alessandra Lisci, Umberto Paciotto, and Salvatore Pinna. Any errors are mine. Thanks to my early readers for your insight: Massimo Paciotto-Biggers, Douglas Biggers, Anthony Polvere, Luciana Milani, James Demby, Sole Martino, Tobias Jones, and Nafia Akdeniz. For my nonstop archaeological questions, grazie Antonello Gregorini, Francesca Cossu, Giorgio Valdes and the Nurnet network, and the many archaeologists and scientists in the field.

An incredible bevy of writers, historians, novelists, poets, and singers in Sardinia awaits an English-speaking readership—I apologize for anyone I have not cited or included. Grazie for the books, Beppe Ferrari, Libreria Vademecum, Libreria Il Labirinto Mondadori and so many other book vendors in Sardinia. Thanks to historians Maria Bonaria Urban, Alessandro Portelli and Fiorenzo Caterini, among many others, for your landmark works, and your patience with my questions. Profound thanks to Paolo Fresu, whose music and words have been a vibrant soundtrack in my life for years.

Deep gratitude to the great crew at Melville House Books. What a joy for a writer to be part of such a passionate, fearless and dynamic publishing house; thank you for all of your work and support, Valerie Merians, Dennis Johnson, Sammi Sontag, Ariel Palmer-Collins, Janet Joy Wilson, Mike Kindgren, Susan McGrath, and Sofia Demopolos. It's a privilege to be back with editor Carl Bromley, who has not only put several of my books in shape and challenged my writing for years, but fielded endless questions with endless patience and humor. Grazie mille, Carl.

To my billie boys, Diego and Massimo, who boarded the boat and shared the journey with us, I look forward to hearing your songs and reading your stories on whatever stage you choose.

And Carla, my jo, who pointed her finger at Alghero and led me on our adventures, who has always turned my dreams into books and given me reasons to believe: *Vine amb a mi, mia bella, vine-hi tu també, que passetjant mirem qui bella que és l'Alguer.*

BIBLIOGRAPHIC NOTES

The epigram from Dickens appeared in his magazine, *Household Words*, in an overview of the island in 1856 and a review of Tyndale's book, *The Island of Sardinia* (R. Bentley, 1849).

The Cossu translation is from *Descrizione geografica della Sardegna, 1799* (Ilisso, 2000), which is not translated in English. Cossu played several administrative roles in the late 1700s, including *censore generale*, and also wrote an important book on agriculture, *La coltivazione de' gelsi e propagazione de' filugelli in Sardegna* (Centro Studi Filologici Sardi, 2002).

PROLOGUE: CROSSING OVER TO SARDINIA

SARDINIA BLUES
Cambosu's *Miele Amaro* (Ilisso, 2004), an anthology of poems, essays and stories, is not translated in English.

To visit Lai's Stazione dell'arte Museum in Ulassai, see: http://www.stazionedellarte.com/.

For an overview of Lai's work in English, see: *Maria Lai and Elena Pontiggia, Art and Connection* (Ilisso, 2017), as well as Anedda's bilingual book on *Maria Lai, Maria Lai. Holding the Sun by the Hand* (5 Continents Editions, 2019).

Serra's travel guide, *Mal di Sardegna*, is not translated in English, but his *Sardegna, quasi un continente* is available in two volumes, *Sardinia, Almost a Continent* (MAGA, 1990).

THREE MAPS AND A PHOTO
Boccaccio's translation is from the sixth day, in the *Decameron* (Everyman's Library, 2009).

For more information on Sabine Rethore's excellent cartography, see: http://www.sabine-rethore.net/engl/artistic%20maps/mediterraneanwit.html.

For more information on Nurnet's amazing geoportal app and map of Sardinia, see: http://nurnet.crs4.it/nurnetgeo/pages/en/homepage.

For general information on Nurnet activities, archives and photos, see: https://www.nurnet.net/.

For more tips on Luca Gonzato's Dipende che Vino's maps, see: https://dipendechevino.com/.

Plutarch's comments are cited widely, including Plutarch, *Roman Lives A Selection of Eight Lives* (Oxford University Press, 2008).

On Nuragic wine, see "Confirming the function of a Final Bronze Age wine processing site in the Nuraghe Genna Maria in Villanovaforru (South Sardinia)," Lovicu, V*itis: Journal of Grapevine Research*, 2020, "Wine in Sardinia. New Archaeological Data and Research Methodology," Loi, *Archaeology and Economy in the Ancient World*, 2020. In Italian: "Gli archeosemi raccontano. L'uva e il vino della Sardegna nuragica," Bacchetta et al., *Sa Massaria Ecologica Storica dei Sistemi di Lavoro Contadino in Sardegna*, and *Il vino in Sardegna* (Ilisso, 2010).

The Sardinian boatmaker in the Americas appears in the chronicles of "A Gentleman of Elvas," and his *Narrative of the Expedition of Hernando de Soto into Florida*, published in Portuguese at Evora in 1557. Project Gutenberg has translations in English.

Abulafia has written several monumental works. *The Great Sea: A Human History of the Mediterranean* (Oxford University Press, 2011) provides a sweeping overview of the region.

Fresu is a jazz legend in Sardinia, Italy and the world. He is also a wonderful author, and his books in Italian include *In Sardegna: Un Viaggio Musicale* (Fertinelli, 2012) and *Poesie jazz per cuori curiosi* (Rizzoli, 2018). More on his music and work is at: http://www.paolofresu.it/it/bio/.

Aru's eclectic work as a singer and songwriter can be found on her official Facebook page: https://www.facebook.com/ClaudiaAruOfficial.

*S'abba tenet memoria/*The water remembers.

This is an English translation from Giacobbe's *Il Mare* (Il Maestrale, 1997).

PART ONE: *S'ABBA TENET MEMORIA* | THE WATER REMEMBERS

1. THE SHIP

Lord Byron's sentiments were published in 1825 after Byron's death, in a compendium of journals maintained by Captain R. N. Benson. See: *Narrative of Lord Byron's Voyage to Corsica and Sardinia, 1821* (British Library, Historical Print Editions, 2011).

Fois has written many novels and collections of essays, several translated in English: *Bloodlines* (Verbs Mundi, 2017), *Memory of Abyss* (Maclehose, 2012), and *The Advocate* (Random House 2004). I refer to his collection of essays, *In Sardegna non c'e il mare* (Laterza, 2013).

Porcacchi's seminal cartography can be found in English, though his book *L'isole più famose del mondo* (1572) remains untranslated: https://collections.library.yale.edu/catalog/2004521.

Vernet's storms can be found at museums and online sites, including the Getty Museum: https://www.getty.edu/art/collection/object/103QT8

Dettori won the Premio Dessi for *Amarante* (Il Maestrale, 1993), still not translated in English.

Roberts played a major role in the lives of Lord Byron and Percy Shelley. Some of his drawings are in Trelawny's *Recollections of the last days of Shelley and Byron* (Ticknor and Fields, 1858), and in Prell's *A Biography of Captain Daniel Roberts* (Strand, 2010).

2. THE LOVE OF ITALY

Jourdan's unhappy book, *L'Ile de Sardaigne,* is available in the original French (E. Dentu, 1861), and Italian, *Gustave Jourdan e la Sardegna* (Tipografia di A. Timon, 1861).

Sardinia has been featured in *National Geographic* magazine numerous times. In 1916, American writer Helen Dunstan Wright (whose husband Charles was a mining engineer in Sardinia) wrote "Little-known Sardinia," followed by Sardinian author Guido Costa (son of the well-known novelist Enrico Costa), "The Island of Sardinia and Its People," in 1923. Pellerano wrote "Where the Sard Holds Sway," in 1926.

Although debate remains on when the original work was written, Von Suchem's *Description of the Holy Land, and of the Way Thither: Written in the Year 1350 A.D.,* has numerous translations, including an updated edition in English by Cambridge University Press in 2013.

The great filmmaker Wertmüller passed away in 2021. *Swept Away* (*Travolti da un insolito destino nell'azzurro mare d'agosto*) came out in 1974 and won the National Board of Review Award as one of the top foreign films. Her *Love and Anarchy* (*Film d'amore e d'anarchia*) was loosely based on Sardinian anarchist Michele Schirru and his plot to assassinate Mussolini.

Actor Halle Bailey posted photos of the Sardinian beach during the filming of *The Little Mermaid* by Disney in 2021.

Sardinia only has a cameo role in the novel, *Catch-22*, but Clooney's miniseries in 2019 was filmed in Olbia and surrounding areas, and parts of Gallura.

Buettner's Blue Zone bestselling phenomenon and health movement, as well as the research by Gianni Pes and Michel Poulain in Sardinia, first appeared in *National Geographic* magazine in November, 2005, "The Secrets of Long Life," and then as a book, *The Blue Zone: Lessons for Living Longer from the People Who've Lived the Longest* (National Geographic Books, 2008). I learned about the Blue Zones in 2010 in Loma Linda, California, one of the featured Blue Zones, when my father traveled there for a special cancer treatment. He handed me Buettner's book, casually mentioning that "a place in Italy" was showcased.

After three decades as the solitary caretaker of Budelli island, Morandi was evicted by national authorities. He moved to Maddalena. In 2019, he published his memoir in Italian, *La poltrona di ginepro. Abbandonare il mondo per la libertà: la mia vita sulla Spiaggia Rosa* (Rizzoli, 2019).

Founded in 1974, the Tenores di Bitti group has performed around the world. Zappa wrote the liner notes for their album, *Intonos* (New Tone Records) in 1994. Peter Gabriel's Real World Record label produced one of their albums, *S'amore 'e Mama*, in 1996.

"Where Kings of the Mountains Are Kidnappers" appeared in the *New York Times* on August 24, 1992, on the kidnapping of the young son of a hotel operator from the Costa Smeralda.

In 1979, the great Italian folk rock singer-songwriter De André and his wife Dori Ghezzi were kidnapped in Sardinia—and held for four months until a ransom was paid. They had established their home in Agnata, in the northern Gallura region, and still remained there after the kidnapping. De André addressed the kidnapping in his song, "Hotel Supramonte," in an album that came out in 1981. He died in 1999, at the age of 58.

Cartier-Bresson's trip to Sardinia in 1962 appeared in *Vogue*, "Sardinia," on April 15, 1963; photos can also be seen at the MOMA in New York City. See also *La fotografia in Sardegna. Lo sguardo esterno 1960–1980* (Ilisso, 2010).

Taylor's story, "A Daughter of Saint Anne," appeared in *The Atlantic Monthly* in March, 1900.

Lord Nelson's letters can be found in various sources, including the multivolume *The Life of Admiral Lord Nelson, K.B., from His Lordship's Manuscripts* (T. Cadell and W. Davies, 1809).

On Nuragic ways to Sardinia in America, see: Mulas, *La Sardegna nuragica. Società, religione, vita quotidiana* (2015, Arkadia), and Carta, "Gershwin in Sardinia," in *Sardinia. Un'isola nell'immaginario anglo-americano*, (2016, Editoriale Scientifica).

3. BALLU TONDU

Atzeni's quotation is a translation from his novel, *Passavamo sulla terra leggeri* (Ilisso, 2000), originally published in Italian by Mondadori in 1996. Atzeni's masterpiece is not translated in English—an oversight that needs to be corrected. Some of his novels are translated in English, French, and other languages, including *Bakunin's Son* (Italica Press, 2008). Most of his work remains in print in Italian, including *Bellas Mariposas* (Sellerio, 2015), and *Il quinto passo è l'addio* (Ilisso, 2002). As one of the godfathers of the Sardinian Literary Spring revival, Atzeni's diverse array of fiction, nonfiction, and poetry has played a major role in Sardinian and Italian literature. There are reams of scholarship and dissertations on Atzeni. I appreciated the work of Gigliola Sulis and Leeds University, "The Island, the Nation, the World. Sergio Atzeni and the post-modern definition of Sardinian ethnic identity," published proceedings from the special conference on Atzeni in Cagliari in 1996, "*Trovare racconti mai narrati, dirli con gioia*," Puggioni's "*Sergio Atzeni e il racconto di foundazione*" (Universita' degli studi di Sassari, 2011–2012). Novelist Paola Soriga wrote a tribute for the *Internazionale*, *"Lo scrittore che ha cambiato il modo di raccontare la Sardegna*," in 2015.

The Sa Domo Manna—Museo Etnografico Villanova Monteleone has good displays on Bastià Pirisi, Remundu Piras and the area's cultural ways. *S'Istranzu avventuradu* (Editrice Sarda F.lli Fossataro) was published in 1969 for the Premio Ozieri.

Bresciani's historical writing on Sardinian dress, *Dei costumi dell'isola di Sardegna: comparati cogli antichissimi popoli orientali* (Uffizio Della Civilta Cattolica, 1850) is available online. Costa wrote about the costumes in his *National Geographic* piece in 1923; a chapter on the dresses and Sardinia by American author Kubly appeared in *The Atlantic Monthly*, July, 1955, from his book, *American in Italy* (Simon and Schuster, 1955).

In *Purgatory*, Dante wrote: "Che' la Barbagia di Sardigna assai, ne le femmine sue più è pudica che la Barbagia dov'io la lasciai." *For the Barbagia of Sardinia / shelters many more modest women / than does that Barbagia where I left her*. Sardinian historian Francesco Casula observed that Dante, among others, often circulated the tale that "the women of Barbagia went with their breasts uncovered," a view that has been contested by other accounts.

Altea's *Edina Altara* (Ilisso, 2005), in Italian, has images of Altara's work. Altara's magazine covers, including her portraits of Sardinian women and their dress, can be found online: http://edinaaltara.blogspot.com/.

Marras's internationally acclaimed designs can be viewed at his website: antoniomarras.com.

The "De Innui Ses" show, featured in *Vogue* on February 21, 2021, can be viewed on YouTube: https://www.youtube.com/watch?v=dgOJxRrKcug.

Images of the Sa Ucca de su Tintirriolu ceramic figures are cited in Cicilloni's "Nuova figurazione antropomorfa di cultura Ozieri da Serra Neula/Puisteris-Mogoro," *ArcheoArte*, 2013. Pottery fragments of dancers from the Grotta di Bonu Ighinu site can be viewed at the Sanna Archaeological Museum in Sassari or online: https://issuu.com/museibook/docs/7_4_20060402095130.

The medieval Church of San Pietro in Zuri, in the district of Ghilarza, is a fascinating place to visit. Consecrated in 1291, the blocks of the church were dismantled, hauled up the valley, and rebuilt in 1923, due to the construction of the Santa Chiara dam. In his chapter on Sardinia in *Cosmographia,* Arquer refers to the popularity of folk dancing. In Italian, see Laneri's *Sigismondo Arquer: Sardiniae brevis historia et descriptio* (Centro di studi filologici sardi, 2007).

4. AGRITURISMO

A bilingual collection (Sardinian-Italian) of Piras' work, *Bonas Noas*, is published in the "i grandi poeti in lingua sarda" series (Edizione della Torre, 1981). There are numerous videos on YouTube on the *gara poetica*. The Sa Domo de sa Poesia

Cantada–the oral poetry museum–also has some excellent exhibits, including online links: https://www.sapoesiacantada.it/poeta/remundu-piras/.

Bourdain's episode on Sardinia appeared on "No Reservations" on September 14, 2009, on Episode 20, Season 5.

Angioni's novel, *Assandira* (Sellerio, 2004) is only available in Italian, as is the rest of his vast body of writing. As one of the main protagonists of the Sardinian Literary Spring, his excellent work deserves translation. Author of numerous essays, novels and poetry collections, written in both Sardinian and Italian, his novel, *Le fiamme di Toledo* (Sellerio 2006), about the life of Acquer, won the Premio Corrado Alvaro and the Premio Mondello.

Mereu's film adaptation of *Assandira*, starring Gavino Ledda, appeared at the Venice Film Festival in 2020, and received a nomination for best film adaptation for the David di Donatello award. Mereu has done several excellent films, including an adaptation of Atzeni's *Bellas Mariposas*.

Gamél Holten's travelogue, *Den Ukendte* (*The Unknown Island*) was published in Danish in 1913. In Italian, see *Sardegna isola sconosciuta*, (Edizioni Iris, 2005).

CNN featured "the world's most dangerous cheese," *casu marzu* in Sardinia, on March 18, 2021. The shepherd's cheese holds a place in the *Guinness Book of World Records* for that same distinction. While we never tried it, we were told it was not dangerous if the maggots were still alive in the cheese.

On the Sardinian language or *limba sarda*, Wagner's *La lingua sarda: Storia, spirito e forma* (A. Francke, Berna, 1951) is considered a seminal text; Sardinian scholarships dates back to Vissentu Porru's *Saggio di grammatica sul dialetto sardo meridionale* in 1811, and his *Nou dizionariu universali sardu-italianu* in 1832. In Italian, see Pittau's longtime work, Bolognesi's *Le identità linguistiche dei sardi* (Condaghes, 2013), among many others. In English, see *Bilingualism and Minority Languages in Europe* (Cambridge Scholars, 2017) and *Language and Identity in Multilingual Mediterranean Settings,* (DeGruyter, 2017). See also the Autonomous Region's cultural department: https://www.sardegnacultura.it/linguasarda/.

Along with Marras's *Antonio Simon Mossa. Un intellettuale rivoluzionario,* (Alfa Editrice, 2008), Mossa's work is online: https://www.archiviosimonmossa.it/

Dante's remark about Sardinians and monkeys can be found in *De vulgari eloquentia* (I, xi, 1-7).

Araolla's *Rimas diversas Spirituales de su Dottore Hieronimu Araolla Sardu Sassaresu* and *Sa vida, su martirio, et morte dessos gloriosos martires Gavinu, Brothu et Gianuari* are online: http://www.sardegnadigitallibrary.it/documenti/17_146_20181123124014.pdf

Tigellius the Sardinian appears in the *Satires* of Horace, around 35 B.C. See B. L. Ullman's essay, "Horace, Catullus, and Tigellius," in *Classical Philology*, July, 1915, and Rowland's "Sardinians in the Roman Empire," in *Ancient Society*, 1974. For all things Roman in Sardinia (in Italian), see Zucca's *Archeologia della Sardegna romana* (Carlo Delfino Editore 2016) and Mastino's chapter, "La Sardegna romana" in *Storia della Sardegna* (Edizioni della Torre, 1998).

The historic chronicles on Sardinian poetry are available online: Madao's *Dissertazioni storiche apologetiche critiche delle sarde antichità* (1792), Smyth's *Sketch of the Present State of the Island of Sardinia* (1827), Casalis's *Dizionario geografico, storico, statistico, commerciale degli stati di S.M. il re di Sardegna* (1833), Mantegazza's *Profili e paesaggi della Sardegna* (1869).

Deledda's *Cenere* has been translated into English, *Ashes* (John Lane, 1908). As the second woman—and first Italian woman, and second Italian—to win the Nobel Prize for Literature in 1926, only a handful of her 33 novels have been translated into English. See *After the Divorce* (Northwestern University Press, 1995) and *Cosima* (Italica Press, 1988). For Deledda's brief Nobel address, visit: https://www.nobelprize.org/prizes/literature/1926/deledda/facts/.

Gramsci's letter on Pirino can be found in his *Letters from Prison* (Columbia University Press, 2011), among various editions in Italian, English and many other languages. Gramsci actually misspelled the poet's name—Pirione, instead of Pirino.

Tyndale has a description of poetic events in *The Island of Sardinia* (Bentley, 1849). For more on oral poetry competitions, in Italian, *Figli delle Muse: La gara poetica sarda e altre forme di poesia orale di improvvisazione* (FrancoAngeli, 2022), by Zizi and Coira. See also Tola's *la Poesia dei poveri* (AMOD Edizioni, 1997), and *La Letteratura in Lingua sarda* (CUEC, 2006).

Check out the website of Sa Domo de sa Poesia Cantada for portraits of women poets, including Chiarina Porqueddu and Maria Farina: https://www.sapoesiacantada.it/poeta/maria-farina/.

Correddu's essay on Piras, "Sa poesia bolu e Remundu Piras," is available online in Italian: https://www.istituto-bellieni.it/sc/sa-poesia-bolu-e-remundu-piras/.

For information on the Ozieri Prize: https://www.premiozieri.it/.

A nice resource of authors, poetry and writing in Sardinian is *Iscritores de Sardigna*: https://www.facebook.com/profile.php?id=100064366045340 and the Sardegna Digital Library: https://www.sardegnadigitallibrary.it/pubblicazioni/.

Boullier published his multivolume research in French, *L'île de Sardaigne: description, histoire, statistique, mœurs, état social* and *Le dialecte et les chants populaires de la Sardaigne* in 1864-65. In Italian: *I canti popolari della Sardegna* (Multigrafica Editrice,1974).

Check out the Sa Razza hip hop group on social media: https://www.instagram.com/quilo_sa_razza/ and https://www.facebook.com/srrazasarda/.

The official website of singer-songwriter Mahmood—Alessandro Mahmood: https://mahmood.it.

5. L'ALGUER

Russo's hit song, "Alghero," is on the *Giuni* album, released in 1986. In 2021, the song was recognized as a *Disco d'Oro*—or gold record—for its sales.

Sardonicus, the pen name of Salvatore Pinna, has publications in Italian and Alguerés, including *Storielline i pennuti, altri animali e qualche pianta* (2017).

For more information on Algherese/Alguerés, and the historic role and revival of Catalan, there is a huge archive of scholarship in Catalan and Italian. One interesting note: the great forger Ignazio Pillito presented poems in Catalano, including some of his own, at a presentation in 1864 at the Jocs Florals de Barcelona literary festival, which renewed interest in Catalan in Alghero. In Catalan, see Armangué i Herrero's *Estudis sobre la cultura catalana a Sardenya* (Institut d'Estudis Catalans, 2001). In Italian, see Sari's *Il catalano di Alghero: una lingua a rischio d'estinzione* (Edicions de l'Alguer, 2018), Budruni's *Breve Storia di Alghero* (Edizione del Sole, 1997), Milanese's *Alghero: Archaeologia di una citta' medievale* (Carlo Delfino Editore, 2013). In English, see Faranelli's "The Invisible Motherland: the Catalan-Speaking Minority in Sardinia and Catalan nationalism," in *Studies on National Movements* (2014), Tufi's "Instances of Emplaced Memory," in *Multilingual Memories: Monuments, Museums and the Linguistic Landscape* (Bloomsbury, 2019), and Chessa's dissertation, "Another Case of Language Death? The intergenerational transmission of Catalan in Alghero," (University of London, 2011).

Alghero has excellent museums on local history, including Museo Archeologico della Città di Alghero, Museo del Corallo di Alghero, and the Museo Diocesano D'arte Sacra at the Cathedral. Check out the website tribute to Pino Piras: https://pinopiras.it/biografia-italiano/

Vuillier's *Les Iles oubliées* (Hachette, 1892), was translated into English, *The Forgotten Isles* (Hutchison, 1896).

While he published first in Barcelona in 1571, Lo Frasso's *Los diez libros de Fortuna de Amor* (1573) became his most famous, thanks to Cervantes. Online, see: https://www.filologiasarda.eu/files/documenti/pubblicazioni_pdf/cfslofrasso/03edizione.pdf.

In 2015, publisher Carlo Delfino Editore put out a beautiful volume on Capo Caccia, *Il Parco Naturale di Porto Conte,* edited by Farris et al.

Fans of Franca Masu maintain a nice website on her diverse work: https://www.francamasu.com.

Rudas's *L'isola dei coralli: itinerari dell'identità (*Nuova Italia Scientifica, 1997) has gone through numerous reprints, most recently part of La Biblioteca della Nuova Sardegna's Capolavori Sardi series. That indispensable series can be found online: https://www.librarything.com/nseries/329090/Capolavori-Sardi-La-Nuova-Sardegna.

The poetry, fiction and nonfiction of Masala have been published in Sardinian and Italian by several publishers, Domus de Janas, Condaghes and Il Maestrale, most recently *Poesias in duas limbas* (2006) and *Quelli dalle labbra bianche* (2010).

6. SARDIGNA

Stiglitz's essay appeared in Italian in *Il Manifesto Sardo* on April 19, 2022. As a longtime archaeologist, he has published widely on the Nuragic and Phoenician periods. See "'Decolonizzare' l'archeologia in Sardegna," Commissione per l'Etica e l'Integrità nella Ricerca del Consiglio Nazionale delle Ricerche, April, 2021. In English, see "Beyond the Nuraghe. Perception and Reuse in Punic and Roman Sardinia," in *Gardening Time: Reflections on Memory, Monuments, and History in Scotland and Sardinia* (Cambridge 2012).

For more information on ancient brews at Nuragic sites like Arrubiu, see "La vite e il vino nella Sardegna nuragica: analisi biochimiche nel nuraghe Arrubiu di Orroli," by Perra et al (Istituto italiano di preistoria e protostoria, 2021).

Online sites for the Ancient Greek writers are plentiful. For Pausanias and Sardinia in English, see: https://www.theoi.com/Text/Pausanias10B.html.

The inscription at the Nuraghe Aidu Entos at Bortigali can be viewed at the Nurnet site: https://www.nurnet.net/mediateca/bortigali-nuraghe-aidu-entos-3/.

To see the Nora stele, visit the National Museum of Archaeology in Cagliari: https://museoarcheocagliari.beniculturali.it/.

A student of pioneering archaeologist Lilliu, Ugas has spent a half century exploring ancient Sardinia, as a professor at the University of Cagliari and investigator on numerous sites. Author of many books, Ugas published *Shardana e Sardegna. I Popoli del Mare, gli alleati del Nord Africa e la fine dei grandi regni (XV-XII secolo a.C.)* in 2016 (Edizioni della Torre). See also Valeria Putzu, *L'impero dei popoli del mare* (Arkadia , 2018).

See Pliny the Elder's comments on Sardinia in English: https://www.perseus.tufts.edu/hopper/text?doc=Perseus%3Atext%3A1999.02.0137%3Abook%3D3%3Achapter%3D13.

A few centuries later, Procopius' work in English can be found online: https://penelope.uchicago.edu/Thayer/E/Roman/Texts/Procopius/Buildings/6*.html.

The informative letters of Pope Gregory to various clergy and leaders in Sardinia have been translated into English. See: http://www.clerus.org/bibliaclerusonline/en%20/eek.htm.

Recent scholarship on the Muslim travelers and conquerors of Sardinia has made a lot of inroads in the last years. In English, see Metcalfe's "Muslim Contacts with Sardinia: From Fatimid Ifrīqiya to Mujāhid of Dénia," in *The Making of Medieval Sardinia* (Brill, 2021), and *A Companion to Sardinian History, 500–1500* (Brill, 2017).

As the legal code of the *judicadu* of Arborea in the late fourteenth century, the Carta de Logu was written in Sardinian. An Italian translation is online: https://www.istar.oristano.it/export/sites/default/.galleries/pubblicazioni/Carta-de-Logu.pdf

In Italian, see Serra's "Il Libellus Judicum Turritanorum e la nascita della prima prosa storiografica in volgare sardo," in *Il Sardo medioevale* (Franco Angeli, 2018).

Toda's work was published in Catalan, *La poesía catalana á Sardenya*, 1889.

I discuss Cesare Casula's histories later in the book, but his works on medieval Sardinia are important reads. In Italian, see *La storiografia sarda ieri e oggi*, (Carlo Delfino Editore, 2009). For a general overview of the Savoyard period, in Italian, see Brigaglia, Mastino, and Ortu's two-part series, *Storia della Sardegna: Dalle origini al Settecento* and *Dal Settecento a oggi* (Laterza, 2002), as well as Brigaglia, Boscolo and Del Piano's *La Sardegna contemporaranea* (Edizioni della Torre, 1976), Francesco Casula's *Carlo Felice e i tiranni sabaudi* (Edizioni Grafica del Parteolla, 2021), and G. Murgia's *Un'isola, la sua storia: La Sardegna sabauda, 1720-1847* (Grafica del Parteolla, 2014).

Calvia's poetry volume, *Sassari Mannu*, was reprinted by Carlo Delfino Editore in 2013.

7. *ISOLARI*

The Atzeni quotation is an English translation from his book of essays, *Raccontare fole* (Sellerio, 1999), on foreign travel writers. The book, alas, is not translated in English.

Soriga has written several novels, in Italian, including *La stagione che verrá* (Einaudi, 2015), and more recently, *Maicolgecson* (Mondadori, 2021)--as in, Michael Jackson.

There's a piazza in Cagliari dedicated to the Tex Willer author, "Galep": https://www.unionesarda.it/news-sardegna/cagliari/cagliari-una-piazza-dedicata-a-galep-il-padre-di-tex-dpp656ob.

On Viale San Vincenzo in Cagliari at the Chapel of the Vincentian nuns, you can also see some of his religious artwork: https://www.sardiniapost.it/cronaca/galep/.

San Salvatore of Sinis feels like a Sardinian Tombstone, Arizona. Actor Nicoletta Machiavelli starred in *Garter Colt*, the spaghetti western filmed there.

You'll need to find your own kiosk newspaper vendors to find all seven books in F. Cesare Casula's *La Storia di Sardegna* (La Nuova Sardegna, 2017), published originally by Carlo Delfino Editore in 1994.

The disastrous *Boom!* film, despite its heavy hitters, is the topic of a new documentary, *A Summer with Joe, Liz and Rich*, by Sergio Naitza: https://filmitalia.org/en/film/170150/.

Cited by virtually every English-speaking travel writer since the early nineteenth century, none of La Marmora's work is translated in English, but the original French editions are online: See *Voyage en Sardaigne* (1826) at https://www.biodiversitylibrary.org/item/183246#page/9/mode/1up and *Itinéraire de l'ile de Sardaigne* (1860): https://www.sardegnadigitallibrary.it/index.php?xsl=2436&s=17&v=9&c=4463&id=220505.

In Italian, La Marmora's books include the three volume *Itinerario dell'isola di Sardegna* (Ilisso, 1997) and *Viaggio in Sardegna* (Fondazione Il Nuraghe, 1926): https://www.sardegnadigitallibrary.it/index.php?xsl=626&id=220645.

There is also a website dedicated to the illustrious La Maramora brothers: http://www. lamarmora.net/en/alberto-la-marmora-biography.html.

Maria Bonaria Urban's *Sardinia in Screen: The Construction of the Sardinian Character in Italian Cinema* (Rodopi, 2013) is a tremendous resource on literature and film in Sardinia—in English. It's truly a landmark text that needs to be translated in Italian, among other languages.

The Varangia crusaders' story is cited in numerous sources, including *The Making of Medieval Sardinia* (Brill, 2021). In French, see "L'émigration anglaise à Byzance après 1066. Un nouveau texte en latin sur les Varangues à Constantinople," Ciggaar, *Revue des études byzantines*, 1974.

Deledda's asides on D'Annunzio, from a letter in 1893, are cited in several sources, including Heyer-Caput's *Grazia Deledda's dance of modernity* (University of Toronto Press, 2008).

Madao's critique of the Swedish traveler is in *Dissertazioni storiche apologetiche critiche delle sarde antichità* (1792). Translated in English in 1784, *An exact description of the island and Kingdom of Sicily, its provinces, towns, and remarkable places . . . To which is added, a short narrative of the island and kingdom of Sardinia*, d'Avity's book is online (The British Library): https://www.google.com/books/edition/ An_exact_description_of_the_island_and_K/MEJiAAAAcAAJ.

Carillo's *Relacion al rey Don Philipe nuestro señor del nombre, sitio, planta, conquistas, christiandad fertilidad, ciudades, lugares y gouierno del reyno de Sardeña*, is online: https://patrimoniodigital.ucm.es/s/patrimonio/item/650700.

While I discuss Emilio Lussu in more detail later in the book, see an American edition of *Road to Exile: The Story of a Sardinian Patriot* (Covici Friede, 1936). The *New York Times* called it "a moving story of moral and physical courage."

According to the American publisher, Amelie Posse-Brázdová's *Sardinian Sideshow* (Dutton, 1933) went through seven printings.

I discuss Lawrence in greater detail in subsequent chapters. *Sea and Sardinia* was first published in excerpts in *The Dial Magazine*, and by Thomas Seltzer in the United States in 1921. Numerous other editions followed; it remains in print (Penguin Classics), among other publications. You can view the original book illustrations by artist Jan Juta online: https://www.gutenberg.org/files/37206/37206- h/37206-h.htm.

8. MONT'E PRAMA

Mont'e Prama has generated a tremendous amount of scholarship—much of it debated, contested, and still incomplete. The official website of the Fondazione Mont'e Prama has a lot of information in English, Italian, French, and German: https://monteprama.it/en/ and the Municipal Museum Giovanni Marongiu of Cabras is online in multiple languages: https://www.museocabras.it/en/museum/.

Nurnet also maintains an archive on Mont'e Prama: https://www.nurnet.net/blog/ monte-prama-2014-2022/.

In English, see "Geophysics-An Essential Tool for Modern Archaeology. A Case from Monte Prama," Ranieri, Trogu, Piroddi, (European Association of Geoscientists & Engineers, 2015), "The Giant Heroes of Mont'e Prama Recovering Ancient Sardinian Heritage," Faedda and Carta, from Columbia University's exhibit: https://montepramaexhibition.italianacademy.columbia.edu/.

In Italian, also see: *Le sculture di Mont'e Prama Conservazione e restauro*, edited by Cobau, which includes Peter Rockwell's "Le tecniche antiche," (Gangemi Editore, 2014). Ranieri's work is also available online in Italian: See "Mont'e Prama, a caccia di antichi Giganti col georadar: le incredibili scoperte di Gaetano Ranieri," in a three-art series on Tiscali Cultura: https://cultura.tiscali.it/news/articoli/monteprama-ranieri-gaetano-intervista-parte-1/ https://cultura.tiscali.it/interviste/articoli/monteprama-ranieri-gaetano-intervista-parte-2/ https://cultura.tiscali.it/interviste/articoli/monteprama-ranieri-gaetano-intervista-parte-3/

PART TWO: *SOS MANNOS* | THE ANCESTORS

This is an English translation of Mura's poem, "Fippo operaiu 'e luche soliana." The original in Sardinian and Italian is online in Tanda's *Un'odissea de rimas nobas* (CUEC, 2003): https://www.yumpu.com/it/document/read/16215642/versione-pdf-sardegna-digitallibrary

Mura has been compared with Spanish poet Federico Garcia Lorca. Tanda called Mura's work, which won the Premio Ozieri, "a true manifesto of the new poetry in Sardinian limba of the twentieth century."

9. POSTCARD FROM SANT'ANTIOCO: THE ARCHER

See above for Atzeni's novel, *Passavamo sulla terra leggeri.*

Bosa is a colorful town on the western coast, famous for its history, arts, and embroidery, among many things. An overview of tourist sites: https://www.sardegnaturismo.it/en/places/nord-ovest/bosa. See also the artistry of Olimpia Melis here: https://www.ilfiletdiolimpiamelis.com/.

The backstory on the "three living and the three dead" is available online at The British Library: https://blogs.bl.uk/digitisedmanuscripts/2014/01/the-three-living-and-the-three-dead.html.

Translated into Italian, *Viaggio in Sardegna* (Ilisso, 1999), Valery's original French work, *Voyages en Corse, a l'ile d'Elbe, et en Sardaigne*, is online: https://www.sardegnadigitallibrary.it/index.php?xsl=2436&s=17&v=9&c=4463&id=220449.

I discuss the *nuraghes* more in detail later in the book—and there is an immense treasury of literature on the Nuragic civilization in Italian and English.

For all things *nuraghe* or *nuraghes*, see Nurnet's online archive: https://www.nurnet.net/mediateca/categorie/nuraghes/.

In English, see *Archaeology and History in Sardinia from the Stone Age to the Middle*

Ages: Shepherds, Sailors, and Conquerors (University of Pennsylvania Museum of Archaeology and Anthropology, 2008) by Dyson and Rowland, *The Periphery in the Center: Sardinia in the Ancient and Medieval Worlds* (Archaeopress, 2001) by Rowland, *The Archaeology of Nuragic Sardinia* (Equinox Publishing, 2016), by Webster, and Blake's "Sardinia's Nuraghi: Four Millennia of Becoming," *World Archaeology*, 1998.

See the *Scientific American*, "The Nuraghi of Sardinia and Similar Structures," August 5, 1899.

In Italian, see *La Sardegna nuragica* (Ilisso, 2000), edited by Lilliu and Pallottino, *Sardegna nuragica* (Il Maestrale, 2009), by Lilliu, *La Sardegna Nuragica, Storia e monumenti* (Carlo Delfino Editore, 2017), and *La Sardegna Nuragica* (Edizioni Della Torre, 2013), by Pittau.

For Sant'Antioco, see: https://visitsantantioco.info/en/la_scoperta/nuraghi-santantioco/ and https://virtualarchaeology.sardegnacultura.it/index.php/it/siti-archeologici/eta-fenicio-punica/necropoli-is-pirixeddu/schede-di-dettaglio/1052-sant-antioco-in-eta-prenuragica-e-nuragica.

For Grutti/Grutt'e Acqua, see: https://www.sant-antioco.it/grutti-acqua-2/.

In Italian, Depalmas' "Le isole minori della Sardegna nella Preistoria," in *Scienze dell'Antichità*, 2016, and Tronchetti's guide to archaeology on Sant'Antioco (Carlo Delfino Editore) is online: https://web.archive.org/web/20111121003637/http://www.sardegnacultura.it/documenti/7_4_20060402095009.pdf.

The collections of the Museo Archeologico Ferruccio Barreca, including the "archer," can be viewed online: https://mabsantantioco.it/il-museo/.

Other sites in Sant'Antioco include the Museo Etnografico "Su magasinu 'e su binu," and Chiara Vigo's Museum of Bisso: https://www.chiaravigo.it/.

Literature on the bronzetti is vast. In Italian, see Depalmas' *Le navicelle di bronzo della Sardegna nuragica* (Gasperini, 2005). Fulvia Lo Schiavo has dedicated decades to Nuragic research. See: "Late Bronze Age Metal Exploitation and Trade: Sardinia and Cyprus," Lo Schiavo with S. Sabatini, *Materials and Manufacturing Processes,* May, 2020, "I Sardi sul mare: le navicelle nuragiche," *La battaglia del Mare Sardonio, Studi e ricerche (*Memoria storica, Mythos, 2000*),* "Dalla storia all'immagine: la navicella dalla Tomba del Duce di Vetulonia," in *Dall'immagine alla storia. Studi per ricordare,* Muscettola, Incontro di Studi, Università degli Studi Federico II, Napoli, 2006, "Interconnessioni fra Mediterraneo e Atlantico nell'età del bronzo: il punto di vista della Sardegna," *Cuadernos de Arqueología Mediterránea*, 2012.

In English, also see: "Neutron-based techniques for archaeometry: characterization of a Sardinian boat model," by Depalmas et al., *Archaeological and Anthropological Sciences*, 2021, *Archaeometallurgy in Sardinia from the origin to the beginning of Early Iron Age* (Montagnac, 2005), and "The Strange Case of the Nuragic Offerers Bronze Statuettes: A Multi-Analytical Study," by Brunetti et al., in *Materials,* 2022,

"Characterisation of Alloy Composition of Protohistoric Small Boat Models from Sardinia (Italy)," *Materials*, 2022, by Iannaccone et al.; and Gonzalez, "Sardinian bronze figurines in their Mediterranean setting," (DeGruyter, 2012): https://www.academia.edu/3633680/Sardinian_bronze_figurines_in_their_Mediterranean_setting.

For a list of bronzetti, see Nurnet: https://www.nurnet.net/mediateca/categorie/bronzetti-nuragici/.

Also, see Bernadini's *Le torri, i metalli, il mare: Storie antiche di un'isola mediterranea* (Carlo Delfino Editore, 2010). For more on Nuragic boats in Crotone, see: https://www.gruppoarcheologicokr.it/navicella-nuragica-del-vii-sec-a-c-presso-il-museo-di-archeologico-di-crotone/.

For more on Nuragic influence on Etruscans, see: *The Etruscan World* (Taylor & Francis, 2014), edited by Turfa, and Haynes' *Etruscan Civilization: A Cultural History* (Getty Publications, 2005). In Italian, see Lo Schiavo's "Il Mediterraneo Occidentale Prima degli Etruschi," in *Gli Etruschi E Il Mediterraneo*, (Commerci E Politica, Orvieto 16-18 Dicembre 2005), Tronchetti's "La Sardegna e gli Etruschi," *Mediterranean Archaeology*, 1988, Pittau's work, including *Origine e parentela dei sardi e degli etruschi* (Carlo Delfino Editore, 1995), and Museo Archaeologico Nazionale's "Miti e simboli di una civiltà mediterranea: la Sardegna Nuragica": https://museoarcheologiconazionaledifirenze.wordpress.com/2014/08/30/firenze-musei-archeologici-nazionali-in-mostra-la-sardegna-nuragica/.

Lai's graphic novel on the archer, with coauthors Tomassi and Fiori, *Il ritorno dell'arciere* (ANNALI di Storia e Archeologia Sulcitana, 2019), is online: https://www.journalchc.com/wp-content/uploads/2019/09/Il-ritorno-dellarciere.pdf%20Il%20ritorno%20dell'arciere.

There's a nice interview with Lai on Nurnet: https://www.nurnet.net/blog/in-esclusiva-nurnet-la-storia-del-recupero-dellarciere-nuragico-di-santantioco-raccontato-dal-protagonista/.

See *The Bulletin of the Cleveland Museum of Art,* vol. 78, Notable Acquisitions (June 1991), and "Pact Will Relocate Artifacts to Italy From Cleveland," November 19, 2008, *New York Times*.

For the British Museum collection, see *Tharros: A Catalogue of Material in the British Museum from Phoenician and Other Tombs at Tharros, Sardinia* (British Museum, 1987). "Bronzes Conjure Up Images of a Fabled Past," October 14, 1990, *New York Times*. For a recent roundup of ancient art seized from art galleries, see "Two Dealers in Pre-Columbian Art Are Indicted," March 3, 2005, *New York Times,* "Looking for a Stolen Idol? Visit the Museum of the Manhattan D.A.," November 21, 2021, *New York Times*, "A Trove of Artifacts Officials Call 'Stolen' Are Returned to Italy," December 15, 2021, *New York Times*.

Auctions for Nuragic bronzetti continue. See: https://www.christies.com/lot/lot-a-sardinian-bronze-worshiper-circa-8th-century-6067620/?from=searchresults&int ObjectID=6067620.

Levi published several works on archaeology in Sardinia, including *L'ipogeo di San Salvatore di Cabras in Sardegna* (Libreria dello Stato, 1949). On the necklace and the Nazi, see "Olbia, Doro Levi: l'ebreo che salvò la collana in pasta vitrea dal Nazismo," January 27, 2020, Olbia.it.

This is an English translation from Susini's collection of poems, *Canti del Nomade* (R. Bemporad, 1928). Along with poetry, Susini also wrote for the theatre, including "Sardi alla mola," which was staged in Cagliari in 1923. He also served as mayor of Sant'Antioco in 1943.

10. RE-STORYING HISTORY

Trouillot's *Silencing the Past: Power and the Production of History* (Beacon, 1995) is a classic on Haitian history—and its interpretations.

Recordings of Marisa Sannia's songs in Italian, Sardinian and Spanish are widely available online. In Italian, see "Marisa Sannia, la prima sarda a Sanremo," in *L'Unione Sarda*, March 13, 2017.

Loddo's activities on social media: https://www.facebook.com/profile. php?id=100072325645330.

In Italian, Nuraghe Seruci featured prominently in the *Archivio storico Sardo*, Volumes 7–9, 1911. Taramelli wrote about Seruci in 1917: *Gonnesa - Indagini nella cittadella nuragica di Seruci (Cagliari)*, in *Monumenti antichi della Reale Accademia dei Lincei*, XXIX. For the official website for Nuraghe Seruci: https://www. facebook.com/nuragheseruciofficial/.

The Nation magazine feature, "Among the Nuraghi," June 1900 was signed by P.T.L.

Porcu's *Hi-Nu-Ra* (Carlo Delfino Editore, 2013) is in Italian.

My play, *Damnatio Memoriae* (in Italian and English, Wings Press, 2015), deals with the Ancient Roman ways of "condemning memory" and literally destroying artifacts of one's existence. The play features Emperor Septimius Severus, who was born in Leptis Magna, in today's Libya, to a Punic family.

See Blake's "Late Bronze Age Sardinia: Acephalous Cohesion from Insularity and Connectivity," *The Cambridge Prehistory of the Bronze and Iron Age Mediterranean* (Cambridge University Press, 2014).

Gracchus's triumphant marking of his devastation is cited in numerous sources in English, including Beard's *The Roman Triumph* (Harvard University Press, 2009), and Moormann's *Divine Interiors: Mural Paintings in Greek and Roman Sanctuaries* (Amsterdam University Press, 2011). For an overview of the Ennius story, see *Silius Italicus' Punica Rome's War with Hannibal* (Taylor and Francis, 2021) by Augoustakis et al., and Casale's "The Poet at War: Ennius on the Field in Silius's Punica,"*Arethusa*, September, 2006.

In Italian, see Caterini's indispensable *La Mano Destra Della Storia: La demolizione della memoria e il problema storiografico in Sardegna* (Carlo Delfino Editore, 2017)

In her earlier cited "Interconnessioni fra Mediterraneo e Atlantico nell'età del bronzo: il punto di vista della Sardegna," Lo Schiavo notes Gomez and Fundoni, "Relaciones del Suroeste con el Mediterráneo en el Bronce Final (siglos XI-X a.C.). Huelva y la isla de Cerdeña," *Anales de Arqueologìa Cordobesa,* 2010 and Fundoni's "Le relazioni tra la Sardegna e la Penisola Iberica nei primi secoli del I millennio a.C.: le testimonianze nuragiche nella, Penisola Iberica," *Anales de Arqueologìa Cordobesa 20,* 2009.

The Danish insight comes from Magna Gunhild Kollund, "Urbanization in Nuragic Sardinia—Why Not?" in *Urbanization in the Mediterranean in the 9th to 6th Centuries B.C.,* Museum Tusculanum Press, 1997.

See above for Lo Schiavo and Sabatini on Cyrus and Sardinia connections.

For the Hacksilber Project, see C. Thompson, and S. Skaggs, "King Solomon's Silver? Southern Phoenician Hacksilber Hoards and the Location of Tarshish," *Internet Archaeology* 35, 2013. The thirteenth century B.C. mining and shipping in Sardinia discovered in the shipwreck was explored in "Incised Late Bronze Age lead ingots from the southern anchorage of Caesarea," by N. Yahalom-Mack et al., in *Journal of Archaeological Science: Reports*, February 2022. Holt's assessment of Nuragic glass was cited in numerous news pieces, including "I primi al mondo a produrre il vetro? Furono i nuragici," July 18, 2021, *La Nuova Sardegna*: https://www.lanuovasardegna.it/regione/2021/07/18/news/i-primi-al-mondo-a-produrre-il-vetro-furono-i-nuragici-1.40512883.

See Ugas's work above in Sardigna section for Shardana research.

For the Viking and Sardinia research, in English, see *Anthropomorphised warlike beings with horned helmets: Bronze Age Scandinavia, Sardinia, and Iberia compared,* by Helle Vandkilde et al. in Praehistorische Zeitschrift, 2021, or in Italian, see "I Vichinghi e i Nuragici, lo strano caso degli elmi, Dalla Danimarca l'ipotesi secondo cui i copricapi con le corna arrivarono dalla Sardegna. L'opinione degli archeologi Fulvia Lo Schiavo e Mauro Perra," January 17, 2022, *La Nuova Sardegna.*

Balmuth's "Archaeology in Sardinia," was in *Journal of American Archaeology,* 1992.

For information on La Sardegna verso l'Unesco, see: https://sardegnaversounesco.org/.

For information on Comitato Civilta Sarda, see https://www.facebook.com/Comitatociviltasarda.

Spano's *Bullettino archeologico sardo,* dating back to 1855, are available online: https://archive.org/details/bullettinoarcheo01sala/mode/2up?ref=ol&view=theater.

The Museo Mediterraneo dell'Arte Nuragica e dell'Arte Contemporanea is online in Italian, "Zaha Hadid, Betile": https://www.regione.sardegna.it/documenti/1_27_20061120100532.pdf.

Antonello Gregorini's *Un Nuraghe per Tutti* (Condaghes, 2017), is in Italian.

Leighton's "Nuraghi as Ritual Monuments in the Sardinian Bronze and Iron Ages (circa 1700–700 B.C.)," is available at *Open Archaeology*: https://doi.org/10.1515/opar-2022-0224.

Il Ponte magazine, in Florence, dedicated an entire issue to Sardinia in 1951. It's an extraordinary document, including some of the leading writers and voices of the day. Lilliu's piece was titled, "Preistoria sarda e civilta' nuragica." An index of the authors—all male—is available online: https://www.sardegnadigitallibrary.it/documenti/1_151_20080904153346.pdf.

11. LAWRENCE OF SARDINIA

Costa's quotation is an English translation from *Racconto storico sassarese del secolo XV,* 1897.

See Casula's *Carlo Felice e i tiranni sabaudi* (Grafica del Parteolla, 2016) in Italian, Sotgiu's *Storia della Sardegna dopo l'Unità* (Laterza, 1986), and Tuveri's *Tutte le opere* (Carlo Delfino Editore, 1990–2002).

Manno's travelogue, *Lettere di un sardo in Italia, 1816–1817,* is online: https://www.sardegnadigitallibrary.it/index.php?xsl=2436&id=220153.

His *Storia di Sardegna* volumes are online, in Italian: https://www.sardegnadigitallibrary.it/index.php?xsl=626&id=205188.

On travel writers in Sardinia, see Corso's *The invention of Sardinia: the idea of Sardinia in historical and travel writing : 1780-1955* (Biblioteca del Viaggio in Italia Studi, 2014). Murgia's *Viaggio in Sardegna: Undici percorsi nell'isola che non si vede* (Einaudi, 2014) is in Italian—and needs to be translated in English. Her novel, *Accabadora* (Counterpoint, 2012) is available in English, as well as *How to Be a Fascist: A Manual* (Penguin, 2020). Balzac's escapade in Sardinia is widely cited in numerous sources, including his own correspondence, *Honore de Balzac, His Life and Writings*, by Sandars (J. Murray, 1904).

Forester's *The Island of Sardinia: the Preface to the Second Edition of Rambles in the Islands of Corsica and Sardinia* (Spottiswoode and Co,1858) is still in print with reproduction publishers. Bouchier's *Sardinia in Ancient Times* (Blackwell; 1917) is still in print. The Baedeker guide carried around by Lawrence is available online: https://archive.org/details/southernitalysi00karl.

See "Notes on Sport in Sardinia," July, 1901 in *Badminton Magazine by* Daniele Vare'.

Wilson cites Lawrence's *Sea and Sardinia* in *The Best of American Travel Writing 2020* (Mariner Books, 2020).

See Crockett's review in the *New York Times,* "Sightseer and Seer in Sardinia," March 15, 1922.

"Frances Mayes Admires Travel Writers, With One Big Exception," appeared in the *New York Times*, September 18, 2022.

Dessi's view on Lawrence took place in his correspondence, available in Italian: *Dessí e la Sardegna i carteggi con "Il Ponte" e Il Polifilo*, (Firenze University Press, 2013).

The citation on Julia Fortunata is online: https://romaninscriptionsofbritain.org/inscriptions/6.

12. PORTO CONTE

Antoine de Saint-Exupéry's *The Little Prince* (Reynal & Hitchcock, 1943) is one the bestselling books in history.   His "Letter to an American," and Philips's photos were published in *Poet and Pilot: Antoine de Saint-Exupery* (Scalo, 1994). More photos are online at *Life Magazine*: https://www.life.com/photographer/john-philips/. For info on the museum, see: https://www.algheroparks.it/vivi-i-parchi/museo-antoine-de-saint-exup%C3%A9ry/.

Sardegna Live did an excellent mini documentary series on *La Nit de San Pasqual,* directed by Marco A. Pani, available online: https://www.youtube.com/watch?v=QemyRGVP7zM.

13. EMPORIUM

The translation in English is from Serra's "Tempus Nostru." Her work is available in Sardinian and Italian, most recently *Lentores* (Soter Editrice, 2019).

Strabo's 2,000-year-old thoughts on Sardinia and thereabouts are available online at numerous sites, including: http://penelope.uchicago.edu/Thayer/e/roman/texts/strabo/5b*.html.

The Museum of Obsidian in Pau and the Historical and Environmental Geomining Park, are worth several days of visiting. In English, see: https://parcogeominerario.sardegna.it/en/ https://parcogeominerario.sardegna.it/en/museum-of-obsidian/.

I discuss Monte d'Accoddi in more detail later in the book, but see *Sperm Whales in the Neolithic Mediterranean: A Tooth from the Sanctuary of Monte d'Accoddi*, by Melis and Zedda (Cambridge University Press, 2021).

There is a significant amount of research on the Phoenicians and Romans at Sant'Imbenia, with some more recent findings on the Nuragic period. The site can be visited online here: https://www.sardegnacultura.it/j/v/258?s=20709&v=2&c=2489&t=1.

For information on the nearby site of Nuraghe Palmavera, which I discuss later, see: https://nuraghepalmavera.it/.

In English, see "Sant'Imbenia (Alghero): further archaeometric evidence for an Iron Age market square," by M. Clemenza et al. in *Archaeological and Anthropological Sciences,* 2021, Marco Rendili's "Sant'Imbenia and the Topic of the Emporia in Sardinia," (Presses Universitaires de la méditerranée, 2018) and "Pottery from Sant'Imbenia: functions vs decorations," IMEKO, 2016.

See earlier references to the Nuragic trade with Iberia, Cyprus, and the Eastern Mediterranean.

In Italian, see Lo Schiavo's, Rendili's "Il Progetto Sant'Imbenia,"*ArcheoArte*, 2012, Lo Schiavo et al, "Il villaggio nuragico di Sant'Imbenia ad Alghero, *Congresso Internazionale di Studi Fenici e Punici,* Tunis, 1995, and *Il Lazio dai Colli Albani ai Monti Lepini tra preistoria ed età moderna*, edited by Troccoli, (Edizioni Quasar, 2009).

The Tarshish connection is still quite contested. In English, Tzilla Eshel from Haifa University's Zinman Institute of Archaeology gives some background, "Tarshish: The Origins of Solomon's Silver," The Torah.com, March, 2022, and in her paper, "Lead isotopes in silver reveal earliest Phoenician quest for metals in the west Mediterranean," PNAS, 2019.

Ptolemy's *Geography* is online: https://penelope.uchicago.edu/Thayer/E/Gazetteer/ Periods/Roman/_Texts/Ptolemy/3/3*.html.

14. TRAVELING WRITERS

Costa is cited above.

Mario de Candia—the Pavarotti of his day, some say—was born Giovanni Matteo De Candia, and his tomb is at the Cimitero in Cagliari. See: https://www. cimiterobonaria.it/scheda/b00028/.

Along with Joyce's *Ulysses*, Mario appears in numerous chronicles on opera, including *The Romance of a Great Singer: A Memoir of Mario* (Smith, Elder & Co., 1910).

All of those Sardinian innovators—from Anedda to Bissiri, Broccu, Angeli, Columbu, among so many others—deserve their own books. In Italian, see *Illustres: Vita, morte e miracoli di quaranta personalità sarde* (Domus de Janas, 2019) by Onnis and Mureddu. A list of notable Sardinians is on Wikipedia: https://en.wikipedia. org/wiki/List_of_people_from_Sardinia.

See earlier entries on Marras. The *New York Times* story, "Quiet Simplicity from Antonio Marras," appeared on Feb. 23, 2006.

See Ledda on historic booksellers in Sardinia: "Per l'attribuzione della Carta de logu del 1560," La Bibliofilia, 2012, and "Studi sul libro tipografico in Sardegna tra Cinque e Seicento," (CUSL, 2012). See also Virdis's "La nascita della Sardegna quale soggetto storico e culturale nel secolo XVI," in *Questioni di letteratura sarda*, edited by Serra (FrancoAngeli, 2012).

You can order used and new books at Libreria Vademecum bookstore: https://www. maremagnum.com/librerie/libreria-vademecum.

Along with Libreria Il Labirinto Mondadori and cyRaNo bookstores in Alghero, check out this list for booksellers in Sardinia: https://www.librimania.it/Sardegna.

For more on the Sardinian Literary Spring, in Italian, see Angioni's *Cartas de logu: scrittori sardi allo specchio* (CUEC, 2007), Broccia's "Letteratura in Limba," *Rom Reykjavik*, 2014. In English, see Broccia's "The Sardinian Literary Spring: An Overview: A New Perspective on Italian Literature," *Nordicum-Mediterraneum* 9, 2014, Dettori's "Regional Identity in Contemporary Sardinian Writing," *Europe Now Journal*, April 2019, and Sulis's "Sardinian Fiction at End of the Twentieth and Beginning of the Twenty-first Century: an Overview and First Assessment," *Incontri Rivista europea di studi italiani*, 2017.

Steiner's "One Thousand Years of Solitude," appeared in *The New Yorker* on October 19, 1987.

Among his many works in Sardinian and Italian, see Paolo Pilllonca's *O bella Musa ove sei tu?* (Domus de janas, 2018). Chatwin's *In Patagonia* (Jonathan Cape, 1977) remains in print. See Shakespeare's biography, *Bruce Chatwin* (Harvill Press, 1999) and *Under the Sun: The Letters of Bruce Chatwin*, with Elizabeth Chatwin (J. Cape, 2010).

Dyer's *Out of Sheer Rage: Wrestling with D. H. Lawrence* (Picador, 2009), is also available in Italian, *Per pura rabbia. Fare a pugni con D.H. Lawrence* (Il Saggiatore, 2021). See Nicklin's "A case for D.H. Lawrence as a father of modern travel writing," in the *Washington Post*, September 2, 2021. Dodge Luhan's story with Lawrence is in *Lorenzo in Taos* (Knopf, 1932). Fancello et al appear in *Cent'anni fa arrivò Lawrence* (Il Maestrale, 2021).

Gramsci's quotation on the miners is cited in numerous sources, most recently Gabass' "Gramsci, Sardinia, and the Southern Question," University of Cluj, 2018, and Dante Germino's *Antonio Gramsci: Architect of a New Politics* (LSU Press, 1990). There is an immense scholarship on Gramsci. For starters, see *The Antonio Gramsci Reader: Selected Writings 1916–1935* (NYU Press, 2000), Hoare's and Sperber's *An Introduction to Antonio Gramsci His Life, Thought and Legacy* (Bloomsbury, 2015), Jean-Yves Frétigné's *To Live Is to Resist* (University of Chicago Press, 2022), Carlucci's *Gramsci and Languages: Unification, Diversity, Hegemony* (Brill, 2013), and Young's "Restless Modernisms: D. H. Lawrence Caught in the Shadow of Gramsci," in *Moving Modernisms: Motion, Technology, and Modernity* (Oxford University Press, 2016). In Italian, see Marras's *Gramsci a Sorgono* (ISKRA, 2014), "Gramsci e la Sardegna. Socialismo e socialsardismo dagli anni giovanili alla grande guerra," by Lussana, in *Studi Storici*, July 2006, *Filosofia de logu: Decolonizzare il pensiero e la ricerca in Sardegna* (Meltemi, 2021), and Gramsci's *Scritti sulla Sardegna* (Ilisso, 2009). In Italian, visit the Istituto Gramsci della Sardegna: http://www.istitutogramscisardegna.it/.

The museum at Gramsci's childhood home in Ghilarza is an important landmark. See online: https://www.casamuseogramsci.it/it/ and https://www.sardegnaturismo.it/en/explore/casa-gramsci.

While I discuss the Sardinian Action Party later in the book, for background information, in Italian: Bomboi's *L' indipendentismo sardo. Le ragioni, la storia, i protagonisti* (Condaghes, 2014), Cubeddu's *Sardisti. Viaggio nel Partito Sardo d'Azione tra cronaca e stori*a (EDES, 2021) and Bellieni's *Partito sardo d'azione e Repubblica Federale. Scritti 1919–1925* (Edizioni Gallizzi, 1985). In English, see Hepburn's "The Polarisation and De-polarisation of Sardinian Nationalism," University of Edinburgh, 2007. The party's official website is here: http://www.psdaz.net/.

Wagner played an important role in Sardinia as a pioneering linguist. The quoted passage is an English translation from *Das ländliche Leben Sardiniens* (Wörter und Sachen, 1921), which was translated into Italian, *La vita rustica della*

Sardegna (Società Editoriale Italiana, 1928) and is available online: https://www.sardegnadigitallibrary.it/index.php?xsl=626&id=218084.

15. UNEARTHING MEMORY
Murgia's quotation is an English translation from *Viaggio in Sardegna*.

The *British Critic* review appeared in vol. 13, in 1799. Azuni's French edition, *Effai fur l'hiftoire géographique, politique et naturelle du royaume de Sardaigne* (Paris, 1798), was translated into Italian, *Storia geografica politica e naturale della Sardegna*, (Società Sardamare, 1950). The website of the Azuni school is here: https://liceoazuni.edu.it/chi-siamo/.

See above on Fresu's vast body of work. The *New York Times* featured "The Trumpeter From Sardinia," on September 5, 2001. The shepherd's quote is an English translation in "Così Berchidda è diventato laboratorio culturale." *Sardinia Post*, August 5, 2022. After three decades, Time in Jazz has been covered in Italian and English in numerous media venues. The *Downbeat* interview with Ted Panken is available online: https://tedpanken.wordpress.com/2018/10/30/a-2012-downbeat-article-with-trumpeter-paolo-fresu-a-2012-blindfold-winefold-test-with-fresu-and-the-complete-interview-for-the-downbeat-article/.

The festival website is: https://timeinjazz.it/associazione/en/.

Gentilcore's *Pomodoro! A History of the Tomato in Italy* (Temple University Press, 2010) features Sardinia. Andrea Manca dell'Arca's work has been reprinted, *Agricoltura di Sardegna* (Ilisso, 2000). Cossu's text is in Sardinian, *Istruzioni po sa cultura e po s ' usu de is patatas in Sardigna* (Stamperia Reale, 1805).

Sciola's official website is: http://www.pinucciosciola.it/ and https://www.psmuseum.it/.

For background, in English, see Marci's *Sciola, the Master of Stone* (CUEC, 2011); in Italian, see *Scolpire il suono, fotografare l'anima – Pinuccio Sciola* (CUEC, 2013).

"Fresu: Quelle sue pietre a Time in Jazz," appeared in *La Nuova Sardegna*, May 15, 2016. Fresu's website has posted the 2011 interview with Sciola http://www.paolofresu.it/upload/press/pdf/fresu-sciola-2011-new-1463386096.pdf.

16. MONTE D'ACCODDI
An English translation of Anedda's "Limba," also appeared in *Modern Poetry Translation:* https://modernpoetryintranslation.com/poem/tongue-limba/. Her work in Italian and Sardinian has been widely translated in English, among other languages. See *Archipelago* (Bloodaxe Books, 2014) and the forthcoming *Historiae* (NYRB Poets, 2023).

Monte d'Accoddi has a growing body of scholarship. In Italian, see Contu's *L'altare preistorico di Monte d'Accoddi* (Carlo Delfino, 2000), which is also available in English. Also see Webster's "Identifying Monte D'Accoddi, Sardinia's 4th-millennium ziggurat," in *Sardinia, Corsica et Baleares Antiquae XVII* (Serra Editore,

2019) and "Topographical and astronomical analysis on the Neolithic "Altar" of Monte D'accoddi In Sardinia." by Pili et al., *Mediterranean Archaeology and Archaeometry*, 2009.

See Graeber's *The Dawn of Everything: A New History of Humanity* (Farrar, Straus and Giroux, 2021).

The dea madre auction was covered widely, including "Mother Goddess Auction: Christie's Halts Sale of 'Stolen' $1M Bronze Age Pagan Icon after Sardinia Campaigns for Its Return," December 2, 2014, *Independent*. For background, in Italian, Giacomo Paglietti, "La madre mediterranea della Sardegna neolitica," *La preistoria in Sardegna* (Carlo Delfino Editore, 2017), Alba's *La donna nuragica: studio della bronzistica figurata* (Carocci, 2005). See above for Murgia's *Accabadora*, and Lilliu and Lo Schiavo citations.

Eleonora of Arborea reappears in the book, as a central figure in the medieval period. For various interpretations of her historic role as a judge, in Italian, see Dessi's *Eleonora d'Arborea, racconto drammatico in quattro atti* (Ilisso, 2010), Onnis' s *Vita, morte e miracoli di quaranta personalità sarde* (Domus de Janas, 2019), Pitzorno's *Vita di Eleonora d'Arborea* (Mondadori, 2010). In English, see Hoe's *Sardinia: Women, History, Books and Places* (Holo Books, 2022).

The Carta de Logu is online, in Sardinian and Italian: https://www.istar.oristano.it/it/materiali/pubblicazioni-istar/carta-de-logu/.

Check out the nice website dedicated to Marianna Bussalai and her writing: http://www.mariannabussalai.org/index.php.

PART THREE: *SA DIE DE SA SARDIGNA* | THE DAY OF THE SARDINIAN PEOPLE

See above for Mura's citations.

17. SARDINIAN CONTADINA

Dessi's quotation is an English translation from the liner notes, "Delirio" (RCA, 1974).

Steinberg's *New Yorker* cover, October 12, 1963, is online: https://digital.library.cornell.edu/catalog/ss:19343332.

See above for Altara citations.

For background on Biasi and to see reproductions of his paintings and drawings, see Altea's "Mediterranizing Gauguin. Giuseppe Biasi's Africa and Sardinia," *Artl@s Bulletin* 10, (2021), and her book, *Giuseppe Biasi*, (Ilisso, 1998), which is also online: https://www.sardegnadigitallibrary.it/mmt/fullsize/2008122013485900474.pdf.

For the latest at the Pinacoteca Nazionale di Sassari, see: https://www.facebook.com/PinacotecaSassari.

For details on the National Archaeological and Ethnographic Museum "G. A. Sanna" of Sassari, see: https://www.sardegnaturismo.it/en/explore/sanna-national-musem.

Julia Carta's story has been chronicled in various places, in Italian, including Pinna's *Storia di una strega: l'inquisizione in Sardegna: il processo di Julia Carta* (EDES, 2000), and Mastino's "Magia e inquisizione nella Sardegna del Cinquecento secondo Tomasino Pinna," Istituzione San Michele, Ozieri, 2017. The town of Bidonì, in central Sardinia, has a museum dedicated to witchcraft, Museo S'omo 'e sa Majarza: https://www.sardegnacultura.it/j/v/258?s=19013&v=2&c=2487&t=1.

For information on the Maria Carta Museum in Siligo, and her incredible career, see these sites: http://www.fondazionemariacarta.it/museo-maria-carta/ and https://comunesiligo.it/contenuti/20784/maria-carta.

Among the vast reports on her concerts and albums, see "Maria Carta, il concerto dimenticato," March 10, 2013, *La Nuova Sardegna*. There are various reprints in Italian of Carta's *Canto Rituale* (Coines, 1975), including the Italian-Spanish edition (Valparaiso Ediciones, 2022).

Gavino Gabriel had an extraordinary influence on twentieth century music and recording in Italy. For more information, in Italian, see Pasticci's *Musica e identità nel Novecento italiano: il caso di Gavino Gabriel* (LIM, 2018). A website dedicated to his work is online: http://www.gavino-gabriel.com/index.php/it/.

For a profile on Bartoli, see "Donna Ninetta Bartoli primo sindaco donna d'Italia": https://www.lacanas.it/novas/2012/donna-ninetta-bartoli-primo-sindaco-donna-ditalia/.

18. THE VALLEY OF THE NURAGHES

Ledda's English translation is from "Un'ode alla mia Madre Terra: per lei farò parlare le pietre," July 4, 2011, *Corriere della Sera*. The history of his studies comes from "Il liceo dei due Presidenti dove Ledda insegna teatro," June 14, 2010, *Corriere della Sera*. The *Drunken Boat* magazine did an interview with Ledda: https://d7.drunkenboat.com/db23/sardinia/gavino-ledda.

Ledda's books have been translated in numerous languages. In English, see *Padre Padrone: The Education of a Shepherd* (Viking, 1979). In Italian and Sardinian, see *Padre Padrone* (Il Maestrale, 2003), *Lingua di falce* (Dalai Editore, 2011), and "Istororra: Su Occhidorzu," in *Cartas de logu. Scrittori sardi allo specchio* (CUEC, 2007).

Day's work on censuses is in Italian or French, including *Villaggi abbandonati in Sardegna dal trecento al settecento: inventario* (Ed. du Centre national de la recherche scientifique, 1973), "La Sardegna come laboratorio di storia coloniale," *Quaderni Bolotanesi*, 1990, "Alle origini della povertà rurale" in *Le opere e i giorni. Pastori e contadini nella Sardegna tradizionale* (Silvana, 1983), "Quanti erano i Sardi nei secoli XIV-XV? *Archivio Storico Sardo*, 1986.

For medieval history, see above for *The Companion to Sardinian History, 500–1500* and *The Making of Medieval Sardinia,* and in Italian, *Sardegna medievale, moderna e contemporanea* (Carlo Delfino Editore, 2021) by Campus et al.

An archive of *Il Messaggero Sardo* newspapers is online: https://www.sardegnadigitallibrary.it/mmt/fullsize/2008080415162400231.pdf.

Clips of Ungaretti and the writers in Sardinia in 1955 can be viewed online at RAI: https://www.teche.rai.it/1955/10/il-viaggio-in-sardegna-di-ungaretti-caproni-reabo-piccioni-ed-altri-intellettuali-nel-1955/.

"A Glimpse of Pre-Tourist Sardinia," appeared in the *New York Times* on August 7, 1955.

For Mackenzie's insight, see "Dolmens and Nuraghi of Sardinia," Papers of the British School at Rome, vol. 6 (1913).

For a prehistoric road map of the Valley of the Nuraghes, see Nurnet: https://www.nurnet.net/mediateca/categorie/nuraghes/.

The official website for Santu Antine nuraghe is online: https://www.nuraghesantuantine.it/.

Santu Antine has a considerable amount of scholarship. For starters, Contu's *Il Nuraghe Santu Antine* (Carlo Delfino Editore, 1988), and for updated research, Foddai's *Il nuraghe Santu Antine e le dinamiche insediative della piana del Riu Mannu* (Carlo Delfino Editore, 2014), and Hoskin's and Belmonte Avilés' *Reflejo del cosmos: atlas de arqueoastronomía en el Mediterráneo antiguo* (Equipo Sirius, 2002) in Spanish.

See the Basilica di Saccargia online: https://www.visit-saccargia.com/.

Mulas's *L'isola Sacra (Condaghes, 2012)* is in Italian. Levi's *Tutto il miele è finito* (Ilisso, 2003) is only in Italian, as well. The proceedings of the 1909 conference, "Dell'uso dei Nuraghi," is online: https://www.sardegnadigitallibrary.it/mmt/fullsize/2009042212415200060.pdf.

For melons and Nuragic times, see "Archaeobotanical analysis of a Bronze Age well from Sardinia: A wealth of knowledge," *Plant Biosystems,* 2014 by Sabato et al, and "Melone, i primi a coltivarlo in Europa furono i sardi in epoca nuragica," *La Repubblica,*" February 18, 2015.

19. GIRL WRITER FOUND DEAD IN MYSTERY CASE

The English translation of Casula's poem is from *Sa Lantia* (Velox, 1950). Regrettably, none of his work is translated in English in book form. Montanaru's great treasury of poetry is available in Sardinian and Italian, including *Montanaru, Boghes, cantos e cantigos. Le liriche di Antioco Casula il miglior poeta di metà Novecento* (Edizioni Della Torre, 2013), *Sos cantos de sa solitudine* (Ilisso, 1998), and *Sas ultimas canzones. Cantigos de amargura* (Ilisso, 1998).

I discuss Casula later in the book, but check out his family home and museum in Desulo: http://www.barbagiamandrolisai.it/english/desulo.html#casula.

For all of his fame, Farina's work was not translated, outside of excerpts or short stories (see "Signor 10," in *The Cosmopolitan*, 1887). In Italian, see *La mia giornata. Dall'alba al meriggio* (S.T.E.N., 1910) for the story on Sassari.

King's comments on Lawrence are in *Sardinian Painting* (Longmans, Green and Co., 1923).

Giles's story filled the crime headlines in newspapers across the States. I relied on various newspaper archive search engines, including the *New York Times* and the *Philadelphia Inquirer*, and the *Byrn Mawr Alumnae Bulletin*, 1937. Her short story, "Apostasy of Anita Fiske," appeared in *A Book of Bryn Mawr Stories* (Jacbos and Co., 1901). In Italian, see "Un'esploratrice in Sardegna," August 8, 1907, *La Nuova Sardegna*, "I funerali di Miss Giles," January 17, 1914, *La Nuova Sardegna*, and *Il Caso Giles* (J. Webber, 2011) by Pintus and Cugia.

20. *FAINÈ*

The English translation of Pintor is from *Storia letteraria di Sardegna* (Timon, 1843). Among his many works in Italian, Pintor also wrote *Storia civile dei popoli sardi* (Casanova, 1877).

Among his several volumes of poetry, see Ruju's *Sassari véccia e nóba* (Ilisso, 2001).

Watch Willie discuss Sardinia on Simpsons: https://www.youtube.com/watch?v=krCwqGfq1tA.

See Letterbox for the Disney *Sardinia* production in 1956: https://letterboxd.com/film/sardinia/.

See Theroux's *The Pillars of Hercules* (G. P. Putnam's Sons 1995) for a "Grand Tour of the Mediterranean," and Richard's *The New Italians* (Michael Joseph, 1994). For more on Piercy's role on the railroads in Sardinia, see Del Piano's "Benjamin Piercy industriale e imprenditore agricolo in Sardegna: la costruzione della rete ferroviaria isolana nell'Ottocento," *Bollettino bibliografico e rassegna archivistica e di studi storici della Sardegna*, 1992, and the Trenino Verde website: https://treninoverdedisardegna.it/history-of-railways-in-sardinia.

The Piercy home is a notable tourist site: https://www.sardegnaturismo.it/it/esplora/villa-piercy.

21. *SA VITTA ET MORTE*

This is an English translation from Araolla's *Sa vida, su martiriu, et morte dessos gloriosos martires Gauinu, Brothu et Gianuari*, available online: https://www.sardegnadigitallibrary.it/documenti/17_146_20181123124014.pdf.

See also *Rimas diversas spirituales* (CUEC, 2006), edited by Virdis.

The English translation is from Pinna's poem, "Nuoro." Her work has been published in various collections, including *La famiglia esclusiva* (Ilisso, 2011) and *Paesaggi d'anima* (Ethos, 2011).

See Gitlin on Deledda, "Literary Resurrection," September 20, 1998, *Chicago Tribune*.

See citations above in Agriturismo on Deledda.

See Steiner above on Satta and the *New Yorker*. Satta's *The Day of Judgment* (Farrar, Straus and Giroux, 1987) is translated in many languages. His novel, *La Veranda* (Adelphi, 2019), is only in Italian.

Ruju's work is in Sardinian and Italian, *Su Connottu* (Il Maestrale, 2008), *Quel Giorno a Buggerru* (Il Maestrale, 2004).

Asproni's *Diario Politico* in Italian was published in six volumes by Giuffrè, from 1974–1983.

See above for Gramsci citations. *Letters from Prison* (Columbia University Press, 2011) are in two volumes; *Prison Notebooks* (Columbia University Press, 2011) are in three volumes.

Casu's *il Vocabolario Sardo-Logudorese-Italiano* (Ilisso, 2002) is also online: http://vocabolariocasu.isresardegna.it/.

See above for citations on Atzeni.

22. *IN SOS LOGOS DE ANGIOY*

See above for Dickens and *Household Words* magazine.

To view "L'ingresso di Giommaria Angioy a Sassari," see: http://old.provincia.sassari.it/sc/salasciuti.wp?pivotContent=SIM2640.

Check out the websites for the various walks: Cammino 100 Torri https://www.cammino100torri.com/ and Cammino Minerario di Santa Barbara: https://www.camminominerariodisantabarbara.org/.

Angioy's memoir is in French, Sardinian, and Italian, *Memoriale sulla Sardegna*, 1799, (Condaghes, 2015). See also in Italian, Pubusa's *Giovanni Maria Angioy e la nazione mancata. I cento giorni che sconvolsero la Sardegna* (Arkadia, 2020), Carta's edited *Su patriottu sardu a sos feudatarios* (CUEC, 2002), Francioni's *Vespro sardo. Dagli esordi della dominazione piemontese all'insurrezione del 28 aprile 1794* (Condaghes, 2001), Enders's *La Sardegna Paraninfa della Pace: e un piano segreto per la sovranità 1712-1714* (Masala, 2011).

Tyndale's English translation of "Su patriotu Sardu a sos feudatario" is online at various sites, including: https://www.antiwarsongs.org/confronta.php?id=5768&ver=105938&lang=it.

See *Monthly Review*'s "Travels in Sardinia," on the French edition of La Marmora's book, 1826.

Lussu's comments can be found in various sources, including *Il pensiero federalista in Sardegna* (Condaghes, 1996), and *Sul Partito d'Azione e gli altri: Note critiche 1939-194: Seconda guerra mondiale* (Ugo Mursia Editore, 2009). As noted above, Lussu was also a prolific author. In English, see *A Soldier on the Southern Front* (Rizzoli, 2014), and Lussu's short story, "Your General Does Not Sleep," May, 1939, *The Atlantic Monthly*, was selected for The Best Short Stories of 1940

(Houghton Mifflin) and appears online: https://www.theatlantic.com/magazine/archive/1939/05/your-general-does-not-sleep/653956/.

In Italian, *Un anno sull'Altipiano* (Einaudi, 2014). For biography, in Italian, see Fiori's *Il cavaliere dei Rossomori. La vita di Emilio Lussu* (Il Maestrale, 2010), and the published papers from the conference, *Emilio Lussu e la cultura popolare della Sardegna* (ISRE, 1983). As I discuss later, the Emilio and Joyce Lussu museum in Armungia contains a great archive: https://www.sardegnacultura.it/j/v/253?s=3566 3&v=2&c=2487&cl=2123&visb&t=1.

For his parliament speeches, see online: https://www.senato.it/application/xmanager/projects/leg18/file/repository/relazioni/libreria/novita/XVIII/Lussu_I_2021.pdf.

See earlier citations on Sardinian Action Party, and in Italian, see also *Storia della Sardegna* (Editore Mursia, 1971) by Raspi, *L 'Indipendentismo Sardo: le ragioni, la storia, i protagonisti* (Condaghes, 2014) by Bomboi.

23. *SU PATRIOTU SARDU*

Bellieni's citation on the song is widely noted, including Cubeddu's "La Sardegna nell'unità d'Italia," Convegno La Sardegna nel Mondo, June 23, 2011. In Italian, see also Bellieni's *La lotta politica in Sardegna dal 1848 ai giorni nostri* (Gallizzi, 1962).

See above on Atzeni's work. On the role of identity, see also *Sergio Atzeni e le voci della Sardegna* (Bononia University Press, 2017), edited by Sulis and Ledda.

On Sardinia and the nation, see Mastino's "Natione Sardus. Una mens, unus color, una vox, una natio," *Archivio Storico Sardo*, 2015, and Gallinari's "From the Medieval Nacio sardesca," *La Nació a l'Edat Mitjana* (Lleida, Pagés, 2020). Livi's chilling book, *Sardi in schiavitù nei secoli XII-XV* (Cesati, 2002) provides an overlooked background on medieval slavery in Sardinia.

For Barella's and Sirigu's flag unveiling, see the interview, "Metto la bandiera sarda in valigia. Andare lontano mi ha reso più forte," *Corriere della Sera*, August 11, 2021.

Numerous sources cite Pope Leo's *vicus Sardorum*, including Tola's *Codice diplomatico di Sardegna* (Tipografia Chirio e Mina, 1847) and Rowland's *The Periphery in the Center: Sardinia in the Ancient and Medieval Worlds* (Archaeopress, 2001).

See above for Lussu's writings on the war and the Sassari Brigade. Bellieni's tribute to Lussu was reprinted by Condaghes in 2019, and online: https://www.sardegnadigitallibrary.it/mmt/fullsize/2009031317254100063.pdf.

To visit the Sassari Brigade museum, see http://turismosassari.it/en/explore/art-and-culture/item/839-historic-museum-of-the-brigata-sassari-a-precious-historic-treasure-in-the-heart-of-sassari.html.

Lobina's novel in Sardinian, *Po cantu Biddanoa* (Ilisso , 2005), is also translated into Italian.

View Delitala's flag for Sardinia in Frongia's book, *Mario Delitala* (Ilisso, 1999).

PART FOUR: *MONTES INSANI* | THE INSANE MOUNTAINS

The English translation is from Mereu's "A Nanni Sulis II," found in several Sardinian and Italian collections, including *Il meglio della grande poesia in lingua sarda* (Edizioni Della Torre, 2008), *Poesias* (Ilisso, 2005), *Poesie complete* (Il Maestrale, 2004).

While Vittorini's *Sardegna come un'infanzia* (Bompiani, 2014) is not translated in English, see also his *Conversations in Sicily* (New Directions, 2000).

For Marconi's Sardinian experiments, see "Inventor Points The Way; Marconi's Latest System of Bending Tiny Radio Waves Around Earth's Curvature Entrances American Engineers," August 21, 1932, *New York Times*.

24. SAVING THE COASTS

For more on monk seals at Grotta del Fico, see: https://www.grottadelfico.it/en/monk-seals/.

See Nivola's "DDT in Sardinia," in March, 1953, *Fortune*. I discuss his art later in the book. For an overview of the malaria campaign, see Tognitti's "Program to Eradicate Malaria in Sardinia, 1946–1950," *Emerging Infectious Diseases*, 2009. News reports abound on the "Emerald Coast" and its decades of development. See also: Corsale's *Surrounded by Water Landscapes, Seascapes and Cityscapes of Sardinia* (Cambridge Scholars, 2016), and the tourist website: https://www.sardegnaturismo.it/en/places/north-east/emerald-coast.

Bandinu's novel, *L'amore del figlio meraviglioso*, (Il Maestrale, 2011) is in Italian.

Soru's comments are from: "Darkness, Silence, and Nature as a Political Plan," 2019: https://www.cca.qc.ca/en/articles/issues/27/will-happiness-find-us/68434/darkness-silence-and-nature-as-a-political-plan.

For background on Soru, "Il Nel progetto di Renato Soru l'identità come risorsa per lo sviluppo della Sardegna," August 6, 2004, *Il Messaggero Sardo*, "Un Programma per cambiare la Sardegna. Insieme," Dichiarazioni del Presidente Renato Soru al Consiglio Regionale della Sardegna, Cagliari, July 27, 2004. In English, see "The Man Who Would Be King," February 18, 2001, *Newsweek*, "Sardinia's coastline protected from developers," September 8, 2006, *Independent*, Lai's "Assessment of the Regional Landscape Plan of Sardinia (Italy): A participatory-action- research case study type," *Land Use Policy*, 2010, and Colavitti et al., "Mind the Gap: Why the Landscape Planning System in Sardinia Does Not Work," *Sustainability,* 2021.

25. POMPÌA

Translations of *Etymologies of Isidore of Seville* are available online: https://sfponline.org/Uploads/2002/st%20isidore%20in%20english.pdf.

For more on food and recipes in Sardinia, in English see Clark's *Bitter Honey: Recipes and Stories from Sardinia* (Hardie Grant, 2020).

See above for citations on d'Avity and *National Geographic*.

Dessí's comments appeared in his correspondence, *Dessí e la Sardegna i carteggi con "Il Ponte" e Il Polifilo* (Firenze University Press, 2013).

On weaving traditions, in Italian, see: *Tessuti: Tradizione e innovazione della tessitura in Sardegna* (Ilisso, 2006). For a nice interview in English on Casa Lussu, see *Domus*: https://www.domusweb.it/en/design/2013/09/04/a_return_to_the_originsthearmungiarugs.html

Pastonesi's *Tortolì, Celu Inferru* (Collage Edizioni, 1991), and the second volume, *Tortolì Saludi e Trigu!* (Collage Edizioni, 1998) is Italian. Soru's quotation on the US bases appeared widely, including "Sardinia Says It's Time for the U.S. Navy to Leave Port," July 17, 2005, *LA Times*, and "U.S. to Shut Base in Italy That Aids Nuclear Subs," November 25, 2005, *New York Times*. In Italian, see Sanna's *La Base Atomica: di al Maddalena-Santo Stefano dall'inizio* (Paolo Sorba Editore, 2008), and Bandinu's *Noi non sapevamo. Lingua, turismo, industria, basi militari, ambiente* (Il Maestrale, 2016). The annual NATO military exercises have been covered extensively, dating back to the March 4, 1952 report in the *New York Times*. The NATO bombing exercises continue, as noted in *L'Unione Sarda* news report, "Defense, exercises continue in the Sardinian Sea," on October 12, 2022.

26. TISCALI

Lilliu's quotation was at the Barumini nuraghe inauguration, a UNESCO World Heritage site. See also Lilliu's and Zucca's *Su Nuraxi di Barumini* (Carlo Delfino Editore, 2001).

On Soru's Tiscali background, see the above citations. There are two decades of news reports on the ups and downs of the company, from the *Wall Street Journal* on April 20, 2000, "Chief of Italian Telecom Tiscali, Soru, Knows What He's Doing," to "Il risveglio di Tiscali, ultima sopravvissuta della new economy," on November 2, 2022 in *il Messaggero*. See also, the company website: https://www.tiscali.com/en/history-and-profile/.

See also Heatherington's *Wild Sardinia: Indigeneity and the Global Dreamtimes of Environmentalism* (University of Washington Press, 2010) for more on the Gennargentu park controversy.

Dessì *Paese d'ombre* (Mondadori, 1973) won the Il Premio Strega, and is translated into English, *The Forest of Norbio* (Harcourt Brace Jovanovich, 1975). He was a prolific author in many genres. In English, see also *The Deserter* (Harcourt, Brace & World, 1962).

Caterini's *Colpi di scure e sensi di colpa: Storia del disboscamento della Sardegna dalle origini a oggi* (Carlo Delfino Editore, 2013) is in Italian. See also Francesco Bussalai's 2021 film documentary, *Àrbores*. On history, Casula's "La distruzione delle foreste sarde," November 26, 2013, on his blog, *Truncare sas cadenas*. In English, see Puddu's "Forest changes over a century in Sardinia," *Agroforest*

Syst, 2012, "8,000 years of climate, vegetation, fire and land-use dynamics in the thermo-mediterranean vegetation belt of northern Sardinia," *Vegetation History and Archaeobotany*, 2021, Pedrotta et al., and Pungetti's "Anthropological approach to agricultural landscape history in Sardinia," *Landscape and Urban Planning*, 1995, and Grove's *The Nature of Mediterranean Europe: An Ecological History* (Yale University Press, 2003).

For classical sources on *insani montes*, see Smith's *Dictionary of Greek and Roman Geography (1854)*. See also, Mastino's "I Montes Insani e gli Ilienses della Sardegna interna: Montiferru, Marghine o Gennargentu?" *Santu Lussurgiu: dalle origini alla Grande Guerra* (Solinas, 2005).

Murenu's poetry has been collected in various editions, including *Tutte le poesie* (Edizioni della Torre, 1990). See above for Mereu's powerful poetry, as well.

To visit *Sa Sedda 'e sos Carros,* see https://oliena.it/en/outdoor/sa-sedda-e-sos-carros/.

On Tiscali archaeological site, see Pais's earlier writings, *La civiltà dei nuraghi e lo sviluppo sociologico della Sardegna* (Dessi, 1911). *Storia della Sardegna e della Corsica durante il dominio* (Ilisso reprint, 1999), Manca's "Tiscali nel nuorese" in *Sardegna Antica,* June 2015, Paulis's "Come ci raccontiamo? Retoriche di un'identità narrata," *Rhesis,* Literature, 2017. For the official websites of the Tiscali site, see https://www.museoarcheologicodorgali.com/ and https://www.sardegnaturismo.it/en/explore/nuragic-village-tiscali.

See above on Atzeni's *Passavamo sulla terra leggeri.* Frau's books include *Le Colonne d'Ercole* (Nur Neon, 2001), and *Omphalos. Il primo centro del mondo* (Nur Neon, 2017). See also, "Was Sardinia home to the mythical civilisation of Atlantis," August 15, 2015, *The Guardian.*

27. BITTI
The English translation is from Brigaglia's, *Il meglio della grande poesia in lingua sarda* (La Nuova Sardegna, 2003), with a preface by Pira.

Sei per la Sardegna (Einaudi, 2014) is in Italian. Not a single book by Pira has been translated into English. In Italian, for background, see *La Sardegna nell'opera di Michelangelo Pira: atti del Convegno in onore di Michelangelo Pira, Quartu Sant'Elena, 1996* (Tema, 1997), and Pira's own *Sardegna fra due lingue* (Edizioni della Torre, 1984), *Rivolta dell'oggetto* (Giuffre, 1978), and *Il villaggio elettronico* (AMOD, 1997), *Sos Sinnos* (Editore della Torre, 1983). The Tenores di Bitti, named after Pira, have a good bibliography online: http://www.tenoresdibitti.com/michelangelopira/bibliografia.htm.

See the Albino Manca museum in Tertenia: http://www.museoalbinomanca.it/.

28. THE BARBAGIA
The English translation is from Satta's "A Vindice mio figlio," *Canti Barbaricini* (Ilisso, 1998). Check out an excellent multilingual website on Satta's work: https://www.sebastianosatta.org/en/.

See above for Mastino's "Ancient Historical Contexts" in *The Making of Medieval Sardinia* for background on the Barbaricini, and in Italian, his chapter "I Sardi Pelliti del Montiferru o del Marghine e le origini di Hampsicora," in *Santu Lussurgiu: dalle origini alla Grande Guerra*, 2005. See also Zucca's "Un Altare rupestre di Iuppiter nella Barbaria sarda," *L'Africa romana* (EDES, 1998).

Cicero's defense of Marcus Scaurus is online at numerous sources: http://www.perseus. tufts.edu/hopper/text?doc=urn:cts:latinLit:phi0474.phi029.perseus-lat1.

See Ruiu's *Maschere e Carnevale in Sardegna* (Imago, 2009) on mask traditions; for photos, see Spironetti's *Senza Mare* (Crowdbooks, 2020). To visit the Museo delle Maschere Mediterranee in Mamoiada, see: https://www.museomaschere.it/orari-info/.

Niceforo's original volume *La delinquenza in Sardegna* (Sandron, 1897) remains in print. His outsized role is covered in D'Agostino's "Craniums, Criminals, and the 'Cursed Race': Italian Anthropology in American Racial Thought, 1861–1924," *Comparative Studies in Society and History*, April, 2002, among numerous studies. See also Sorge's *Legacies of Violence: History, Society, and the State in Sardinia* (University of Toronto Press, 2015). Cagnetta's *Inchiesta su Orgosolo* has been published in book form, *Banditi a Orgosolo* (Ilisso, 2022). Gramsci's article is found in *The Postcolonial Gramsci* (Routledge, 2012).

For Scorsese on De Seta, see "Vittorio De Seta obituary," *The Guardian*, December 11, 2011. Saviano's report appeared in "Saviano: così De Seta mi insegnò a combattere il male con l' arte," October 31, 2008, *La Repubblica*.

Bouchier's *Sardinia in Ancient Times* (Kessinger, 2010), published in 1917, remains in print.

Recent DNA studies include "Genomic history of the Sardinian population," *Nat Genet*, 2018, by Chiang et al., and "Genetic history from the Middle Neolithic to present on the Mediterranean island of Sardinia," *Nature Communications*, 2020, by Marcus et al.

For the websites for the Romanzesu and Santa Cristina complexes, see: https://www.romanzesu.sardegna.it/ and https://www.pozzosantacristina.com/en/.

Among the vast archives on sacred wells in the Nuragic period, in English see Depalmas's "Water and Cults in Nuragic Sardinia," *Water* 5, Wiley Interdisciplinary Reviews, December 2017, and M. Webster's thesis, "Water Temples of Sardinia: Identification, Inventory and Interpretation," (Uppsala Universitet, 2014). In Italian, see Moravetti's *Il santuario nuragico di Santa Cristina* (Carlo Delfino Editore, 2003), Zucca's *Viaggio nell'archeologia della provincia di Oristano* (E.P.T., 2004), Fadda's *Il villaggio nuragico Su Romanzesu* (Carlo Delfino Editore, 2006).

In Italian, see Laneri's "Giovanni Arca e il Bellum marchionicum," *Multas per gentes: studi in memoria di Enzo Cadoni* (EDES, 2000), and Arca's *Barbaricinorum libelli* (CUEC, 2005).

29. ASPRONI, GARIBALDI, AND THE PRINCE OF SATIRE

This is an English translation of Mazzini's article in *L'Unita' Italiana,* June 5, 1861. See also Murgia's "Giuseppe Mazzini e la Sardegna," Malta Historical Society, 2005.

White Mario's comments are in *The Birth of Modern Italy: Posthumous Papers of Jessie White Mario* (T. Fischer Unwin, 1909). For Garibaldi's letter to Lincoln, see "The Italian Liberals to President Lincoln,"August 30, 1863, *New York Times.* Parks' *The Hero's Way* (W. W. Norton, 2021) is translated in Italian, *Il cammino dell'eroe. A piedi con Garibaldi da Roma a Ravenna* (Rizzoli, 2022). To visit the Garibaldi museum, see: https://www.garibaldicaprera.beniculturali.it/

On Asproni, see Puligheddu's *Giorgio Asproni. Nel nome della Rivoluzione. Un protagonista sardo nel Risorgimento italiano* (Ilisso, 2017), Puddu's "Giorgio Asproni a 80 anni dalla morte," October 3, 1956, *La Nuova Sardegna,* and "Giorgio Asproni e sa die de sa Sardigna. Il ricordo del grande Bittese in un discorso del 1979 di Armando Corona," Fondazione Sardinia: http://www.fondazionesardinia.eu/ita/?p=13160.

Pau's *Sas gamas de Istelai* (Condaghes, 2004) is only in Sardinian. Mele's work is included in the "I grandi poeti in lingua sarda" series, *Diego Mele* (Edizioni della Torre, 1984). See also *Il Parnaso sardo del poeta bernesco estemporaneo teologo Diego Mele* (Ledda, 1922).

Bandinu's prolific writing in Sardinian and Italian include, *Lettera a un giovane sardo* (Editore della Torre, 1996), *Il re è un feticcio* (Ilisso, 2005), *La scena nascosta* (Il Maestrale, 2021), *Lettera a un giovane sardo sempre connesso* (Domus de Janas, 2017).

30. L'ATENE BARBARICINA

See above for Fois's work.

For all the great museums in and near Nuoro, see: https://www.comune.nuoro.it/vivere/cultura/17.

See Medas' *Paskedda: Torramus a su connottu* (Edizioni Abbà, 2021).

Along with Satta and Ruju on the Buggerru strike and Sardinian mining history, see Murtas' "Buggerru, dopo l'eccidio il primo sciopero generale," November 16, 2021, *La Nuova Sardegna,* Rollandi's *Miniere e minatori in Sardegna* (Editore della Torre, 1981). For the Museum of the Miners: https://www.comunebuggerru.it/it/amministrazione/luoghi/luogo/Museo-del-minatore/.

Ciusa's work is in Nuoro, Cagliari, Rome, among other places. Bossaglia's *Francesco Ciusa* (Ilisso, 1990) and Altea's *Francesco Ciusa* (Ilisso, 2004) provide excellent background. Photographer Vittorio Alinari has a nice look at Ciusa's "La Madre dell'ucciso" in his book, *In Sardegna: Note Di Viaggio* (Fratelli Alinari, 1915).

Along with Nivola's memoir, *Memorie di Orani* (Ilisso, 2003), see Altea's *Costantino Nivola* (Ilisso, 2004). In English, the *New York Times* recently did a nice portrait,

"When Reviving a Forgotten Sculptor's Reputation Is a Family Affair," June 2, 2021. See also "The Crumbling Art of Costantino Nivola, a Picasso for the People," March 12, 2020, *Atlas Obscura*. Visit the Nivola museum here: https://museonivola.it/en/.

Giacobbe's work is available in Italian and Danish, including *Diario di una maestrina* (Il Maestrale, 2003), *Gli arcipelaghi* (Il Maestrale, 2017) *I ragazzi del veliero* (Il Maestrale, 2017).

For the extraordinary Orgosolo murals, see: https://www.sardegnaturismo.it/en/silent-voice-orgosolo-murals.

See above citations for Deledda. Visit her museum here: http://www.isresardegna.it/index.php?xsl=565&s=16&v=9&c=4094&nodesc=1.

PART FIVE: *SEDD'E SU DIAULU* | THE DEVIL'S SADDLE

This is an English translation from Atzeni's title poem, *Due colori esistono al mondo: Il verde è il secondo* (Il Maestrale, 1997).

31. THE CONSUL

The translation is from Agus, *Un tempo gentile* (Nottetempo, 2020). Her novels in English include *While the Shark is Sleeping* (Saqi, 2014), *From the Land of the Moon* (Europa Editions, 2010).

Soriga's *Sardinia Blues* (Bompiani, 2008) is not translated in English. Other works in Italian include *Nelle mie vene* (Bompiani, 2019), *NuraGhe beach. La Sardegna che non visiterete mai* (Laterza, 2011).

Dickinson's "Letters from a Farmer in Pennsylvania" are online: https://history.delaware.gov/john-dickinson-plantation/dickinsonletters/pennsylvania-farmer-letters/.

For Navoni's correspondence with the American leaders of the day, see: https://founders.archives.gov/search/Author%3A%22Navoni%2C%20Francois%20de%22.

For more on Eaton, see Reid's *To the Walls of Derne William Eaton, the Tripoli Coup, and the End of the First Barbary War* (Naval Institute Press, 2017), Wright's *The First Americans in North Africa: William Eaton's Struggle for a Vigorous Policy Against the Barbary Pirates, 1799–1805* (Princeton University Press, 1945). Eaton's correspondence on the Porcile case is online: https://founders.archives.gov/documents/Madison/02-08-02-0060.

Schirru's case was followed widely in the international press, including "Schirru Composed At His Execution: Naturalized American Executed by Fascist Firing Squad Refused Chaplain's Comfort," May 30, 1931, *New York Times,* and "American Is Shot For Plot On Il Duce," May 29, 1931, *New York Times*. In Italian, see Fiori's *L'anarchico Schirru. L'uomo giustiziato per aver pensato di uccidere Mussolini* (Garzanti, 2010).

32. *SA MUNDANA CUMMEDIA*

The English translation is from Poddighe's *Sa Cummedia Mundana* (Domus de Janas, 2014). An English translation for the full poem is here: https://www.academia. edu/25151003/Salvatore_Poddighe_Salvatore_Poddighe_SA_MUNDANA_ CUMMEDIA_A_MUNDANE_COMEDY_Prima_Parte_First_Part.

Visit the Museo del Tesoro e Area Archeologica di Sant'Eulalia: http://www.mutseu. org/it/index.html.

Among his vast body of works in Sardinian and Italian, see Carta Raspi's *Sardegna Terra di poesia* (Fondazione Il Nuraghe, 1929), *Storia della Sardegna* (Mursia, 1971), *Una civiltà che risorge: la Sardegna nuragica* (Fondazione Il Nuraghe, 1955). See also: *Raimondo Carta Raspi: storico, editore, organizzatore culturale* (Insula, 2020).

See Garzia's *Mutettus cagliaritani* (EDES, 1977). On Gramsci and Garzia, see Carlo Figari's "Il primo articolo di Gramsci" online: http://www.carlofigari.it/il-primo-articolo-di-gramsci/.

See above on Lussu citations. Also, Lussu's "Avvenire della Sardegna" essay, which appeared in *Il Ponte* magazine in 1951, is online: http://www.fondazionesardinia. eu/ita/?p=1852.

33. OF STELES AND ISLANDERS

The English translation is from Zucca's "Storiografia del problema della 'scrittura nuragica'" (*Bollettino di Studi Sardi, 2012*).

Visit the National Archaeological Museum in Cagliari: https://www.cagliariturismo. it/en/places/places-of-art-and-culture-319/university-of-cagliari-official-department-148/national-archaeological-museum-43.

For the ancient menhirs and archaeological sites, visit Pranu Muttedu in Gona: http://www.pranumuttedu.com/ and Biru 'e Concas in Sorgono: https://www. sardegnaturismo.it/en/explore/biru-e-concas.

See the Mont'e Prama citations above.

For directions to literally thousands of Nuragic sites, see Nurnet's geoportal: http://nurnet.crs4.it/nurnetgeo/.

Other sites include:

Barumini: https://comune.barumini.ca.it/contenuti/174415/area-archeologica-nuraxi.

Genna Maria: http://www.gennamaria.it/.

Arrubiu: http://www.nuraghearrubiu.it/.

Losa: https://www.nuraghelosa.net/.

La Prisgiona: https://www.gesecoarzachena.it/?page_id=1220.

Serra Orrios: https://www.museoarcheologicodorgali.com/siti-di-interesse/siti-gestiti/ serra-orrios.

34. ON THE RIM OF THE WORLD

In a self-proclaimed "exile" in Sardinia, Quasimodo's poems on Sardinia are online: https://www.luigiladu.it/Articoli/ppulina_quasimodo.htm.

See Porta Flavio here: http://www.visitiglesias.comune.iglesias.ca.it/it/vacanza/biglietteria-online/ and http://www.minieredisardegna.it/LeMiniere.php?IdM=51&IdCM=&SID=.

For background on Carloforte, see Vallebona's *Carloforte. Storia di una colonizzazione* (Editore della Torre, 2013), *Cronache inedite o poco note di alcuni fatti avvenuti in seguito all'invasione tunisina sull'isola di San Pietro, 1798–1803* (Edizioni della Torre, 2003), and Toso's *Isole tabarchine. Gente, vicende e luoghi di un'avventura genovese nel Mediterraneo* (Le Mani 2014). To visit the Island of San Pietro, see: isoladisanpietro.org .

On Antas, see Zucca's *Il Tempio di Antas* (Carlo Defino Editore, 1989), and more recently, Zucca's edited volume, *Il tempoi del Sardus pater ad antas: Fluminimaggiore, sud Sardegna. Monumenti Antichi* (Bretschneider Editore, 2019), and Melis's "Miti (antichi e moderni) sulla Sardegna: Sardus Pater," *Theologica e Historica*, 2013. In English, see Terpstra's "Mediterranean Silver Production and the Site of Antas, Sardinia," *Oxford Journal of Archaeology*, 2021.

EPILOGUE: THE DESIRE TO RETURN

Aristotle's reference to Sardinia in *Physics IV, II*, is widely cited. In English, see also Minunno's "A note on Ancient Sardinian incubation (Aristotle, Physica IV 11)," *Ritual, Religion, and Reason. Studies in the Ancient World in Honour of Paolo Xella* (Münster, 2013), and in Italian, see Mastino's "Aristotele e la natura del tempo: la pratica del sonno terapeutico davanti agli eroi della Sardegna," *I riti della morte e del culto di Monte Prama-Cabras, Convegni Lincei 303* (Bardi Edizioni, 2015).

Ortu's reference is in "Establishing Power and Law in Medieval and Modern Sardinia," *A Companion to Sardinian History, 500–1500* (Brill, 2017).

Tirso de Molina's *Cigarrales de Toledo* (1621) and comments are cited in numerous sources, including Para's "La Sardegna in alcune fonti letterarie e paraletterarie spagnole di età moderna," *Archivio Storico Sardo, Convegno Internazionale di Studi* (Edizioni AV, 2019).

Dessí's quotation is from *Dessí e la Sardegna i carteggi con "Il Ponte" e Il Polifilo* (Firenze University Press, 2013). Valdès's quotation is from his article online at Nurnet, "Minoici e Micenei in Sardegna," February 21, 2015: https://www.nurnet.net/blog/minoici-e-micenei-in-sardegna/.

To visit Nuraghe Palmavera, see: https://nuraghepalmavera.it/.

For more on the Nuragic meeting huts, see Mulas's and Zedda's "Orientation of the Nuragic Meeting Huts," *Mediterranean Archaeology and Archaeometry*, Vol. 16,

2016, Stiglitz's "Migrant Images. Travel Memories in Nuragic Sardinia," *Medea*, July, 2016, and Gonzalez's "Anarchy in the Bronze Age? Social organization and complexity in nuragic Sardinia," *Social organisation and complexity in Sardinia* (Routledge, 2019).

See above for Montanaru's citations. Online editions of his works are also at the Sardegna Digital Library: https://www.sardegnadigitallibrary.it/index.html.